SAVING INDIA
from INDIRA

SAVING INDIA from INDIRA
THE UNTOLD STORY OF EMERGENCY

MEMOIRS OF J.P. GOYAL

Edited by **RAMA GOYAL**

Forewords by
ARUN JAITLEY AND MEGHNAD DESAI

RUPA

Published by
Rupa Publications India Pvt. Ltd 2019
7/16, Ansari Road, Daryaganj
New Delhi 110002

Sales Centres:
Allahabad Bengaluru Chennai
Hyderabad Jaipur Kathmandu
Kolkata Mumbai

Copyright © Rama Goyal 2019

The views and opinions expressed in this book are the author's own and the facts are as reported by him/her which have been verified to the extent possible, and the publishers are not in any way liable for the same.

All rights reserved.
No part of this publication may be reproduced, transmitted, or stored in a retrieval system, in any form or by any means, electronic, mechanical, photocopying, recording or otherwise, without the prior permission of the publisher.

ISBN: 978-93-5333-395-9

Second impression 2022

10 9 8 7 6 5 4 3 2

Printed in India

The moral right of the author has been asserted.

This book is sold subject to the condition that it shall not, by way of trade or otherwise, be lent, resold, hired out, or otherwise circulated, without the publisher's prior consent, in any form of binding or cover other than that in which it is published.

Dedicated to
WE, THE PEOPLE OF INDIA,
especially to Shivam and Rishabh,
grandsons of Shri J.P. Goyal
and
representatives of the future generation of India,
in the hope that it never becomes
I, THE OWNER OF INDIA

—Editor

Contents

Foreword by Arun Jaitley ix
Foreword by Meghnad Desai xi
Preface xv
Acknowledgements xxv
Abbreviations and Acronyms xxvii

1. Why This Book? 1
2. Rescuing Raj Narain's Election Petition 9
3. Indira Nehru Gandhi Versus Raj Narain:
   The Battle in the Supreme Court 27
4. Proclamation of Emergency and Its Aftermath 43
5. Meeting the Leaders in Jail 54
6. Differences among the Lawyers 76
7. Taming of the Judiciary by Indira Gandhi 90
8. The Historic Election Case at the Supreme Court 101
9. Thwarting the Ploy of the Chief Justice of 'Indi(r)a' 114
10. 'Judicial Suicide' and Other Excesses during
    the Emergency 134
11. The People Versus Indira Gandhi:
    Democracy Restored at Last 150

Appendices:
Appendix I: Proclamation of Emergency and
               Press Censorship 160
Appendix II: Excerpt from 'Interim Report I'
               of the Shah Commission of Inquiry 163
Appendix III: Statutes and Amendments 181
Appendix IV: Correspondence 236

Index 241

Foreword
by Arun Jaitley

Shri J.P. Goyal, Senior Advocate, was in the forefront of the battle against the Emergency. He was an old Socialist and an ardent follower of Dr. Ram Manohar Lohia. He was ideologically committed to his belief and value system. Starting his career as an Advocate-on-Record, he finally became a designated Senior Advocate in the Supreme Court of India and had the privilege of serving as a member of the Rajya Sabha (1982–88).

Before and during the Emergency, he was not merely a witness to history but an active participant in the making of history. He was a key lawyer for Raj Narain in the famous election case against Mrs. Indira Gandhi. He had the privilege of appearing with Shri Shanti Bhushan both in the Allahabad High Court and the Supreme Court of India. He also had an opportunity to appear for many of the detenus in the *habeas corpus* case during the Emergency. There were several cases relating to the conditions of detention of the detenus with which he was associated. An effort was made during the Emergency by the government to get the Kesavananda Bharati judgement reviewed by the full court presided by the Chief Justice. As a participant in that case, he also had an opportunity to watch the legendary performance of Nani Palkhivala for one and a half days before the Full Court questioning the very need for the constitution of the Full Bench. The Bench was dissolved on day three.

Having witnessed the ups, downs and manoeuvres in all these cases, he was one who was fully competent and uniquely placed to write his memoirs and leave it for the benefit of the future generations. He used to visit the jails frequently to get in touch with the leaders amongst the political detenus. While spending his professional time on legal cases involving the performance of his public duties, he made a lot of personal sacrifices. He recorded his views before his demise but could not publish them. His daughter Ms Rama Goyal has now taken the initiative to put before the public this account of one of the active participants of the dark era, which is recorded for the benefit of history. His personal account as a public book will be a valuable addition to any library.

I wish the author and this publication all the very best.

Arun Jaitley
2, Krishna Menon Marg
New Delhi 110 011
29 June 2018

Foreword
by Meghnad Desai

This is a gem of a book, an heirloom that would have been lost except for the efforts of Rama Goyal to retrieve it from her father's files and prepare it for publication. J.P. Goyal was a Supreme Court Senior Advocate (in the lawyers' *varna* system, a top-level Brahmin). He fought for many years cases on behalf of his clients, the most famous of whom was Shri Raj Narain who has earned his place in Indian political history as the person who took the then prime minister, Indira Gandhi, to court, questioning her election in 1971. The repercussions of that case led to the declaration of the Emergency by Indira Gandhi (with the help of a pliable President) on 25 June 1975.

The bulk of the book is a detailed record dictated by Shri Goyal and gives his account of the tough and long fight that he and his lawyer colleagues waged in the Allahabad High Court and the Supreme Court of India to defend the Constitutional rights of the citizens of India from predations by an authoritarian Prime Minister. Even before the Emergency was declared, Indira Gandhi had perverted the judiciary by superseding three Supreme Court judges to promote Shri A.N. Ray as Chief Justice. Thus, the spirit of the Constitution was already violated. She had also, before the declaration of the Emergency, used her massive parliamentary majority to amend laws with retrospective effect to escape the likely consequences of her actions. (Documentary details are provided in the appendices of this book.) The Allahabad High Court decided against Indira Gandhi and declared her election void. On appeal to the Supreme Court, she won a stay order but with a caveat that pending the final judgement she could continue

to sit in Parliament and be prime minister but could not vote in Parliament. This was when she declared an Emergency despite the fact that given her party's majority in Parliament she did not need to vote.

Shri Goyal gives us a blow by blow account as an insider who fought this insidious development. He gives a brilliant account of how a determined bunch of half a dozen lawyers prevented the Supreme Court from reversing the historic 1973 Kesavananda Bharati judgement of the Supreme Court that protected a core of the Constitution against amendments. This is a rare treat, since it is an example of non-violent resistance against arbitrary power, a true *satyagraha*.

Even so, the most disturbing thing about the Emergency, as this account demonstrates, is that it was perfectly legal. The Constitution of India was drafted by the Constituent Assembly but it retained many aspects of the colonial Constitution as drafted in the Government of India Act, 1935. The apparatus of repression, including suspension of many Fundamental Rights citing danger to the security of the nation as a reason, is retained in fact from the British Raj. The declaration of an External Emergency in 1971 (war with Pakistan over Bangladesh) was hardly remarked about. The 1975 Emergency compounded the crisis by citing internal security. Neither was necessary.

The Westminster system of parliamentary democracy lacks a true separation of powers, which the American Constitution has developed to perfection. A prime minister with sufficient majority in the House of Commons can virtually do whatever s/he likes, including declaring war. As there is no written Constitution, it is convention and the Royal Prerogative of a hereditary monarch as Head of State that can halt the British prime minister in extreme circumstances, though no such need has arisen in centuries. The second chamber, the House of Lords, has no power to stop the prime minister, except to make him/her unable to prolong the life of a Parliament beyond five years.

India awoke to life without freedom, and in some cases, no life at all.

Indira Gandhi had won the election to the Lok Sabha from the Rae Bareli parliamentary constituency in 1971, soon after which an election petition was filed against her by Raj Narain, her principal opponent in that constituency, to set aside her election. Shri J.P. Goyal, my father, born in Nala village in 1926 in the then Muzaffarnagar district of Uttar Pradesh (UP), had enrolled as a lawyer at Allahabad High Court in 1952 and began practising in the Supreme Court of India in 1959, became Advocate-on-Record, and was designated as Senior Advocate in 1979 by the Supreme Court of India. He had been Raj Narain's advocate since 1960 and played a principal part in the prosecution of Raj Narain's case against Mrs. Indira Gandhi and in subsequent legal matters during the Emergency period thereafter. He played a most crucial role in the events leading up to Mrs. Indira Gandhi losing the election case filed against her in the Allahabad High Court. At one stage, pursuing the election petition had been virtually rendered futile after a perverse and seemingly motivated order of the then presiding judge in the Allahabad High Court, wherein the judge recalled his own order without any reference. It was Goyal's persistence in the Supreme Court that restored propriety in the pending case that otherwise had been rendered futile. He played a central role in ensuring that the Fundamental Rights, as enshrined in the Constitution of India, were preserved and not trampled upon by a thirteen-judge Bench wrongfully constituted by the then Chief Justice of India, A.N. Ray, presumably at the behest of Mrs. Indira Gandhi. A most crucial manoeuvre, that he was an integral part of and privy to, thwarted a diabolic design of the then Chief Justice of India to strike down the landmark 1973 Kesavananda Bharati judgement, which protected the basic features of the Constitution of India from amendments. During the Emergency period, Goyal took an active role in meeting the Opposition leaders in jail as well as those that were

'Uxbridge, UK, and did not pursue the matter with him any further, relegating it to the back of my mind. The papers thus came as a revelation to me. When I showed the papers to my brother, Rameshwar Prasad Goyal, who is a lawyer in the Supreme Court of India, he told me that our father had indeed told some people in the Supreme Court about his having written these papers. It is these papers that are now being published in the present book.

One intriguing question that comes to mind is why my father, after writing his account in 1979, did not publish these papers. I can only surmise that he was not interested in publicity as such and wrote these papers primarily to record the correct version of events while they were still fresh in his mind. Perhaps he did not publish them as he did not wish to offend his colleagues who, in his assessment, had not made the right decisions on the proper course of action to be followed in the sensitive cases leading up to and during the Emergency. Whatever may be the reason, I feel it is my duty as a citizen of this country and as Goyal's daughter to publish these papers as a matter of historical record. If some egos are hurt, then so be it.

Nearly 80–85 per cent of the current adult population in India was either born after the period with which this book is concerned or was very young (less than ten years old) when the proclamation of the Emergency was made in 1975. They may, therefore, not be familiar with the events that took place then. Others may not be well-versed in law and the various Articles and Amendments in the Constitution of India. For their benefit, I have added, in Editor's Notes at the end of each chapter and Appendices to the text, explanatory notes, references, legal citations and details of the various Articles and Amendments in the Constitution mentioned in the text, as well as excerpts from the Shah Commission Report detailing the events leading up to the proclamation of the Emergency. The unpublished 'JP Papers' and the 'Emergency Files' provided information for many of the explanatory notes. In many places in the book, Goyal is very

critical of some colleagues, judges, persons and political parties. I have retained these also as it is a matter of record in historic cases. Another caveat needs to be noted. As there are no verbatim records of the court proceedings, many of the arguments in the court have been put in first person without any loss of meaning for better readability and to give a first-hand experience to the reader. Similarly, conversations between the lawyers and judges and political leaders have at times been put in first person without any loss or additions in meaning. This book describes the theatre of events as they actually unfolded, in the words of J.P. Goyal. As mentioned above, these papers were dictated by Goyal to his typist sometime in 1979 from his recollection of the events. As this is a memoir or a personal account of events as they unfolded, I have deliberately left the language more or less unchanged to reflect Goyal's words and thoughts, including the respectful formal use of the prefixes 'Shri' and 'Smt' in addressing colleagues as well as opponents.

When the election petition of Raj Narain against Mrs. Gandhi was filed in 1971, I was an eight-year-old child. While I was then too young to understand the nuances of this case, I was aware even then of something important going on. I recall seeing the cover of files labelled 'Raj Narain versus Indira Priyadarshini Nehru Gandhi' on my father's office table and being childishly elated by my 'discovery' of the full name of Mrs. Indira Gandhi, including the name 'Priyadarshini' that I was not aware of then as it was not commonly used while referring to her. I remember the ventilator windowpanes in our residence being covered with black carbon paper to ward off any intrusive observation by the Intelligence Bureau (IB) officials who were often stationed in a jeep outside our house, which served as a residence-cum-office for my father. Some colleagues and relatives of my father who happened to be in government service during that time, especially during the Emergency period, stopped visiting us lest they come into the bad books of the government and be penalized. Such was the fear generated during the Emergency. My mother, who was then a teacher in the Government Girls' Senior Secondary School, Pandara Park, New Delhi, was under constant stress that she may be targeted by the government due to her husband being a lawyer for Raj Narain against the prime minister. Teachers of all government-aided schools, including my mother, were under severe threat of demotion unless they met the sterilization campaign targets imposed on them by the government.

I was, at the time, studying in a boarding school in Dehradun and would return to Delhi for two-month-long vacations in the summer and winter. During the summer vacation of 1974, I recall my father being under immense financial pressure, impacting his physical health and state of mind. Young children are often wont to put their parents on a pedestal and any perceived fall from that pedestal can leave a lasting impression on their minds. When leaving for my boarding school at Dehradun after that summer vacation, as I said goodbye to my father, I had the feeling that he was dying and that I would not see my father again. I was under such severe strain that about two weeks into the school term, I had a premonition that my father was dead and went to my house mistress and told her, 'I know my father is dead and I want to make a telephone call home.' Upon learning of this, my father immediately rushed to Dehradun along with my mother to meet me and pacify me that he was indeed alive. As my father has written in his papers, Chief Justice A.N. Ray, who had been brought in as Chief Justice by Mrs. Indira Gandhi by superseding three senior judges of the Supreme Court, used to dismiss cases being argued by my father, as my father had organized the All-India Convention of Lawyers protesting against the appointment of A.N. Ray as Chief Justice. This led to my father's law practice taking a hit and dwindling, and consequent financial hardships and mental tension to the family. All this happened in the backdrop of the case against Mrs. Gandhi and the rigours of the Emergency.

Arrests of Opposition leaders, including JP and Raj Narain, were made usually at night. For sometime after the imposition of the Emergency, there was apprehension that, along with the Opposition leaders, the lawyers of Raj Narain may also be arrested. Goyal reckoned this to be unlikely as then Mrs. Gandhi would have no face left to show to the world. Even though the Indian press had been muzzled by her with press censorship, the foreign press would report that she had arrested even the lawyers representing her opponent Raj Narain, who had already been arrested. This would have cast aspersions on the fairness of the trial and democracy in India. Nevertheless, at the behest of Raj Narain, who believed that Mrs. Gandhi could do anything and even arrest his lawyers, and if that were to happen it would be very difficult to prosecute his legal case against her, for some time as a precaution, Goyal began sleeping in a different place away from his residence at night, either in the houses of some friends or in his house at Neeti Bagh in New Delhi that was then under construction. I often accompanied my father in these nightly sojourns and as a child, it was exciting for me to go 'underground' with my father. While I was aware that something wrong was happening in the country, I could not understand the full extent of the damage that was sought to be done to our rights and freedoms enshrined in the Constitution and the reign of terror that was unleashed then, especially during the Emergency period.

Press censorship was imposed on 26 June 1975 after the imposition of the National Emergency. While some newspapers buckled under the pressure of censorship, some others remained defiant, prominent among the latter being *The Indian Express* and *The Statesman*. *The Indian Express* responded by leaving its lead editorial space blank in the first edition of the newspaper to be published after the imposition of the Emergency. Others tried to circumvent the censorship and to protest in novel ways, such as the cleverly worded obituary, 'D'OCracy—D.E.M., beloved husband of T. Ruth, loving father of L.I. Bertie, brother of Faith,

Hope, Justicia, expired on June 26', which appeared in the Bombay edition of *The Times of India* on 28 June 1975. As under the press censorship, it was difficult to get the full and correct news from any one newspaper, Goyal began getting a number of newspapers from different regions in the country in the hope that some newspaper, however small or regional, may have carried some important news which might have slipped past the censor's watch. Each day, around forty newspapers would arrive at our residence. These were read by men employed as newsreaders by my father. Their task would be to read the newspapers and mark out any important news to be told to my father or for him to read later on. As a child, I remember thinking that these newsreaders had the best job in the world—to read newspapers, thus acquiring knowledge, and get paid for it!

Unwittingly, I became a witness to history being made. Knowing the importance of the case and the events as they unfolded, my father used to often take me along with him wherever he could so that I could become aware of the happenings in the country. He arranged for me to be present in the Supreme Court of India on 23–24 June 1975 when the Indira Nehru Gandhi versus Raj Narain case was heard in the court of Justice V.R. Krishna Iyer, whose judgement on 24 June 1975 was a catalyst for the imposition of the Emergency on the night of 25–26 June 1975. I witnessed the crowd of people and the press that had gathered in the Supreme Court to hear the judgement that day. I recall my father telling other lawyers about his conversation with N.A. Palkhivala in the corridor outside Justice Krishna Iyer's chambers while waiting to hear his judgement. The Emergency was imposed the next day, after which Palkhivala immediately resigned from being a counsel for Mrs. Gandhi.

In light of the above, it is sad that the Supreme Court of India did not give my father, Shri J.P. Goyal, the respect of having a Full Court Condolence Reference for him after his demise on 11 September 2013, even though he had been designated as

Senior Advocate by the Supreme Court of India in 1979 and, as will be apparent upon reading this book, worked very hard to uphold the rule of law and democracy and the independence of the judiciary. M.N. Krishnamani, the President of the Supreme Court Bar Association (SCBA) at the time of my father's demise, was then away in the United States of America (USA), and had informed some Supreme Court lawyers by telephone that there would be a Full Court Reference for my father. A few months after my father's demise, new office bearers of the SCBA, with P.H. Parekh as the new President, were elected. There might have been some laxity during this changeover in sending the required information for the Full Court Reference to the Supreme Court judges. It seems that the office bearers of the SCBA initially delayed in sending the required information to the judges and then later preferred to not send it at all, so that the initial delay itself was not to be noticed by the judges who would then not question the office bearers about the delay. As a result, my father was denied a Full Court Reference in the Supreme Court of India. Perhaps there may be still time to rectify this.

The Emergency of 1975–77 is the darkest chapter in recent Indian history, especially in the post-Independence period. It is a history that needs to be told and retold, so that we, the people of India, remember how close the nation had come to losing its precious democracy, as we resolve to strengthen and value democracy in India.

Rama Goyal
New Delhi
19 April 2019

Acknowledgements

I must thank a friend, who wishes to remain unnamed, for encouraging me to get my father Shri J.P. Goyal's papers published and for providing many valuable suggestions. Without his encouragement and support, this publication may not have been possible. M.G. Devasahayam, who was the District Magistrate and the Inspector General of Prisons in the Union Territory of Chandigarh during the period of Jayaprakash Narayan's detention in Chandigarh during the Emergency, provided some very helpful clarifications and tips and gave permission to quote excerpts from his book *JP in Jail: An Uncensored Account* (2006). Dr. N.M. Ghatate, Senior Advocate, Supreme Court of India, provided some very interesting anecdotes and gave permission to quote excerpts from his book *Emergency, Constitution and Democracy: The Indian Experience* (2011). Neera Chhabra, Chief Librarian, and V. Arunachalam, Librarian, in the Judges' Library, Supreme Court of India, provided valuable assistance in locating relevant copies of the *All India Reporter* (AIR) for cross-checking case citations. Anju Gagneja, Chief Librarian, Mazhar Khan, Senior Assistant Librarian, and Dipender Singh Sajwan, Assistant Librarian, in the Legislature Cell, Supreme Court of India, were very helpful in locating relevant Government *Gazettes* for cross-checking various government orders. At the National Archives of India, archivists Udey Shankar and Hitendra Kumar and all other staff were very helpful and swiftly located files and books related to the Emergency and Parliamentary Debates. The Indira Gandhi National Centre for Arts (IGNCA) provided access to the digital files named 'JP Papers', which were given to them by the Patna-based Braj Kishore Memorial Institute, founded by Jayaprakash

Narayan (JP) and Dr. Rajendra Prasad. I would especially like to thank Professor B.B. Mandal, the Secretary of the Braj Kishore Memorial Institute, for promptly granting me permission to quote from the 'JP Papers', and for his enthusiastic response to the publication of these memoirs. The National Archives of India also granted permission to quote from the Emergency Files and to print the Proclamation of Emergency on 25 June 1975 and other relevant material. Clippings from newspapers were sourced from the Nehru Memorial Museum and Library (NMML) in New Delhi. Thanks are due to all of the above organizations and people.

I would like to thank Jeffrey Hyland in the Commonwealth Parliamentary Association (CPA) Headquarters Secretariat in London for his prompt assistance in sourcing photographs from the CPA Isle of Man branch and for obtaining permission for me to print them in this book. Thanks are due to the CPA Isle of Man branch for granting me permission to do so. I must also thank Rupa Publications for publishing this book.

Needless to say, none of the above-mentioned persons and organizations are responsible for anything written in this book. Above all, I thank my parents, late Shri J.P. Goyal and late Shrimati Mithlesh Kumari Goyal, for whom service to the nation was above all. Fortunately, my father took out time from his busy law practice to write these memoirs, for which I am very grateful.

Abbreviations and Acronyms

ADM	Additional district magistrate
AIIMS	All India Institute of Medical Sciences
AIR	*All India Reporter*
Asstt.	Assistant
BLD	Bharatiya Lok Dal
c/o	care of
CBI	Central Bureau of Investigation
CIA	Central Intelligence Agency
CID	Crime Investigation Department
Congress (O)	Indian National Congress (Organization)
Congress (R)	Indian National Congress (Requisitionists)
CPC	Civil Procedure Code
CPI	Communist Party of India
CPI (M)	Communist Party of India (Marxist)
CrPC	Code of Criminal Procedure
CWC	Congress Working Committee
DC	District Commissioner
DIG	Deputy Inspector of Police
DISIR	Defence and Internal Security of India Rules
Distt	District
DLT	*Delhi Law Times*
DM	District magistrate
DMK	Dravida Munnetra Kazhagam
DSP	Deputy Superintendent of Police
EM	Executive Magistrate
GOI	Government of India
IAF	Indian Air Force
IAS	Indian Administrative Service

IB	Intelligence Bureau
IGP	Inspector General of Police
IIC	India International Centre
ILR	*Indian Law Reports*
Ins.	Inserted
JP	Jayaprakash Narayan
LLB	Bachelor of Laws
MISA	Maintenance of Internal Security Act, 1971
MLA	Member of the Legislative Assembly
MP	Member of Parliament
OSD	officer on special duty
PGIMER	Postgraduate Institute of Medical Education and Research
RLR	*Rajasthan Law Reporter*
SCBA	Supreme Court Bar Association
SCC	*Supreme Court Cases*
SCR	*Supreme Court Reporter*
Sd/-	Signed
SLP	special leave application
Smt	Shrimati
SP	Superintendent of Police
Subs.	Substituted
Supdt.	Superintendent
UK	United Kingdom
UP	Uttar Pradesh
USA	United States of America
VIP	Very Important Person
Vs/vs	Versus/versus
w.e.f.	with effect from

1
Why This Book?

Shri Lal Bahadur Shastri's death on 11 January 1966 was a very unfortunate event in the history of India.[1] He was a person who truly represented the common man of India. In my view, an even more unfortunate event in the history of India was the installation of Smt Indira Gandhi as the prime minister of India after Shri Lal Bahadur Shastri's demise. The history of India over the last several hundred years has been witness to many unfortunate events that led to misrule in the country. It would be fair to say that Indians themselves were responsible for the imposition and continuation of oppressive foreign rule in India. This was made possible because of internal strife and hatred among Indians towards each other.[2] A similar thing happened on the death of Shri Lal Bahadur Shastri. There was internal strife in the ruling Congress party, ultimately leading to the then president of the Congress party, Shri K. Kamaraj, and his colleagues installing Smt Indira Gandhi as the prime minister, favouring her over Shri Morarji Desai, who had the rightful claim, not only due to his being a senior member of the party but also because of his ability.

Another unfortunate aspect for the country was that after Independence in 1947, the Opposition in this country had an almost nil presence in Parliament, even though the combined Opposition parties had got the mandate from the majority of voters. The Opposition was a divided house and the Congress party, which represented only a minority of voters, ruled on account of the fact that the various political parties in the Opposition could not come to an understanding and work together. The highest percentage of votes in the Lok Sabha elections obtained by the Congress party, even in Jawaharlal Nehru's time, was about 48 per cent of the total votes polled.[3] Thus, more than 50 per cent people of this country who went to the polls had voted against the Congress party.

Towards the end of 1970, Smt Indira Gandhi gave the call of '*garibi hatao*' (remove poverty) and thought that she had convinced people that she would indeed remove poverty. Even though the Lok Sabha election was due in February 1972, nevertheless, without any rhyme or reason, she dissolved the Lok Sabha on 27 December 1970 and declared that General Elections would be held in February 1971, one year ahead of time. She used lofty words without fulfilling any word of it. This shows that Smt Indira Gandhi was not for maintaining democratic institutions and held elections much before the stipulated time when people were under a delusion, in order to come to power again for her own benefit and for the benefit of her party. The majority of the people in this country are hero-worshippers and believed that Nehru's daughter would deliver the goods and remove poverty. In the General Elections of 1971, the Congress party was returned to the Lok Sabha with a huge majority.[4] The Opposition was virtually routed. Here again, it must be pointed out that the Congress party got only 43.68 per cent of the total votes polled. Thus, even in the 1971 General Election with the so-called 'Indira wave', the Congress party could not secure even half of the votes polled.

Smt Indira Gandhi used to say that she had the will of the people behind her. Vast funds for the Congress party were collected from companies and wealthy individuals under implied threat or coercion.[5] Many people gave money to the party under the impression that the Congress party would continue to rule for all times to come and that it was the only way of getting advantage out of the Congress party government. Defections from the Opposition were encouraged, with the result that some important members of the Opposition joined the Congress party. Only hardliners among the leaders and workers of the Opposition did not do so. In my judgement, the country was ruled by the Congress party during this period more with a view to benefit its party members, who made their own money without doing anything.[6] Most of the members of the Congress party in this country after Independence, in my view, have been self-seekers and promoters.[7] At present, things are coming out revealing that those who were once at the helm of affairs made money out of funds of the public for their own benefit and devoured the money of the public. In all religious faiths, the saying is that if the 'king' himself is corrupt and immoral, his administration cannot possibly be good or proper.

During Indira Gandhi's regime of over eleven years from February 1966 onwards till she was ousted in March 1977, it was apparent that she wanted to remain in power by hook or by crook. Dr. Ram Manohar Lohia,[8] one of the greatest leaders that this country has produced and with whom I was closely associated since 1960 onwards till his demise in 1967, used to say that the Nehru family members would work under the garb of democracy till it suited them and when it did not, they would discard it. At that time, people did not believe him and many people even laughed at his insinuations. But I see that his words have come true.

Much can be said about the working of the government under Smt Indira Gandhi. A number of books have been written by various authors regarding the Emergency, the excesses committed thereunder, and related matters.[9] However, I feel that certain essential aspects have not been touched upon in these books. One such book which I will mention is titled *The Case That Shook India*, written by Prashant Bhushan, the son of Shri Shanti Bhushan, the Union minister for law and justice in the Morarji Desai government. I am sorry to say that some of the things have not been correctly or fully mentioned therein. I can say that I felt the necessity of writing this book after the said book was written. However, in my book, I will focus on some selective aspects related to the legal case leading up to the imposition of the Emergency in 1975, and thereafter. It is my endeavour in writing the present book to place before the public certain facts that I have personally known and experienced, have knowledge of, and was privy to.

EDITOR'S NOTES

1   This was also the view of Nani A. Palkhivala, who wrote: 'The rot in public life began after the death of Lal Bahadur Shastri and has been increasing at a galloping rate.' N.A. Palkhivala, *We the Nation: The Lost Decades*, New Delhi: UBS Publishers Distributors Ltd, 1994, p. 219.

2   Dr. Bhimrao Ramji Ambedkar, chairman of the Drafting Committee of the Indian Constitution, appointed by the Constituent Assembly, stated in his last speech to the Constituent Assembly on 25 November 1949: 'On 26th January 1950, India will be an independent country (*Cheers*). What would happen to her independence? Will she maintain her independence or will she lose it again? This is the first thought that comes to my mind. It is not that India was never an independent country. The point is that she once lost the independence she had. Will she lose it a second time? It is this thought which makes me most anxious for the future. What perturbs me greatly is the fact that not only India has once before lost her independence, but she lost it by the infidelity and treachery of some of her own people. In the invasion of Sindh by Mahommed-Bin-Kasim, the military commanders of King Dahar accepted bribes from the agents of Mahommed-Bin-Kasim and refused to fight on the side of their King. It was Jaichand who invited Mahommed Gohri to invade India and fight against Prithvi Raj and promised him the help of himself and the Solanki Kings. When Shivaji

was fighting for the liberation of Hindus, the other Maratha noblemen and the Rajput Kings were fighting the battle on the side of Moghul Emperors. When the British were trying to destroy the Sikh Rulers, Gulab Singh, their principal commander sat silent and did not help to save the Sikh Kingdom. In 1857, when a large part of India had declared a war of independence against the British, the Sikhs stood and watched the event as silent spectators. Will history repeat itself? It is this thought which fills me with anxiety.' See 'Constituent Assembly of India Debates (Proceedings)—Vol. XI', Friday, 25 November 1949, available at Lok Sabha, Parliament of India website http://164.100.47.194/Loksabha/Debates/cadebatefiles/C25111949.html, accessed 20 June 2018.

3 In the General Elections of 1951–52, the first Lok Sabha elections after Independence in August 1947, the Indian National Congress party, under the leadership of Jawaharlal Nehru, got 44.99 per cent of the valid votes polled, winning 364 seats out of 489 seats. The Socialist Party got the second highest number of votes at 10.59 per cent of the valid votes cast but could win only twelve seats. The Communist Party of India (CPI) won the second highest number of seats with sixteen seats, but with only 3.29 per cent of the valid votes polled. In the General Elections held in 1957 to the Second Lok Sabha (1957–62), the Indian National Congress party got 47.78 per cent of the total valid votes polled, and in the General Elections held in 1962 to the Third Lok Sabha (1962–67), it got 44.72 per cent of the valid votes polled. The Fourth Lok Sabha elections held in 1967 saw the Indian National Congress party get 40.78 per cent of the total valid votes polled. In 1969, there was a split in the Indian National Congress party into two parts, namely the Indian National Congress (Requisitionists) or Congress (R), which sided with Indira Gandhi, and the Indian National Congress (Organisation) or Congress (O) led by K. Kamaraj. In the elections held in 1971, the Indian National Congress (R) party polled 43.68 per cent

of the valid votes cast while it got 34.52 per cent of the valid votes cast in the 1977 elections. Source: 'Election Results—Full Statistical Reports', Election Commission of India, available at http://eci.nic.in/eci_main1/ElectionStatistics.aspx, accessed 18 April 2018.

4   Polling for the General Elections took place in March 1971. The Indian National Congress (R) won 352 seats out of elections to 518 constituencies. The Communist Party (Marxist) won the second highest number of seats, with only twenty-five seats. The 'Grand Alliance' of a few parties—the Indian National Congress (Organisation), Bharatiya Jana Sangh, Praja Socialist Party, Swatantra Party and Samyukta Socialist Party—could together win only fifty-one seats. [Source: 'Statistical Report on General Elections, 1971' to the Fifth Lok Sabha, Vol. I (National and State Abstracts and Detailed Results), Election Commission of India, New Delhi, available at http://eci.nic.in/eci_main/StatisticalReports/LS_1971/Vol_I_LS71.pdf, accessed 27 May 2018.] Speaking in the Rajya Sabha on 21 July 1975, Home Minister K. Brahmananda Reddy, referring to the 1971 elections, stated '…at the time of the election and before the election, what was known then and even now also as the Grand Alliance of some parties who had no common ideology or programme had been formed to defeat the Congress party at the polls. And you saw the result. These parties thought that elections mean only a political game or even a manoeuvre of combining some votes or splitting some votes. Therefore, certain parties which had combined into a grand alliance were dazed and in fact even stunned at the result of the elections.' See 'Parliamentary Debates Rajya Sabha, Official Report', No. 1, 21 July 1975, pp. 47–48, in *Rajya Sabha Debates*, Vol. 93, Nos. 1–16, 1975, Rajya Sabha Secretariat, New Delhi.

5   That vast amounts of funds were collected under coercion or extortion by the Congress party leaders has been widely commented upon. The 'permit–licence–quota Raj' was used to

procure vast funds by for the party. Stanley A. Kochanek writes: '...the period after 1969 was characterized by one member of the Indian Parliament as the era of "briefcase politics," a phrase used to describe the transfer of vast amounts of black money in the form of cash into the coffers of the Congress party.' See, Stanley A. Kochanek, 'Briefcase Politics in India: Congress party and the business elite', *Asian Survey*, Vol. 27, No. 12, December 1987, pp. 1278–1301, p. 1290. C.S. Pandit writes: 'Often representatives of trade and industry were called up by him (L.N. Mishra, foreign trade minister) to Delhi and asked to produce specified amounts. Those who declined were threatened with possible raids by people of the Revenue Intelligence and Enforcement Directorate, which are now operating under the Cabinet Secretariat. In Bombay financial circles stories started circulating of the amounts secured by the foreign trade minister under such threats. Others who came forward willingly with whatever was asked for, received concessions beyond their imagination to expand their business and amass further resources. A number of new stars were born on the industrial firmament of India during this time.' See, C.S. Pandit, *End of an Era*, New Delhi: Allied Publishers Pvt Ltd, 1977, p. 70. Indira Gandhi's biographer Krishan Bhatia writes that donations had become more like extortions: 'The money that Indira's senior Cabinet colleagues collected for the parliamentary elections in 1971 and state elections the following year allegedly amounted to tens of millions of rupees and usually changed hands on the basis of a clear *quid pro quo*. At times ministers deliberately talked publicly about non-existent government plans to nationalize or regulate a particular industry or trade with the intention of creating nervousness among the people concerned. This naturally encouraged the flow of contributions, especially as the apparent threat ceased once the interest concerned had paid up.' See, Krishan Bhatia, *Indira: A Biography of Prime Minister Gandhi*, London: Angus and Robertson, 1974, p. 267.

6. On Sanjay Gandhi's coterie of supporters, Coomi Kapoor writes, '...they were committed not to any ideology but to self-advancement.' See, Coomi Kapoor, *The Emergency: A Personal History*, New Delhi, Penguin Books India, 2015, p. 218.
7. Writing about Sanjay Gandhi's pet project, Maruti, Coomi Kapoor states, 'The tale of Maruti is replete with examples of extortion, string-pulling to bend rules, and blackmail.' See, Coomi Kapoor, *The Emergency: A Personal History*, New Delhi, Penguin Books India, 2015, p. 212.
8. Dr. Ram Manohar Lohia was a frequent visitor to Shri J.P. Goyal's law chambers in the Supreme Court of India. Sushil Jain, a lawyer colleague of Shri J.P. Goyal, narrated to the editor that on one such occasion, Dr. Ram Manohar Lohia discussed how to use parliamentary language to say not-so-complimentary or derogatory things in Parliament.
9. K.R. Malkani, *The Midnight Knock*, New Delhi, Vikas Publishing House, 1978; Vinod Mehta, *The Sanjay Story*, New Delhi: Jaico Publishers, 1978; Kuldip Nayyar, *The Judgement*, New Delhi: Konark Publishers, 1977; Uma Vasudev, *Two Faces of Indira Gandhi*, New Delhi: Vikas Publishing House, 1977; Janardana Thakur, *All the Prime Minister's Men*, New Delhi: Vikas Publishing House, 1977; Prashant Bhushan, *The Case That Shook India*, New Delhi: Bell Books, 1978; Soli J. Sorabjee, *The Emergency, Censorship and the Press in India, 1975–77*, New Delhi: Central News Agency (Pvt) Ltd, 1977.

2
Rescuing Raj Narain's Election Petition

Smt Indira Gandhi was a candidate of the Indian National Congress (R) in the 1971 Lok Sabha elections for the Rae Bareli constituency. Shri Raj Narain of the Samyukta Socialist Party was her main opponent in this election. Mrs. Indira Gandhi won the election. I happened to be a counsel for Shri Raj Narain since 1960 in his legal matters in all forums, including those in the Supreme Court. I first appeared for Shri Raj Narain before the Chief Election Commissioner of India in a petition filed by him under Articles 191 and 192 of the Constitution against Shri Kamalapati Tripathi. Since then, I have had the privilege of being Shri Raj Narain's lawyer and a man who has always been consulted by him in legal matters.

After the 1971 elections, Shri Raj Narain consulted me regarding the filing of an election petition against Smt Indira Gandhi. The draft of an election petition was prepared by Shri B. Solomon, an advocate of the party[1] from Lucknow, on Shri Raj Narain's behalf and this draft was shown to me. Shri Raj Narain wanted me to handle this case and file the case at Allahabad. I expressed my inability to do so as it was very difficult for me to go from Delhi to Allahabad on all the dates for hearing that would come up in the case. I suggested that it would be better if a local advocate at Allahabad were to be engaged so that the case may not lapse in default due to non-prosecution. I also told him that Shri R.C. Srivastava, a lawyer who had been consistently doing cases for the Opposition, was already there in Allahabad and if he wanted a senior lawyer, Shri Shanti Bhushan may be engaged as he was a lawyer of the Congress (O) and also a good lawyer. I suggested the name of Shri Shanti Bhushan, as Shri S.C. Khare, who was at one time the advocate handling most cases for the Opposition, had by that time joined the Congress party. Shri S.N. Kacker, another leading advocate of the Allahabad High Court, was the Advocate General of Uttar Pradesh (UP) at that time. Shri Raj Narain told me that he had no money to pay Shri Shanti Bhushan's fees. I told Shri Raj Narain that I could not ask another advocate not to charge fees but I hoped that when an approach would be made to Shri Shanti Bhushan, he would not charge any fees. Shri Raj Narain then approached Shri C.B. Gupta, former chief minister of Uttar Pradesh, who asked Shri Shanti Bhushan to do the case free of charge. In this way, Shri Shanti Bhushan was introduced in the case and Shri R.C. Srivastava was chosen to assist as the junior advocate in the case.

Shri Raj Narain, from time to time, used to keep me informed about the progress of the case at Allahabad. The election petition was listed before Justice W. Broome in the Allahabad High Court.[2] On behalf of Shri Raj Narain, an application was made for interrogatories, requiring Smt Indira Gandhi to answer certain questions on oath by way of affidavits.[3] The said application was argued in the Allahabad High Court. Various objections were advanced on her behalf that interrogatories should not be issued in election matters. However, Justice Broome rejected those objections and directed Smt Indira Gandhi to reply to certain interrogatories regarding Shri Yashpal Kapur, her election agent, who was, at one time, her secretary in the government, and other matters.[4] Against the order of Justice Broome, Smt Indira Gandhi filed a special leave petition (SLP) in the Supreme Court.[5] I had filed a caveat on behalf of Raj Narain and opposed the SLP and the application for stay.[6] Special leave to appeal was granted to Smt Indira Gandhi but I objected to the stay being granted to her.

At that time, the Chief Justice of India had formed various Benches to hear different categories of cases. For example, there was an Election Bench to hear election appeals, a Labour bench to hear labour appeals, and a Tax Bench to hear tax cases. The appeal came up for hearing before the Election Bench, which was presided over by Justice K.S. Hegde and also comprised Justice A.N. Grover and Justice H.R. Khanna. Arguments were heard for about one and a half days. Shri C.K. Daphtary, counsel for Smt Indira Gandhi, wanted to place certain rulings from cases in England that in election cases, interrogatories could not be issued. I placed reliance on a ruling that I had discovered in which the Supreme Court had held that the Civil Procedure Code (CPC) was applicable to election cases, and as interrogatories were also part of the CPC, there was no reason as to why interrogatories could not be issued in election cases, unless it was barred by the Legislature. As there was no such bar, the court issued interrogatories. The learned judges were against the contentions of Shri Daphtary and concurred with me. Shri Daphtary insisted that she should not be asked to give replies to the interrogatories. I argued that it was ridiculous that a prime minister who claimed to represent a country as vast as India should say to the court that she would not answer certain questions merely because they went against her. The learned judges were apparently impressed and ordered that Smt Indira Gandhi would have to answer the interrogatories but they would be kept in a sealed cover during the pendency of the appeal in the Supreme Court.[7] Justice Hegde incidentally suggested to Shri Daphtary that it would be in the interest of his client if the appeal was withdrawn rather than it be dismissed on merits.[8] A fortnight's time was taken by Shri Daphtary to consult Smt Indira Gandhi who, at that time, had gone to the United States of America (USA). The appeal was listed again for hearing after two weeks and it was withdrawn. The result was that the order of Justice Broome, issuing interrogatories to Smt Indira Gandhi, was confirmed by the Supreme Court, or in other words, became final.[9]

About a month thereafter, it was surprising that one day the same Justice Broome, who had given an elaborate judgement in favour of Shri Raj Narain and against Smt Indira Gandhi, on his own motion,[10] one day in court, when there was no occasion for it, told Shri Shanti Bhushan that paragraph 5 of the election petition was vague, even though the written statement on behalf of Smt Indira Gandhi had already been filed and issues had already been settled and framed without any objections.[11] The advocates for Shri Raj Narain were surprised and contended that paragraph 5 was not vague. Shri Shanti Bhushan said that if it was indeed vague, an application for amendment would be made, and it was made the same day. Justice Broome then passed three orders.[12] He dismissed the application for amendment, holding that it was belated. He struck off some of the important interrogatories that he had already issued to Smt Indira Gandhi, regarding Shri Yashpal Kapur and other matters, and passed an order holding that Shri Yashpal Kapur ceased to be a government servant effective from 14 January 1971 after he had tendered his resignation on 13 January 1971 from the office he had been holding, even though his resignation was accepted by the President of India on 25 January 1971. Shri Yashpal Kapur became Smt Indira Gandhi's election agent on 1 February 1971, and when she went to Rae Bareli to file her nomination papers on the same day, he also sat on the dais from which she made a public speech. Shri Yashpal Kapur had been in the Prime Minister's Secretariat since 1966, first as her officer on special duty (OSD) and later as her political advisor. Earlier also, in the General Election of 1967, he had resigned from government service just before the election and became Smt Indira Gandhi's election agent. After the election, he was again reinstated in his post. It was apparent that this time also, in the General Election of 1971, this camouflage and subterfuge was going to be done, but as Shri Raj Narain had filed the election petition after the election, Shri Yashpal Kapur was not reinstated immediately after the election but instead, later on in 1972, he was made a member of the Rajya Sabha from UP.

CHALLENGING THE ORDERS

After these three orders were passed by Justice Broome against Shri Raj Narain and in favour of Smt Indira Gandhi, Shri Raj Narain's election petition had almost become dead and Shri Shanti Bhushan said there was nothing left in the case now. The only thing left to do was to sign the order of the dismissal of the petition. When Shri R.C. Srivastava suggested that Shri Raj Narain should go in appeal to the Supreme Court against these three orders, Shri Shanti Bhushan had differences with him and said that there was no use of going to the Supreme Court and let the election petition be dismissed finally and only thereafter a regular appeal may be filed in the Supreme Court by Shri Raj Narain. However, Shri R.C. Srivastava and Shri Raj Narain did not agree with Shri Shanti Bhushan. Shri Raj Narain requested Shri Shanti Bhushan to get the appeal filed in the Supreme Court and to argue the matter there. Shri Shanti Bhushan said that there will be nothing achieved in the Supreme Court and the Supreme Court will not do anything. However, the papers of the case were given to me sometime towards the end of November 1971 for filing any challenge to the orders in the Supreme Court. I drafted three SLPs with stay applications.

Soon thereafter, Pakistan attacked Indian Air Force stations on 3 December 1971, thus dragging India into war with its neighbour. After Bangladesh was formed as a result of this war with Pakistan,[13] I suggested to Shri Raj Narain that as something had been achieved by the formation of Bangladesh and bifurcation of Pakistan, it would be in the fitness of things to withdraw the election petition against Smt Indira Gandhi. Shri Raj Narain told me that Shri Atal Bihari Vajpayee was also of the same view and that he would consult his colleagues and let me know. By that time, an SLP had not yet been filed against the aforesaid three orders of Justice Broome.

It was in the month of January 1972 that Shri Raj Narain told me that he had received information from an authentic source that foul play had been played by Smt Indira Gandhi and she had approached the brother of Justice Broome in England and had asked him to influence his brother to pass an order in her favour. It was also told to me that Justice V. Bhargava, a retired judge of the Supreme Court, was made the chairman of the Sugar Industry Enquiry Commission by Smt Indira Gandhi, joining it on 16 September 1971, and in turn he was asked to go to Allahabad and persuade Justice Broome to decide the matter in favour of Smt Indira Gandhi and against Shri Raj Narain. Justice Broome was considered to be a very independent judge with an impeccable reputation. I had happened to appear before him when he was district judge in Meerut and again in the Allahabad High Court. Under these circumstances, it was difficult for me to believe what was being conveyed to me. However, taking into consideration the facts as they have been stated above—that Justice Broome struck off the same interrogatories that had already been almost confirmed by the Supreme Court, in respect of which the SLP had been withdrawn by Indira Gandhi and an elaborate judgement had been given by Justice Broome, and even though it was not pointed out on behalf of the other side by means of an application that paragraph 5 of the election petition was vague, and even though issues had already been settled and framed—it did not appear reasonable as to why a judge without any rhyme or reason would reopen an issue for which there was no occasion. Man may commit errors and he may show his weakness. I do not say anything against Justice Broome but I have been agitated about Justice Broome's conduct in the case as not being above board.

When Shri Raj Narain told me about the above-mentioned facts, I was very agitated, and said that we should file an SLP in the Supreme Court and that if Smt Indira Gandhi had tried to interfere with the working of the judiciary, it was my duty as a lawyer to ensure that such mischief was undone. Three SLPs were then filed along with the stay applications. Special leave to appeal was granted to us and ultimately, the three appeals came up for hearing before a Bench consisting of Justice K.S. Hegde, Justice Jaganmohan Reddy and Justice K.K. Mathew. Arguments went on for several days. Shri C.K. Daphtary and Shri S.C. Khare were the main counsels on Indira Gandhi's side, while Shri S.V. Gupte, who later became the Attorney General of India,[14] and I were the counsels on Shri Raj Narain's side along with Shri R.C. Srivastava, Shri S.S. Khanduja and other lawyers. Ultimately, our appeals were allowed and the Supreme Court granted an interim stay order. This is how the case was restored again and this is how Shri Shanti Bhushan got the opportunity of arguing the election petition, as otherwise, according to him, there was nothing left in the case.

The Supreme Court held that paragraph 5 of the election petition of Shri Raj Narain was not vague. Interrogatories regarding Shri Yashpal Kapur and other important matters that had been struck off by Justice Broome were restored by the Supreme Court. We insisted that Justice Broome's observation that Shri Yashpal Kapur ceased to be a government servant as soon as he made the application for his resignation should also be set aside. Otherwise, we would be in difficulty in the High Court. We relied on two judgements of the Supreme Court, namely in the case of *Raj Kumar vs Union of India*[15] and in the case of *State of Punjab vs Amar Singh Harika*.[16] The court agreed with us and held that Shri Yashpal Kapur continued to be a government servant till his resignation was accepted by the President of India on 25 January 1971, and the view taken by the Allahabad High Court was incorrect. We also argued that the order of the President of India accepting Shri Yashpal Kapur's resignation was published in the *Government Gazette* on 6 February 1971 and the matter should be looked into in light of the election law, as the general public would understand that Shri Yashpal Kapur ceased to be a public servant only on 6 February 1971 when it was published in the *Government Gazette*. The Supreme Court said in its judgement on 15 March 1972 that this aspect of the matter would be gone into by the Allahabad High Court.[17] At that time, no one in the country realized the importance of the judgement of the Supreme Court as it was an interlocutory stage. I, however, was convinced that now the case would be decided against Smt Indira Gandhi as the Allahabad High Court was bound by the observations of the Supreme Court. The said judgement of the Supreme Court is reported in 1972 AIR 1302, 1972 SCR (3) 841 (*Raj Narain vs Smt Indira Nehru Gandhi and Anr*).

It is interesting that regarding the two stages when the cases came up to the Supreme Court and Shri Raj Narain won and I appeared and Shri Shanti Bhushan did not appear, there is no mention of this fact in Shri Prashant Bhushan's book, *The Case That Shook India* (1978), lest his father Shri Shanti Bhushan's image be diminished. On pp. 11–12, regarding the interrogatories, Shri Prashant Bhushan has mentioned the following: 'In the Supreme Court, the case went before Justices Hegde, Khanna and Vaidyalingam. After some arguments were heard by the bench on this matter, the appeal was withdrawn by Khare on the advice of the bench.' Similarly, on pp. 14–15, Shri Prashant Bhushan has given a special liberal treatment to the three appeals that were filed by Shri Raj Narain in the Supreme Court and which were allowed, and on account of that order only the case was sent back to the High Court and Shri Shanti Bhushan had an opportunity of arguing the case before Justice J.M.L. Sinha. No mention of advocates' names as to who appeared on Shri Raj Narain's side and who appeared on the side of Smt Indira Gandhi has been made. Whereas throughout the book on almost each page, Shri Prashant Bhushan has given the name of his father and tried to build up his image as a big lawyer. I may inform Shri Prashant Bhushan that there were stages in the case where only the so-called junior lawyers have succeeded. It is not incidental that the so-called junior lawyers who won the case at a very crucial stage have even their names omitted in the book. The junior lawyers do not bother for their publicity. However, the publicity in Shri Prashant Bhushan's book is intended to build up the image of his father Shri Shanti Bhushan and nothing else, which should not be done at the cost of others. It pained me very much that Prashant Bhushan has degraded all the lawyers who appeared with Shri Shanti Bhushan and has tried to build up the image of his father Shanti Bhushan. Shri Prashant Bhushan is a young man who has just passed LLB and he might be about twenty-one to twenty-two years of age at the time of this writing. In 1971, when the case was started at Allahabad, he might have been only thirteen to fourteen years of age. I do not understand how this minor boy was so vigilant at every stage that he was listening to the talks of Shri Raj Narain and Shri Shanti Bhushan with so much attention. I do not dispute the right of a person, whether minor or major, to write a book, but it can very well be presumed that the various matters that Shri Prashant Bhushan has mentioned in the book must have been told to him by Shri Shanti Bhushan, from whom he must have collected much information. At a number of places in the above-mentioned book, allegedly written by Shri Prashant Bhushan, it is stated that during the case Shri Shanti Bhushan felt like this and that etc.; it cannot be done unless information was elicited from Shri Shanti Bhushan extensively on various matters. In chapter 2, titled 'The Petition', it has been mentioned that after 'some junior lawyer had done the initial drafting of the petition, Shri Raj Narain took the draft' to Shri Shanti Bhushan on 22 April 1971 (p. 7). There is no mention of the name of the lawyer who had done the initial drafting. An impression has been created in that chapter that the drafting of the junior lawyers was not proper and it was only Shri Shanti Bhushan who put the most important paragraphs in that petition. This is nothing but the image building of Shri Shanti Bhushan and denigration of the so-called junior lawyers who had worked so hard in the case. In chapter 2, titled 'The Petition', Shri Prashant Bhushan has stated that to Shri Shanti Bhushan, the petition seemed to be more of a channel of propaganda than an election petition. An impression has been given in that chapter as if Shri Raj Narain was filing the election petition only as a propaganda stunt. The relevant passage from the book (p. 8) is as follows: 'To Bhushan the petition seemed to be more of a vehicle for propaganda than an election petition. He also did not believe the first allegation, which was the main charge in the petition. So he told Raj Narain that he would only argue the case if it was treated as a serious election petition and not as a propaganda stunt.' To my mind, this is nothing but denigration of Shri Raj Narain, the election petitioner in the case.

INSIDE THE BLUE BOOK

After the Supreme Court judgement, the matter was reopened in the Allahabad High Court. In the meantime, Justice Broome had retired in March 1972 and Justice K.N. Srivastava ultimately took over the case. There were certain documents that the petitioner Raj Narain wanted to exhibit, and in respect of which the government took the plea of special privilege to prevent him from doing so.[18] One of these documents was known as the 'Blue Book', entitled 'Rules and Instructions for the Protection of the Prime Minister When on Tour or Travel'. During the time of Shri Jawaharlal Nehru and Shri Lal Bahadur Shastri as prime ministers, the instructions in this Blue Book were that when the prime minister went on tour in any state, the state government concerned would provide protection for the prime minister's speeches and arrange the prime minister's meetings at the state government's own expense, excluding election meetings. Thus, the expenses incurred on election meetings were not to be incurred from the state exchequer. However, for ensuring the safety of the prime minister, the state government was to make arrangements for rostrum, lights, seating arrangements, etc., and the Congress party was asked to pay the expenses incurred thereon. In the year

1969, when Smt Indira Gandhi was the prime minister, she got the said instructions changed and the word 'except' was changed into the word 'including'.

Section 71(6) of the Blue Book originally read as follows:

> It has been noticed that the rostrum arrangements are not always properly made because the hosts are sometimes unable to bear the cost. As the Prime Minister's security is the concern of the State, all arrangements for putting up the rostrum and barriers at the meeting place will be borne by the State whatever may be the occasion for which the public meeting is called, *except* election meetings. (emphasis added)

Smt Indira Gandhi got it amended on 19 November 1969 to the following:

> It has been noticed that the rostrum arrangements are not always properly made because the hosts are sometimes unable to bear that cost. As the security of the Prime Minister is the concern of the State, all arrangements for putting up the rostrum, the barriers etc. at the meeting place *including* that of an election meeting will have to be made by the State Government concerned. (emphasis added)

The state governments thus had to spend huge sums of money for the election meetings of the prime minister that were not government functions or for public purposes, but for her own private purpose or for the purpose of her political party.

The case went on in the Allahabad High Court. When the question of privilege of this Blue Book was placed before the Allahabad High Court, Justice K.N. Srivastava rejected the contention placed on behalf of the state of UP and wrote an elaborate judgement which held that the Blue Books must be exhibited and no privilege can be claimed for them.[19] Against that order, the state of UP filed an SLP in the Supreme Court.[20]

FOCUS ON THE SUPREME COURT

The SLP involved the question of interpretation of Sections 123 and 162 of the Indian Evidence Act, 1872 and no constitutional question was involved therein.[21] But the Chief Justice of India, A.N. Ray, got it listed before a Bench of five judges presided over by him. The cause list of the Supreme Court of that day would show that only this case, viz. *State of Uttar Pradesh vs Raj Narain*, was listed before five judges and thereafter other cases were listed before three judges.[22] It is widely believed that Justice A.N. Ray—who was brought in as the Chief Justice of India in April 1973 after superseding three eminent judges of the Supreme Court, namely Shri J.M. Shelat, Shri K.S. Hegde (who later became the speaker of the Lok Sabha), and Shri A.N. Grover,[23] was playing in the hands of Smt Indira Gandhi.[24] It is my information that he used to have private dinners with Smt Indira Gandhi at her residence. He cannot be regarded as a judge when he was acting on her directions.[25] At that time, the Election Bench was a different Bench, of which the Chief Justice was not a member. In order to grant himself jurisdiction in the matter, he constituted a five-judge Bench for the limited purpose of admission of that SLP. Shri Raj Narain asked me to file a caveat to oppose the SLP. I suggested that we should not file a caveat but simply watch the proceedings because sometimes it is tactless to file a caveat and appear before the Supreme Court. There have been occasions when the learned judges, instead of asking questions to the petitioner's counsel, immediately ask questions to the respondent's counsel and in this way sometimes the special leave to appeal is granted. I watched the proceedings of that day in that case. Mr. Fali S. Nariman, the Additional Solicitor General of India at that time, appeared for the state of UP.[26] Some members of the Bench were reluctant to grant special leave to appeal. In that event, Chief Justice A.N. Ray, without consulting the other judges, ordered notice to show cause as to why special leave to appeal not be granted.[27]

When the matter came up after notice, Shri V.M. Tarkunde, who was a former judge of the Bombay High Court and a leading Senior Advocate of the Supreme Court of India, and I appeared for Shri Raj Narain. Shri Niren De, the Attorney General at the time, appeared for the state of UP. I told Shri Tarkunde, 'I have no faith in this Chief Justice, and I assure you that when we go to the court, he will not hear the Attorney General and he will call upon us and will grant special leave to appeal.' My prophecy came true. The Chief Justice immediately called upon Shri Tarkunde and told him, 'After all, it is an important matter and we must admit it and decide.' Despite our best efforts in the case, special leave to appeal was granted. The Chief Justice fixed the date for the hearing of the appeal on a day that suited him. He was to go abroad and fixed a date falling after his return from abroad. At the hearing of the appeal, Shri Shanti Bhushan and I appeared. Shri R.C. Srivastava, the junior counsel in the case at Allahabad (later the Additional Advocate General of UP), also came. I told them that I had no faith in the Chief Justice and that it would be good if we made a protest that it was not a constitutional case and question why five judges were going to hear the case. I further told them that this was being done just because the Chief Justice wanted the case to be decided by him in favour of Smt Indira Gandhi.

I know my friend Shri Shanti Bhushan from the time I joined the Bar at Allahabad in 1952. I do not have anything to say against him. He is a sincere, hard-working and intelligent man, but sometimes I have not appreciated his approach to the problems. He told me that he was against all this and did not agree with me. He also advised me that I should have faith in all judges. Earlier, I had spoken to Shri Raj Narain and he also shared my view that we should not argue before a Bench presided over by Chief Justice A.N. Ray. There were occasional differences between me and Shri Shanti Bhushan regarding the conduct of the case. Though Shri Shanti Bhushan did not agree with our proposals, Shri Raj Narain and I did not want to annoy him. Hence, the case was argued in the Supreme Court for five days. The judgement dated 20 March 1974 of Justice K.N. Srivastava of the Allahabad High Court[28] was set aside and the appeal of the state of UP was allowed.[29] However, some observations were made in the judgement that the judge could see the documents in-camera and could decide as to which document could be exhibited. Fortunately, the matter was now to come up before a very independent judge, Shri J.M.L. Sinha in the Allahabad High Court, and a number of documents that were relevant in the case got exhibited.[30]

EDITOR'S NOTES

1   Samyukta Socialist Party.
2   The election petition was filed in April 1971.
3   'Affidavit' refers to a written statement confirmed by oath or affirmation, for use as evidence in court.
4   *Raj Narain vs Smt Indira Gandhi & Ors* on 14 September 1971, AIR 1972 All 41.
5   'Special leave petition' refers to a petition to be granted special leave to appeal by the Supreme Court granted by Article 136 in the Constitution of India, 1949. The Supreme Court may, in its discretion, grant special leave to appeal from any judgment, decree, determination, sentence or order in any cause or matter passed or made by any court or tribunal in the territory of India, except to any judgment, determination, sentence or order passed or made by any court or tribunal constituted by or under any law relating to the armed forces.
6   'Caveat' refers to a notice that certain actions may not be taken without informing the person who gave the notice. 'Stay' refers to the act of temporarily stopping a judicial proceeding through the order of a court.
7   'Pendency': Suspense; the state of being pendent or undecided; the state of an action, etc. after it has been begun, and before

the final disposition of it. See, 'The Law Dictionary: *Featuring Black's Law Dictionary Free Online Legal Dictionary 2nd Ed.*', https://thelawdictionary.org/pendency/, accessed 26 March 2019.

8   'Merits of a case' refers to the intrinsic rights and wrongs of a case, outside of any technical, procedural, or emotional considerations or biases.

9   That the appeal was withdrawn during the course of the hearing is also mentioned in the Supreme Court judgement *Raj Narain vs Smt Indira Nehru Gandhi and Anr* on 15 March 1972, 1972 AIR 1302, 1972 SCR (3) 841.

10 'Motion' refers to a written or oral application made to a court or judge to obtain a ruling or order directing that some act be done in favour of the applicant. 'On its own motion' refers to actions by a judge taken without a prior motion or request from the parties concerned.

11 Code of Civil Procedure, 1908, Schedule I, Order XIV, Rule 1, as amended up to date, defines the meaning of settlement and framing of issues. 'Framing of Issues: (1) Issues arise when a material proposition of fact or law is affirmed by the one party and denied by the other. (2) Material propositions are those propositions of law or fact which a plaintiff must allege in order to show a right to sue or a defendant must allege in order to constitute his defence. (3) Each material proposition affirmed by one party and denied by the other shall form the subject of distinct issue. (4) Issues are of two kinds: (a) issues of fact, (b) issues of law. (5) At the first hearing of the suit the court shall, after reading the plaint and the written statements, if any, and after examination under rule 2 of Order X and after hearing the parties or their pleaders, ascertain upon what material propositions of fact or of law the parties are at variance, and shall thereupon proceed to frame and record the issues on which the right decision of the case appears to depend. (6) Nothing in this rule requires the court to frame and record issues where the defendant at the first hearing of the suit makes no defence.'

12 These orders were passed on 27 November 1971 and 22 December 1971.
13 The India–Pakistan war lasted for thirteen days from 3 December 1971 to 16 December 1971, leading to the break-up of Pakistan and formation of a new country, Bangladesh, in what was earlier known as East Pakistan.
14 Shri S.V. Gupte was the Attorney General of India during the period 1 April 1977 to 8 August 1979.
15 *Raj Kumar vs Union of India* on 18 April 1968, 1969 AIR 180, 1968 SCR (3) 875.
16 *State of Punjab vs Amar Singh Harika* on 6 January 1966, 1966 AIR (SC) 1313.
17 *Raj Narain vs Smt Indira Nehru Gandhi and Anr* on 15 March 1972, 1972 AIR 1302, 1972 SCR (3) 841.
18 'Special privilege' refers to a special and exclusive legal advantage or right such as a benefit, exemption, power or immunity; a privilege granted (as by a law or Constitution) to an individual or group to the exclusion of others and in derogation of common right.
19 *Raj Narain vs Smt Indira Nehru Gandhi and Anr* on 20 March 1974, AIR 1974 All 324.
20 The state of UP filed an SLP in the Supreme Court in April 1974.
21 For Sections 123 and 162 of the Indian Evidence Act, 1872, see the websites https://indiankanoon.org/doc/208203/ and https://indiankanoon.org/doc/1762984/, respectively.
22 'Cause lists' are the schedule of cases to be heard by the courts on the following day(s). The cause lists give details such as the court number, the Bench dealing with the cases, and the case details like case number, petitioner/respondent, respective advocates, etc.
23 After the retirement of Chief Justice S.M. Sikri on 26 April 1973, Justice J.M. Shelat was entitled to appointment as the Chief Justice of India. After Justice J.M. Shelat's retirement due on 16 July 1973, Justice K.S. Hegde would have become Chief

Justice of India, and after Justice K.S. Hegde's retirement in June 1974, the office of Chief Justice of India would have devolved on Justice A.N. Grover, who would have retired in February 1977, a few days after the retirement of Justice A.N. Ray on 29 January 1977. Thus, in the normal course of appointments, Justice A.N. Ray would never have become the Chief Justice of India. Thus, the supersession of three judges—Justice J.M. Shelat, Justice K.S. Hegde, and Justice A.N. Grover—by the Government of India under Prime Minister Indira Gandhi made it possible for Justice A.N. Ray, the next seniormost judge after the three superseded judges, to become Chief Justice of India.

24 Replying to a letter written by Jayaprakash Narayan, in which the latter had raised the issue of the independence of the judiciary, Prime Minister Indira Gandhi, in a letter dated 9 June 1973, referring to the appointment of Chief Justice A.N. Ray superseding three senior judges, stated: 'The seniority principle had led to an unduly high turnover of chief justices. I take it that no one maintains that the rule of law is safeguarded only by the principle of seniority. In the appointment of a new Chief Justice, we have only freed ourselves of a convention which had the sanction neither of the Constitution nor of rationality. It would be atrocious to think that the independence of the judiciary is thereby affected. The outcry and controversy which have attended the appointment seem to be wholly misplaced.' Letter No. 400-PMO/73, 'JP Papers', File 12, unpublished, Cultural Informatics Lab, Indira Gandhi National Centre for the Arts, New Delhi and Braj Kishore Memorial Institute, Patna. S. Mohan Kumaramangalam, minister of steel and mines, speaking in the Lok Sabha on 2 May 1973 on the appointment of the Chief Justice of India, stated: 'Firstly, it is not an essential pre-condition to the proper working of the democratic system that the Chief Justice must be appointed on the basis of seniority, but on the contrary, such a practice can only lead to harmful consequences, as the wrong man may well be appointed by the accident of seniority,

and seniority often means that no judge will serve for a long enough period to give continuity and leadership to the court.' Lok Sabha Debates No. 48, 2 May 1973, p. 391, in *Lok Sabha Debates* (Fifth Series), Vol. XXVII, 19 April to 4 May 1973, Lok Sabha Secretariat, New Delhi.

25. Nani A. Palkhivala writes, 'The poisoning of the well-spring of justice began in 1973 when the three seniormost judges of the Supreme Court, who were independent enough to decide against the executive in Kesavananada's case, were superseded upon the Chief Justice's office falling vacant.... The government expressly proclaimed that it wanted "committed" Judges—committed to the ideology of the ruling party. That began an era of a judiciary made to measure. The Government looked out for pliant Judges.' See, N.A. Palkhivala, *We the Nation: The Lost Decades*, New Delhi: UBS Publishers Distributors Ltd, 1994, p. 219.

26. Fali S. Nariman was Additional Solicitor General of India from May 1972 to 25 June 1975 and resigned from this position on 26 June 1975 after the imposition of the Emergency in the late hours of 25 June 1975.

27. 'Notice to show cause' refers to a court order that requires one or more of the parties to a case to justify, explain, or prove something to the court or to appear before the court and explain why a certain course of action should not be taken against it.

28. *Raj Narain vs Smt Indira Nehru Gandhi and Anr*, Election Petition No. 5 of 1971, 20 March 1974, AIR 1974 Allahabad 324 (V 61 C 82).

29. *State of UP vs Raj Narain & Ors*, 24 January 1975, 1975 AIR 865, 1975 SCR (3) 333.

30. Jagmohan Lal Sinha was appointed in the Allahabad High Court as an additional judge with effect from 3 January 1970 and permanent judge on 25 August 1972, from which position he retired on 12 May 1982. Justice K.N. Srivastava retired in June 1974.

3

Indira Nehru Gandhi Versus Raj Narain: The Battle in the Supreme Court

Ultimately, arguments in the case started at Allahabad and continued for a number of days. The complete attention of Shri H.R. Gokhale, the then law minister, and Smt Indira Gandhi was on the case. I was told that Shri H.R. Gokhale and Shri Siddhartha Shankar Ray, the then chief minister of West Bengal, were the persons in charge of the case on behalf of Smt Indira Gandhi, giving her advice from time to time. On 3 October 1974, the Supreme Court, in the case of *Kanwar Lal Gupta vs Amar Nath Chawla & Ors*, 1975 AIR 308, 1975 SCR (2) 269, held that the expenses incurred by a political party for a candidate would also be considered to be the expenses incurred by that candidate. Accordingly, the appeal of Shri Kanwar Lal Gupta was allowed and the election petition of Shri Amar Nath Chawla was set aside. This judgement of the Supreme Court clearly hit Smt Indira Gandhi in her election case. In order to undo the effect of this judgement, the Congress party got the Representation of the People (Amendment) Act, 1974[1] passed by the Parliament. It gave retrospective operation to the Amendment and it was provided therein that the expenses incurred by a political party for a candidate will not be treated to be the candidate's expenses. Despite protests by the Opposition, this legislation was passed by the Parliament, merely for the sole purpose of giving benefit to Smt Indira Gandhi in the election case. Raj Narain challenged the *vires* of this legislation in the Allahabad High Court by way of a writ petition.[2] Niren De, then Attorney General of India, went to

Allahabad to argue on behalf of the government. Arguments in the case closed on 23 May 1975 and the judgement was reserved.

At that time, Shri Raj Narain and I were in Allahabad, along with Shri Shanti Bhushan and Shri R.C. Srivastava. We sat together and chalked out a programme that if we lose now we lose, but if we win, then we must file a caveat in the Supreme Court so that Smt Indira Gandhi may not get an *ex parte* stay order.[3] When Shri Raj Narain came to Delhi, he sent me a *vakalatnama*[4] duly signed by him, so that if he was not available in Delhi at the time of the judgement, I could do the needful by filing a caveat.

THE JUDGEMENT AND ITS AFTERMATH

On 12 June 1975, Justice J.M.L. Sinha delivered the judgement declaring the election of Smt Indira Gandhi as 'void'. On certain points the case was decided against us, but on other points, the case was decided in our favour. It was so arranged that immediately after the pronouncement of the judgement the result could be conveyed to me and Shri Raj Narain by telephone. I was sitting in my chamber in the Supreme Court waiting for the verdict. I got the news at 10.08 a.m.

Immediately, I telephoned Shri Faqir Chand, the Deputy Registrar of the Supreme Court, and told him that Smt Indira Gandhi had lost the case and I was sending my caveat through my clerk. I also told him that nothing should be done orally or in writing until I was heard. Immediately thereafter, the caveat was filed. At that time, Justice V.R. Krishna Iyer was the vacation judge in the Supreme Court. Within one and a half hours, we got the news that Smt Indira Gandhi had obtained a stay order for twenty days, which was granted by Justice J.M.L. Sinha. The stay order was obtained through misrepresentation made on her behalf by her advocate Shri S.C. Khare. It was given in writing that as it was a question of election of the leader of the party and the office of the prime minister was involved, some time would be taken by the Congress party to elect another leader. This order was passed *ex parte* by Justice J.M.L. Sinha while our advocate Shri R.C. Srivastava, who was in Allahabad at that time, was not heard. Shri Shanti Bhushan was in Bombay at that time. I was told by Shri R.C. Srivastava that after Justice J.M.L. Sinha passed the said stay order in his chambers at the instance of Shri S.C. Khare, immediately thereafter the learned judge went to his residence. Our advocate, while knowing that the stay order had been passed without a hearing, went to the learned judge's residence and told him that the order was passed without hearing him, but the learned judge did not change his order. Smt Indira Gandhi engaged Shri N.A. Palkhivala as her Senior Advocate and Shri J.B. Dadachanji and Co. as junior advocates. The order of Justice J.M.L. Sinha was that the stay order would continue for twenty days or till the time when the appeal was filed in the Supreme Court by Smt Indira Gandhi, whichever took place earlier.

The procedure in the Supreme Court for filing appeals and petitions is that the petitions and appeals should be filed at the filing counter and not directly before the court. Thereafter, these petitions or appeals are sent to the relevant departments/sections, viz. constitutional, labour, civil, criminal, etc., and thereafter, after properly scrutinizing the papers, they are sent up to the Assistant Registrar. The case is then registered and listed. I told Shri Dadachanji, the junior counsel of Indira Gandhi in the case, that we were not going to accept any procedure that was different from the procedure prescribed in the Supreme Court Rules, and that he could not present the appeal and the stay application in the court but must file his appeal and the stay application in the office of the court, and that only after it was adjudged as proper in terms of procedure would it be listed.

Shri Dadachanji must have conveyed my attitude in the matter to Shri H.R. Gokhale and Smt Indira Gandhi. I told Shri Dadachanji that it was a question of principle and no distinction should be made between a high profile person and a common litigant. After all, justice and prescribed procedure is common for all and dispensable not for one only. Further, if by presenting the appeal on the filing counter, the stay order passed by Justice J.M.L. Sinha stood vacated, the heavens would not fall. At the most, the stay order would stand vacated and Smt Indira Gandhi would have to resign from the office of the prime minister. After all, she was held to have committed corrupt practices in her election and the practice in all democratic countries had been that a person who was adjudged by the court to have committed acts of corruption could not hold high office.[5]

Shri N.A. Palkhivala must have been told by Shri Dadachanji about my attitude on the subject. Shri Shanti Bhushan, who was staying at the Taj Hotel in Bombay, arguing a case in the Bombay High Court, was persuaded by Shri Palkhivala not to stick to the procedure of the Supreme Court. Shri Shanti Bhushan, without consulting me, agreed to whatever Shri Palkhivala had said. He telephoned me from Bombay to tell me that Shri Palkhivala had said that I had a rigid attitude in the matter. He suggested that we should be graceful and not fight on minor technicalities. I told Shri Shanti Bhushan that since he was the leader in the case and I did not have much to say, he should do whatever he liked, and that my mind was not working on the lines suggested by him. I told him that he was putting Smt Indira Gandhi at a very high position in the Supreme Court, which is the temple of justice. Suppose the case was that of any other member of the Legislature in place of Smt Indira Gandhi, then he would have filed his appeal and the stay application at the filing counter only and not in the court. I told Shri Shanti Bhushan that it was the practice of the Supreme Court that no appeal or petition had so far been filed in the Supreme Court directly. Shri Shanti Bhushan told me that he had given his word to Shri Palkhivala and that I should not resist.

The next day, I telephoned Shri Shanti Bhushan and told him

that though it was his order, I was not happy about him agreeing with Shri Palkhivala. He said that I should not repeat the same thing again, and once a thing had been settled I should not reopen it again and again. Shri Dadachanji telephoned me, saying, 'I believe some jyotishi (astrologer) told Smt. Indira Gandhi that mention should be made on Friday, the 20th of June 1975.' I said I would be available in the court, and the matter was mentioned on that day. Shri Shanti Bhushan had not returned from Bombay then. I represented Shri Raj Narain while Shri Palkhivala and Shri Dadachanji represented Smt Indira Gandhi on the other side. On that very day, just to show her popularity and her force, at the time when mention was being made in the court, a rally was arranged at the Boat Club near India Gate in New Delhi, which was addressed by Smt Indira Gandhi. Shri Sanjay Gandhi was also there and a number of persons from different parts of the country were brought in trucks to Tilak Marg and the Supreme Court to raise slogans. It appears that all this was done just to influence the judge that Smt Indira Gandhi was all-powerful in this country and he must be careful in deciding the case. It may be pointed out that after the Emergency was revoked, Justice V.R. Krishna Iyer had made a statement that he and his wife were pressurized and were under duress to decide the case in favour of Smt Indira Gandhi.[6]

At 10.30 a.m., the mention was made amidst this atmosphere. I told the learned judge that we on this side in good grace would not create any technical difficulties and would assist the court in justice, as desired by the other side. I agreed that the appeal and the stay application be presented in open court before the learned judge on Monday, 23 June 1975, which was proposed to be fixed in the case. I was afraid, however, that if the voluminous papers were to be placed before the judge on that day he would say that he had not read the brief and, therefore, he would adjourn the matter for one or two days to study the case. Then the other side would pray that an *ex parte* stay order (full stay order) be granted, as was granted by Justice J.M.L. Sinha. The practice of the Supreme Court in the matter of election petitions and appeals for the last twenty-four years had been that in an election case, where the election had been set aside by the High Court, the Supreme Court never granted a full stay order. I was apprehensive that if the papers were presented before the Supreme Court, the learned judge may grant a full stay order and this would set a bad precedent for other cases.

I suggested to the court that unofficially we could exchange the papers beforehand and a paper book could be constituted.[7] The paper book could be sent to the learned judge's residence on Sunday, 22 June 1975, by lunchtime, so that he could read the brief and the matter could be argued. My statement before the court was not appreciated by my colleagues Shri P.N. Lekhi and other lawyers who were there at that time. I said that I could not do anything as Shri Shanti Bhushan had already made a commitment to Shri Palkhivala. They were agitated as to why on behalf of Shri Raj Narain we had agreed to Smt Indira Gandhi presenting her petition before the court. My friends told me that this amounted to recognition of the personality cult, against which we had been fighting all these years. I had taken into confidence all my colleagues before I made the statement before the court. *The Statesman* of 21 June 1975 commented on my statement, stating that on behalf of the Opposition, good grace had been shown and it was now up to Smt Indira Gandhi to show good grace in the same vein.

Shri Raj Narain was not in Delhi on the day the mention was made in the court as he had gone to Patna. He came to Agra from Patna and telephoned me from there on 20 June itself. The news of my statement before the court had reached Agra as it was announced on the radio. Shri Raj Narain said that I should not have made such a statement that Smt Indira Gandhi could place her papers before the court when others could not do so. I informed him that my actions were as per the instructions of Shri

Shanti Bhushan who had been put on my head by him and that I had been asked to take this position by Shri Shanti Bhushan. We had to file our counter affidavit by the evening of the next day, i.e. Saturday, 21 June 1975. Shri Raj Narain suggested that I fly to Bombay by the evening flight and that Shri Shanti Bhushan and I should sit together and prepare the counter affidavit. I immediately went to Bombay and joined Shri Shanti Bhushan there at about 9 p.m. In the meantime, Shri Raj Narain had come to Delhi and telephoned Shri Shanti Bhushan in my presence. He asked Shri Shanti Bhushan as to why I had made such a statement in the court and if these were his instructions. Shri Shanti Bhushan confirmed that I had made the statement under his instructions. Shri Raj Narain was annoyed with this, but Shri Shanti Bhushan said that we should not be on technicalities and that whatever we had done was in good grace. He, however, did not take into consideration that Smt Indira Gandhi was into self-promotion and lacked grace. This has been my point of view about her, with which unfortunately Shri Shanti Bhushan did not agree.

We prepared the counter affidavit. As there was very little time, it was thought that the matter should be cyclostyled in Bombay itself.[8] We contacted the law firm Gagrat & Co., but unfortunately the whole thing could not be cyclostyled in time. I had to miss my appointed flight and took a later flight back to Delhi. The rest of the work was done in the Bharatiya Lok Dal (BLD) office and, therefore, Shri Raj Narain's affidavit was sworn at about midnight, following which the counter affidavit was served on Shri Dadachanji at about 1 a.m. The press was also there and the contents of our counter affidavit were published in the newspapers of 22 June 1975. The rejoinder affidavit was filed on 22 June itself on behalf of Smt Indira Gandhi and the matter came up for hearing the next day, 23 June 1975, before Justice V.R. Krishna Iyer.

THE DAY OF THE HEARING

There were large crowds in the Supreme Court on the day of the hearing. It was very difficult even for the lawyers to reach the court. There were twelve lawyers on our side and the opposite side had a similar number of lawyers. The parties were given five seats each for their *pairokars*.[9] I had put Shri Madhu Limaye, Shri Jyotirmoy Bosu, Shri Shyam Nandan Mishra, Shri Rabi Ray, and Shri Piloo Mody as Shri Raj Narain's *pairokars* in the case. They were sitting just behind us on the second bench with Shri Raj Narain. On behalf of Smt Indira Gandhi, her elder son Rajiv Gandhi was also present. Some chief ministers were also brought to be present in the court on behalf of Smt Indira Gandhi. With great difficulty, we, the lawyers, entered the court.

Shri Palkhivala started the arguments. Such stay applications in the Supreme Court required only one or two minutes. The arguments on the stay application surprisingly took place, however, and went on up to 5.05 p.m.[10] The court had to sit beyond time and without any lunch interval.[11] The crowd was so large that if the judge had to go to his chambers there would be no space for him to come out of the court and it would have been a security risk. Therefore, it was decided that nobody would move and the court would go on hearing the case even during the lunch interval.[12] Shri Palkhivala began the arguments on the merits of the appeal. My colleagues and I were agitated about it. I told Shri Shanti Bhushan, who was sitting in second place, that he should immediately stand and tell the court that the merits of the appeal cannot be gone into for the hearing of the stay application and this is not the matter of argument. I also told him to tell the court that as for the last twenty-four years the practice of the Supreme Court in cases like the present one had been to give only a limited stay order, the same routine order should be passed in this case also. Shri Shanti Bhushan, however, did not agree with me. Despite my insisting a number of times, Shri Shanti Bhushan did not stand up and heard all the arguments of Shri Palkhivala on merits. He did not at all tell the court, contrary to what was desired not only by me but my other colleagues as well as the pairokars who were sitting behind us. Shri Jyotirmoy Bosu and Shri Madhu Limaye, who were sitting just behind me, also told me a number of times to tell Shri Shanti Bhushan that the case should not be heard on merits as this was not the matter of argument and that he should not allow Shri Palkhivala to argue on the merits of the appeal on the office of the prime minister which was not at all involved in the case. Shri Jyotirmoy Bosu also told me to tell Shri Shanti Bhushan that the same routine order that had been passed for the last twenty-four years by the Supreme Court should be passed in this also. Unfortunately, Shri Shanti Bhushan did not pay any heed to our views and kept on hearing Shri Palkhivala. The Supreme Court in all election appeals had until then been ordering that no fresh election will take place and the candidate who had lost the election in the High Court will sign the register of the Parliament only on such days so as to not incur disqualification. He/she was not allowed to draw any salary or allowances as an MP. It should have been stressed on our behalf that similar orders should have been passed and if the court wanted to hear the appeal on merits we should have protested and told the court we were not prepared for it. I am sure that if we would have agreed to halt we would not have allowed Shri Palkhivala to argue the case for so long on merits. Seeing that this was an appeal against the judgement of the Allahabad High Court that had declared the election of a candidate as an MP void, we should have protested that the question of the office of the prime minister was not at all involved. However, on our side also, when the arguments were presented they were also made on merits and on the involvement of the office of the prime minister. This was the second mistake, according to me, committed by our side, after the first that I was compelled to make on 20 June 1975, as outlined above, in the name of not sticking on technicalities. The orders were reserved and it was ordered that the learned judge would deliver the judgement at 3.30 p.m. the next day (24 June 1975) in his chambers. Shri Shanti Bhushan returned to Bombay where he was arguing a case in the High Court there.

The next day, 24 June 1975, crowds started collecting in the premises of the Supreme Court about two hours before the orders were to be delivered. The Registrar of the Supreme Court had directed that only four lawyers could enter the learned judge's chambers—two from our side and two from the other side, namely Shri Shanti Bhushan and myself on our side and Shri Palkhivala and Shri Dadachanji on the other side. As there was a big crowd on the lawns of the Supreme Court and it was very difficult to get through, the Registrar had requested us to be in front of the learned judge's chambers at least fifteen minutes before the orders were to be delivered. On our side, I reached there, and on the other side, Shri Palkhivala and Shri Dadachanji reached there. We stood in the corridor in front of Justice Krishna Iyer's chambers, whose doors were closed.

The doors of Justice Krishna Iyer's chambers were to open only at 3.30 p.m. The entire crowd, including members of the Indian and foreign press, was waiting on the lawns of the Supreme Court. There were huge crowds even outside the Supreme Court premises and on the roads. When we were standing outside the chambers of the learned judge, I spoke to Shri Palkhivala and told him that I was of the view that democracy cannot be maintained in this country unless people get equal opportunities in the matter of elections. I also told him that how could it be called equality, particularly when the prime minister of the country had the means within the limited period allotted for election campaigning to address even ten to twenty meetings in one day and have the opportunity of using government planes without any cost to herself or her own party, whereas the leaders of the Opposition sometimes could not even afford to have a bullock cart for the purpose of election campaigns. After all, the importance of the means of election campaign during the period prescribed for it cannot be minimized. I told him that I knew the difficulties of finances and the means of the Opposition parties, and if the prime minister, the high office of the ruling party, is given some facilities at the expense of the government exchequer to have an upper hand in the matter of election campaign, where even government servants and officers are used, then how was it possible to change the government of the day. Shri Palkhivala, who has been a very good friend of mine and whom I respect as a man believing in human liberties and democracy, heard me very attentively without any comment. Shri Palkhivala and I had worked together on different occasions earlier, particularly in the matter of holding of the All India Convention of Lawyers on 11–12 August 1973 in Ashoka Hotel, New Delhi, condemning the supersession on 25 April 1973 of the eminent judges Shri J.M. Shelat, Shri K.S. Hegde and Shri A.N. Grover by Shri A.N. Ray, who was expected to deliver the goods to Smt Indira Gandhi and who, in fact, performed what was desired of her.

At 3.30 p.m., the doors of Justice Krishna Iyer's chambers opened. We entered inside the learned judge's chamber. He had got cyclostyled a number of copies of his judgement, which contained twenty-three cyclostyled pages each. We were given the said cyclostyled copies. The judge read out the operative portion of the order. In the said order, though he had observed that the merits of the appeal could be gone into only at the time of the hearing of the appeal, he also observed that he had hesitated to prolong the 'absolute stay' granted by the Allahabad High Court as the High Court's finding, until overruled, held good. Even though the office of the prime minister was not involved in the election petition filed by Smt Indira Gandhi, nevertheless the learned judge gave an elaborate order and held that she could still continue in the office of the prime minister. However, she could not participate in the parliamentary proceedings as an MP but as the prime minister, she could speak in Parliament (without a right to vote).

This order created a great complication.[13] When I came out to go to my chamber with the order, a crowd of members of the press waiting on the lawns of the Supreme Court surrounded me and it was very difficult to get out of the crowd. It must have taken more than an hour for me to come out of the crowd and reach my chamber. It being the summer season, I was fatigued during this hour and sat outside my chamber for some time.

A DECISIVE RESOLUTION

I received a telephone call from Shri Raj Narain from his residence in Delhi on 8, Dr. Bishambar Das Marg. He asked me to bring the order and explain the same to the political leaders who had gathered at that time in Delhi at Shri Morarji Desai's house at 5, Dupleix Road. I went to Shri Raj Narain's residence and from there we went to Shri Morarji Desai's place. Shri Jayaprakash Narayan and Shri Morarji Desai were sitting together. I read out the relevant portions of the order to the leaders of the Opposition gathered there. Shri Piloo Mody thereafter asked me to accompany him to a room, where Shri Asoka Mehta, Shri L.K. Advani, Shri Piloo Mody and I drafted the resolution that was to be released to the press by the Coordination Committee of five Opposition parties, namely the Congress (O), the Bharatiya Lok Dal, the Jana Sangh, the Socialist Party and the Akali Dal.

The salient features of that resolution were that Smt Indira Gandhi had not got a full stay order from the Supreme Court and under the circumstances she could not remain the prime minister. She was found to be guilty of corrupt practices, and even Justice Krishna Iyer in his order had indirectly brought up the issue of political propriety and democratic dharma, saying that it would be better to observe judicial silence on it.[14] It was pointed out that the principles and practice in democratic countries had been that if a person was under a cloud of suspicion, then he or she must vacate the office held by him or her. By the said resolution, a sort of advice was given to Smt Indira Gandhi that she should quit the high office of the prime minister. The said resolution was published in the newspapers of 25 June 1975.[15]

In the evening of 25 June 1975, there was a large meeting at New Delhi's Ramlila Maidan, which was addressed by Shri Jayaprakash Narayan and other leaders. In that meeting, Shri Jayaprakash Narayan declared that if Smt Indira Gandhi did not quit the office of the prime minister with grace, the Coordination Committee would be compelled to undertake a peaceful satyagraha against her continuance in that office.[16] Shri Raj Narain also addressed the meeting, which ended at about 9 p.m.

Shri Raj Narain went to his residence thereafter. From there, he telephoned me and requested me to come to his residence, where he wanted to talk to me on many issues. I reached there at about 10–10.30 p.m. We discussed many connected issues, political as well as about the case. We sat together till about midnight. I wanted to leave for my residence but Shri Raj Narain said that it was not proper for me to go at that late hour. He said that some foul play may be done by the other side if I went out at that odd hour as I was appearing for him in the case and the other side could not be relied upon. Under these circumstances, I was asked by Shri Raj Narain to spend the night at his residence. I telephoned my wife at home and informed her that I would not be coming back home that night.

EDITOR'S NOTES

1. For Representation of the People (Amendment) Act, 1974, see Appendix III.1.
2. *Vires*: Latin, meaning power or authority
3. *Ex parte*: Latin, meaning 'for one party', referring to motions,

hearings or orders granted on the request of and for the benefit of one party only. 'Ex parte stay order' refers to temporarily stopping a judicial proceeding through the order of a court which has been obtained on the request of and for the benefit of one party only.

4   Vakalatnama: Authority in writing given by a litigant to a lawyer to represent the litigant in court.

5   In fact, Dr. Chenna Reddy, chief minister of Andhra Pradesh, and D.P. Mishra, chief minister of Madhya Pradesh, were made to relinquish their offices by Indira Gandhi when two High Courts set aside their elections on the ground of corrupt practices pending the decision of the Supreme Court on their appeals there.

6   This is also mentioned in an article by T.R. Andhyarujina, Senior Advocate, Supreme Court of India, and former Solicitor General of India and Advocate General of Maharashtra: 'Many years later, Justice Iyer revealed the pressure under which he was put to decide in favour of Indira Gandhi. On the day of the high court judgment in June 1975, then Law Minister H.R. Gokhale telephoned him and wanted to personally meet him, obviously to influence him to grant an unconditional stay of the judgement of the high court. Justice Iyer told him on the phone that as the prime minister had engaged an advocate (later N.A. Palkhivala), the appeal should be filed in the Supreme Court registry and there was no need to meet him.' See T.R. Andhyarujina, 'Justice for the Helpless', *The Indian Express*, 6 December 2014, available at http://indianexpress.com/article/opinion/columns/justice-for-the-Helpless/, accessed 14 January 2018.

7   'Paper book' refers to a collection of all the case appeal papers of an appellant compiled in order, including the index, memo of parties, list of dates, plaint with grounds of appeal, affidavits etc., which are stitched together loosely with a paper cover. It resembles a book, and hence, the name.

8   Cyclostyle: an early device for duplicating handwriting, in which

a pen with a small toothed wheel pricks holes in a sheet of waxed paper, which is then used as a stencil.
9   *Pairokar*: Purveyor/Representative in a legal matter.
10 The court started its sitting at 11.30 a.m.
11 This was unprecedented at that time.
12 Piloo Mody, however, managed to get out during the lunch interval to have his lunch. See 'Court Skips Lunch, Not Piloo', *Hindustan Times*, New Delhi, 24 June 1975, p. 1.
13 *Indira Nehru Gandhi (Smt) vs Raj Narain & Anr* on 24 June, 1975, 1975 AIR 1590, 1975 SCC (2) 159.
14 Justice Krishna Iyer observed, 'Legality is within the Court's province to pronounce upon, but canons of political propriety and democratic dharma are polemical issues on which judicial silence is the golden rule.' *Indira Nehru Gandhi (Smt) vs Raj Narain & Anr* on 24 June 1975, 1975 AIR 1590, 1975 SCC (2) 159.
15 '5 Opposition Parties Demand Resignation', *The Statesman*, Delhi, 25 June 1975, p. 1.
16 Derived from the Sanskrit words *satya* (meaning 'truth') and *agraha* ('insistence' or 'holding firmly to'), the word *satyagraha* denotes a philosophy and practice that came to be associated with the passive non-violent struggle most notably adopted by Mohandas Karamchand Gandhi against the British rule in India. The peaceful *satyagraha* was supposed to begin on 29 June 1975. In a letter to Prime Minister Indira Gandhi dated 21 July 1975, Jayaprakash Narayan explained the planned *satyagraha*:

> The programme was for a selected number of persons to offer Satyagraha before or near your residence in support of the demand that you should step down until the Supreme Court's Judgement on your appeal. The programme was to continue for seven days in Delhi, after which it was to be taken up in the States. And, as I have said above, it was to last only until the judgement of the Supreme Court.

I do not see what is subversive or dangerous about it. In a democracy the citizen has an inalienable right to civil disobedience when he finds that other channels of redress and reform have dried up. It goes without saying that the Satyagrahi willingly invites and accepts his lawful punishment. This is the new dimension added to democracy by Gandhi. What an irony that it should be obliterated in Gandhi's own India.

It should be noted—and it is a very important point—that even this program of Satyagraha would not have occurred to the Opposition had you remained content with quietly clinging on to your office. But you did not do it. Through your henchmen you had rallies and demonstrations organized in front of your residence begging you not to resign. You addressed these rallies and justifying your stand advanced spurious arguments and heaped calumny on the head of the Opposition. An effigy of the High Court Judge (Justice J.M.L. Sinha) was burnt before your residence and posters appeared in the city suggesting a link between the judge and the CIA. When such despicable happenings were taking place every day, the Opposition had no alternative but to counteract the mischief. And how did it decide to do it? Not by rowdyism, but by orderly Satyagraha, self sacrifice.

—'JP Papers', File 2-2, unpublished, Cultural Informatics Lab, Indira Gandhi National Centre for Arts, New Delhi and Braj Kishore Memorial Institute, Patna.

4
Proclamation of the Emergency and Its Aftermath

Two cots, one for myself and the other for Shri Bhrigunath,[1] were put on the rear lawns of Shri Raj Narain's residence. I went to bed. At about 3 a.m., I was woken up by Urmilesh Jha, who was the former secretary to Dr. Ram Manohar Lohia and was at that time working as a secretary to Shri Raj Narain. He told me that the entire house was surrounded by the police and that Shri Jayaprakash Narayan had been arrested at the Gandhi Peace Foundation.[2] Shri Bhrigunath also woke up. Urmilesh Jha told me that Shri Raj Narain, who was inside, had asked me not to get up, otherwise the police might arrest me too. I got up nevertheless. I saw policemen all around. I could not restrain myself and entered the room where Shri Raj Narain was surrounded by the police. He introduced me to the police officers while making preparations to go with them. A warrant was served on Shri Raj Narain, who showed the same to me. It was under Section 3 of the Maintenance of Internal Security Act, 1971 (MISA) and signed by Shri Sushil Kumar, District Magistrate (DM), Delhi.[3] I found that the receiver of Shri Raj Narain's telephone was put off the hook. I rebuked the police officers for doing so, and told them that they could only arrest Shri Raj Narain and not interfere with other facilities in the house such as the telephone. Urmilesh Jha told me later that Shri K.S. Radhakrishna, Secretary of the Gandhi Peace Foundation, had told him over the phone that Shri Jayaprakash Narayan had been arrested. Shri Raj Narain had his bath and packed some books to take along with him. In the early hours of the morning, he was taken away in a car by the police in my presence. After he left, Smt T. Lakshmi Kantamma, an MP, who was later a member of the Working Committee of the Janata Party, arrived at Raj Narain's residence.[4] Shri Era Sezhiyan, who was the leader of the Dravida Munnetra Kazhagam (DMK) in the Lok Sabha at that time and who was living in the neighbourhood, also arrived there. They both enquired about all that had happened.

The *Statesman* and the *Hindustan Times*, Delhi's two leading newspapers at the time, somehow appeared the next day, though other papers could not appear. The main news was that the President of India had declared National Emergency on account of internal disturbances under Article 352 of the Constitution of India.[5] I went to my residence. Immediately after reaching, I received a phone call from someone from the *Hindustan Times* who asked for my reaction to the proclamation of the Emergency. I dictated my views on the telephone, stating that there was no national emergency and it was only Smt Indira Gandhi's own personal emergency as she was in trouble and could not get a full stay order from the Supreme Court. I further stated that as Smt Indira Gandhi, according to democratic norms, must vacate the office she was holding, she had done this mischief merely to keep herself in office. I said that democracy was finished in this country,[6] and that she ought to have resigned on the day when she was found to have committed corrupt practices by Justice J.M.L. Sinha on 12 June 1975.

DESTRUCTION OF DEMOCRATIC VALUES

We came to know that the power connections of almost all the newspapers in Delhi and outside were disconnected at the instance of the government. On 27 June, there was no newspaper. Along with the Emergency, censorship of the press was introduced, and newspapers were to be published under censorship.[7] In the beginning, for one or two days, the newspapers protested in various ways. The Delhi edition of *The Indian Express* on

28 June 1975 kept the editorial column blank as a mark of protest.[8] It is said that pressure was exerted on the members of the press to write editorials favourable to the government.

Many political leaders and workers of the Opposition were arrested overnight on 25–26 June, and in the following days.[9] It was a reign of terror in the country. It was not even known to the relations of a detenu as to where the arrested person had been put away.[10] The detenus could not write freely to anyone. Even if a letter was written, it was censored by the jail authorities and there was no guarantee that the letter would reach its destination.[11]

As I was the resident lawyer in Shri Raj Narain's case in Delhi and Shri Shanti Bhushan was away in Bombay, friends and relatives of almost all the Opposition leaders and workers started coming to me for advice as to what was to be done and how to have interviews with the detenus, especially since the whereabouts of the detenus were not known to them. Shri Jayaprakash Narayan's brother Shri Rajeshwar Prasad, who was residing in Bombay, also came to Delhi and met me to seek advice on what to do. I telephoned the then Union Home Minister Shri K. Brahmananda Reddy and Shri Om Mehta, who was then the minister of state for home, personnel and parliamentary affairs.[12] I also telephoned the DM, Shri Sushil Kumar. For a number of days, nobody was allowed to talk to them. The modus operandi was that whenever any phone call was made to them for any purpose connected to the detenus, the secretaries and officers would tell the caller that the minister or officer was absent. Sometimes, the minister or officer was alleged to be in the bathroom for a number of hours! I was very agitated to see before my eyes the destruction of all values of democracy in the country.

THREATENING TO BOYCOTT THE CASE

I started threatening the advocates on the other side that we would boycott this case under these circumstances, when it was not even known as to where my client had been taken away. Shri N.A. Palkhivala resigned from Smt Indira Gandhi's case on 26 June 1975 itself. However, J.B. Dadachanji continued to be her Advocate-on-Record. I told Shri Dadachanji on the telephone that Justice Krishna Iyer had said in his judgement that on the opening day of the Supreme Court after the summer vacations, i.e. 14 July 1975, there would be a mention before the court about fixing a date of hearing and that by that time, the paper books would be ready, but I was not agreeable to participate in the case under the circumstances. It may be pointed out that within the period of limitation, we had also filed our cross-appeals on those points in the case that had been decided against us in the judgement passed by Justice J.M.L. Sinha.[13] The appeal filed by Smt Indira Gandhi was numbered Civil Appeal No. 887 of 1975 (*Indira Nehru Gandhi vs Raj Narain & Anr*) and the cross-appeal filed by us on behalf of Raj Narain was numbered as Civil Appeal No. 909 of 1975 (*Raj Narain vs Indira Nehru Gandhi*). In the afternoon of 26 June, Shri V.M. Tarkunde telephoned and requested me to give him a copy of the judgement of Justice J.M.L. Sinha, which he wanted to study. He told me that he had come from Srinagar. I told him about the arrest of Shri Jayaprakash Narayan and other leaders and about the declaration of the Emergency. He did not know anything at that time. He was surprised about all that had happened

I was secretly told that Shri H.R. Gokhale was in charge of Smt Indira Gandhi's appeal in the Supreme Court and everything was being done in consultation with him. As mentioned earlier, I had threatened J.B. Dadachanji that we were going to boycott the case as our client was under detention and I was not even told about his whereabouts or allowed to meet him. It appears that Shri Dadachanji communicated this to Smt Indira Gandhi and Shri H.R. Gokhale. Ultimately, on 4 July 1975, I received a letter from the Delhi Administration to the effect that I could meet Shri Raj Narain in Rohtak Jail the following day.

SETTING UP MEETINGS IN ROHTAK

Through a source, I came to know that Shri Piloo Mody, Shri Chandra Shekhar,[14] Shri Sikander Bakht, Shri Biju Patnaik and Shri K.R. Malkani, among others, were also lodged in Rohtak Jail. I, along with Urmilesh Jha and Chander Shekhar, the office secretary of the Bharatiya Lok Dal, reached Rohtak and met Shri N.K. Garg, the DM, for arranging my interview with Shri Raj Narain. As I had instructions from relatives and friends of a number of incarcerated leaders to meet them, I asked the DM to show me the rules framed by the state government regarding interviews with detenus under MISA. I found that Rule 14(4) of the Haryana rules,[15] relating to detention of detenus, allowed a detenu to have an interview with an advocate of his choice. The interview was to be held in the presence of a jail official or police officer, but out of their hearing.[16]

Acting under this rule, I wrote separate letters to Shri Asoka Mehta, Shri Chandra Shekhar, Shri Biju Patnaik, Shri K.R. Malkani, Shri Sikander Bakht and Shri Piloo Mody to the effect that I had been instructed by their friends and relatives to give them legal advice regarding the validity or otherwise of their detention and that if they wanted to meet me they should express their intention on that very letter. Letters were addressed to them through the DM, Rohtak, who forwarded the same to them in jail. When each one of them expressed their consent to meet me and their consent was received by the DM, he arranged an interview with them. He told me that he would give thirty minutes time for the interview of each detenu. I told him that what was the use if I was to be not allowed to sit with all the detenus at one time and be expected to render separate advice to each detenu every time. I asked him to allow me to sit with all the detenus together. He agreed to this procedure.

EDITOR'S NOTES

1. Bhrigunath, a long-standing associate of Raj Narain, had signed the latter's nomination form in the election to the UP Legislative Assembly in 1952 from Banaras (South) constituency.
2. This was not the first time that Jayaprakash Narayan had been arrested. He had been to jail a number of times and had been inhumanly tortured during the freedom struggle against the British rule in India. During the Quit India Movement he, along with Dr. Ram Manohar Lohia and Aruna Asaf Ali, took charge of the ongoing stir when all the senior leaders had been arrested. He was held in such high regard that Mahatma Gandhi made it clear to the British that unless both Jayaprakash Narayan and Dr. Ram Manohar Lohia were unconditionally released the negotiations with the Cabinet Mission of 1946 would not start. Given this ultimatum, the British released both Jayaprakash Narayan and Dr. Ram Manohar Lohia in April 1946.
3. For Section 3 of the Maintenance of Internal Security Act, see Appendix III.2.
4. Smt T. Lakshmi Kantamma was an MP continuously from 1962 to 1977 from the Indian National Congress party. However, she opposed Indira Gandhi when the latter imposed the Emergency and became an important leader of the Janata Party, serving as the party's All India General Secretary.
5. For Article 352, see Appendix III.3. For government decisions immediately after the proclamation of the Emergency, see Appendix I.
6. In this context, M.G. Devasahayam recounts a conversation with Jayaprakash Narayan, wherein the latter states: "'Shrimati Indira Gandhi is like my daughter. She had played in my lap. Why she is doing all these things? His (sic) father, Pandit Jawaharlal Nehru would have rather died than doing all these things. Where was Pandit Nehru and where his daughter Shrimati Indira Gandhi is?" Then, he asked how ironic it was that the plant of democracy

so fondly nurtured by two stalwarts of Nehru family should be uprooted by their very offsprings. He further said, "How it was in the Gandhian era and what dream we had for this country? What has it come to?" Then with a sigh, he said, "I should not even take the names of Mahatma Gandhi and Indira Gandhi in the same breath." He was never bitter about Indira Gandhi, he was only sad.' See 'JP Papers', File 2-1, unpublished, Cultural Informatics Lab, Indira Gandhi National Centre for the Arts, New Delhi and Braj Kishore Memorial Institute, Patna.

7   See Appendix I for details of government orders on press censorship.

8   Its sister publication, *The Financial Express*, on 28 June 1975, in its first edition after the imposition of the Emergency, reproduced Rabindranath Tagore's poem 'Where the mind is without fear and the head is held high', concluding with the prayer 'Into that heaven of freedom, my Father, let my country awake'.

9   Even in the face of these arrests, some Opposition leaders displayed great wit and poise. Dr. N.M. Ghatate writes about the arrest of Shyam Nandan Mishra and Atal Bihari Vajpayee: 'When the Internal Emergency was declared, Atalji, Advaniji, Shri Shyam Nandan Mishra and Shri Madhu Dandavate, all M.P.s, were in Bangalore in connection with Parliamentary work and were staying in the MLA (Member of Legislative Assembly) Hostel. When the Karnataka police came to arrest them, Shyam Babu was doing his morning yoga. When the police entered his room, he was doing his *Sirsasan* (headstand) and when he was informed about his arrest, Shyam Babu staying in the same position asked the police, "Where is the arrest warrant?" As the Police did not have any such warrant, they said they were arresting them under Section 151 of Cr.P.C. (Code of Criminal Procedure), where police have power to arrest without warrant if they have an apprehension that a person is likely to commit cognizable offence such as murder, dacoity, house breaking etc. Shri S.N. Mishra objected to such arrest as they were respected

leaders of political parties and asked them to get the proper arrest warrants. He said, "I will not come unless you bring the warrant." So they went back and prepared a warrant which read "Shri S.N. Mishra, M.P., son of so and so, ..." There was another S.N. Mishra who was also an M.P. from UP whose father's name was inserted in the warrant. ... When Shyam Babu read the warrant, he said, "I am not that father's son." So the police respectfully asked, "What is your father's name, Sir?" He replied, "Why should I tell you? Find it from the Parliament's Directory." It was 10 o'clock by then, and the police had not even taken their morning tea. The Police Inspector then told Atalji, "If Shri Mishraji does not come, we will have to physically take him to the Police Station." At that time, Atalji told, "Shyam Babu, let us go to our *Sasural* (father-in-law's house)." In the Indian culture the son-in-law gets a royal treatment at in-laws place.' Dr. Ghatate also writes that when he went to Bangalore jail to see the above-mentioned leaders, he '...was surprised to see Atalji wearing warm jail clothes. I exclaimed, "Atalji what is all this!" and he replied, "Now Indira Gandhi will feed me and Indira Gandhi will give clothes. I am not going to spend a penny from my pocket." See Dr. N.M. Ghatate, *Emergency, Constitution and Democracy: An Indian Experience*, New Delhi: Shipra Publications, 2011, pp. 37–39.

10 Detenu: a person in custody; detainee; used commonly in India.
11 Jayaprakash Narayan wrote, in a letter to V.M. Tarkunde dated 15 September 1975, 'Can you believe it, out of the 20 letters I have written in the ten weeks of detention as many as 19 have not been delivered! I consider this to be a serious and unlawful deprivation of a detenu's right. I wish you consider this matter from the legal aspect and do the needful.' See 'JP Papers', File 8, unpublished, Cultural Informatics Lab, Indira Gandhi National Centre for Arts, New Delhi and Braj Kishore Memorial Institute, Patna. M.G. Devasahayam, the jailor of Jayaprakash Narayan in Chandigarh, writes of Jayaprakash Narayan being

dismayed over his letters not reaching the addressees. Referring to Jayaprakash Narayan's meeting with his brother-in-law S.N. Prasad on 20 July 1975, Devasahayam writes: 'On coming to know that Prasad had not received the letter written by JP to him on 7 July 1975, JP got quite upset. He was wondering what the Delhi Administration was doing with the letters. ... He said he was surprised and distressed to find that his brother-in-law had not received the letter he had written to him on the seventh. He was wondering why should the government feel reluctant in sending letters, which are purely private in nature. I told him that Delhi Administration had sent the letters to GOI. He just smiled and did not say anything.' See M.G. Devasahayam, *JP in Jail: An Uncensored Account*, New Delhi: Roli Books Pvt Ltd, 2006, pp. 50–53. Dr. N.M. Ghatate writes of letters to and from K.R. Malkani not reaching his wife: 'In early August, 1975 when I went to meet Malkani at the Hissar Jail, his wife told me that she had not received any letter from her husband. When Mr. Malkani came to meet me in the Jailor's office, he was in a sulky mood and told the Jailor, "Start your tape recorder" and started criticizing the government for imposing fake Emergency etc. He also told me that he had not received any reply from his wife, though he had sent several letters. ... After he had gone back to his cell, I asked the Jailor why they were not receiving any letters. He replied, "Sir, Mr. Malkani writes 'My dear Sundari' and the letters are full of criticism of Mrs. Indira Gandhi and Emergency which I have to censor and what remains is only 'Your Kewal'. Similar are Mrs. Malkani's letters so how can I send them to Mrs. Malkani or her letters to Mr. Malkani? But added if Mrs. Malkani sends any sweets etc. I will immediately deliver them to Mr. Malkani." See Dr. N.M. Ghatate, *Emergency, Constitution and Democracy: An Indian Experience*, New Delhi: Shipra Publications, 2011, p. 50.

12 Om Mehta was in fact considered to be even more powerful than K. Brahmananda Reddy. In a letter dated 7 July 1975, Chandra

Shekhar wrote to Union Home Minister K. Brahmananda Reddy: 'My predictions have come true. I am your prisoner. ... Convey my compliments to your Deputy "Om", who is enjoying powers perhaps more than you.' See 'JP Papers', File 8, unpublished, Cultural Informatics Lab, Indira Gandhi National Centre for Arts, New Delhi and Braj Kishore Memorial Institute, Patna.

13 'Cross-appeal' refers to a request filed by an opposing party (respondent) to a higher court to review a decision made by a lower court.

14 Chandra Shekhar was one of the few Congress party leaders who had the courage to ask Mrs. Indira Gandhi to step down from the position of prime minister given the adverse judgement of Justice J.M.L. Sinha on 12 June 1975, notwithstanding the stay granted to her. In the night of 25–26 June 1975, '...a large party of police was sent to surround his house. They told him they had a message for him, to telephone a certain number. Indira answered. She told him she was declaring emergency. He was to issue a statement of support and she would make him No. 2 in her cabinet. If he did not then the police were there to take him into detention under the MISA powers. He said give me five minutes, He packed his bag and surrendered to the police there and then. He was kept in solitary confinement for eighteen months.' See 'Minutes of conversation between Allan and Wendy Scarfe and Shri M.G. Devasahayam—16.3.1994 in Room 419, Hilton Hotel, Melbourne, Australia', in 'JP Papers', File 9, unpublished, Cultural Informatics Lab, Indira Gandhi National Centre for Arts, New Delhi and Braj Kishore Memorial Institute, Patna.

15 Haryana Detenus (Conditions of Detention) Order, 1971, Haryana Government, Home (Jails) Department, *Haryana Government Gazette (extraordinary), Part III*, 11 December 1971.

16 These rules relating to interviews of detenus with advocates were amended further on 9 July 1975, soon after J.P. Goyal's interviews with Jayaprakash Narayan and Raj Narain and other leaders in

jail on 5–6 July 1975. The Home Ministry issued a directive to chief secretaries of all states and Union Territories that interviews with lawyers for professional consultation relating to detention should be in the presence and hearing of an officer nominated by the detaining authority or any other authority.

5
Meeting the Leaders in Jail

I entered the jail. In one big room on the first floor of the jail, one table and six chairs were placed. Shri Asoka Mehta, Shri Chandra Shekhar, Shri Raj Narain and one Sikh leader were seated there. Shri Piloo Mody could not come to the first floor; he maintained that it would be difficult for him to climb up the stairs. However, he asked me to tell his wife to arrange for an air conditioner for him in jail.[1] When we reached the first floor, two officers appointed by the DM sat at a distance. They could only see us, but could not hear anything of our conversation. Humorously, Shri Asoka Mehta asked me to preside. I told him, 'You are the president, not I.'

I had taken copies of the proclamation of the Emergency, the notification issued by the President suspending Fundamental Rights, and other papers. My view was that even though there were certain technical defects in the proclamation of the Emergency and the issue of the notification suspending Fundamental Rights, if we challenged these in court, the government could rectify those errors and our purpose of approaching the court to quash the proclamation of the Emergency and notification suspending Fundamental Rights would not be served. After discussion, my advice was not to go to court. I said that Mahatma Gandhi never went to the courts for his release and that it was a political matter, which had to be fought politically.[2] All the leaders gathered there agreed. I continued to have discussions with them for over two hours. Shri Chandra Shekhar, who was robed in saffron-coloured clothes, did not utter a single word. However, I was fully conscious that he also was agreeing with my suggestions. It was lunchtime and we dispersed. I was offered lunch in the jail itself. We came to the ground floor in the office of the Superintendent of Jail and there, lunch was served to me. Shri Biju Patnaik also came there to meet me. I spoke to him and Shri Raj Narain, who was already seated there. I was informed while speaking to them that the interviews with Shri Sikander Bakht and Shri K.R. Malkani had been cancelled. It appears that instructions were sent from Delhi not to allow them to be interviewed by me.

I found that all the leaders whom I met were in high spirits. They were of the opinion that Smt Indira Gandhi had destroyed democracy, and had made so many arrests, against all norms of civilized human behaviour, only to keep herself in power by hook or crook. Shri Raj Narain in confidence told me there that Shri Jayaprakash Narayan had been put in detention in the Postgraduate Institute of Medical Education and Research (PGIMER, commonly referred to as the PGI) at Chandigarh. I asked him how he knew about this. He told me that he was giving me definite information and that this information was given to him by a police officer who had accompanied Shri Jayaprakash Narayan to the PGI, Chandigarh.

After my interviews at Rohtak Jail, I went to meet the DM, Shri N.K. Garg, at his residence to thank him. I found that he was surrounded by the Superintendent of Police (SP) and other police officers and they were deep in discussion. It appeared that the DM was very displeased with me. He was troubled that he had allowed me an interview with so many leaders. After thanking him, I went along with my colleague to the house of Chand Ram, who was also under detention.[3] We stayed there for some time and then came to Delhi.

FIGHTING FOR SHRI JAYAPRAKASH NARAYAN

Arriving in Delhi, we went straightaway to Shri Raj Narain's residence, from where I telephoned the DM of Chandigarh, Shri M.G. Devasahayam, an Indian Administrative Service (IAS) officer.[4] I told him that I had instructions from Shri Rajeshwar Prasad, the brother of Shri Jayaprakash Narayan, to give the latter legal advice regarding his detention and that I wanted to meet him and asked whether it would be convenient for me to come the next day (Sunday). The DM immediately told me that I could make the necessary application for an interview even on Sunday at 9 a.m. Thus, it was confirmed that the information I had received from Shri Raj Narain that Shri Jayaprakash Narayan was detained at the PGI at Chandigarh was correct. I immediately telephoned Shri Rajeshwar Prasad at the Gandhi Peace Foundation and told him that Shri Jayaprakash Narayan was detained in the PGI at Chandigarh and that he should accompany me the next morning to Chandigarh. I also telephoned Shri V.M. Tarkunde and asked him to accompany me. However, he said that he had a consultation scheduled the next day and, therefore, he would not be in a position to go with me. However, I insisted that he should go along with us. I wanted to take him along with a positive purpose. He and I had differences regarding the filing of *habeas corpus* petitions. He was of the view that Shri Rajeshwar Prasad, as next of kin, could file a *habeas corpus* petition on behalf of Shri Jayaprakash Narayan in the Delhi High Court. I stuck to the view that I had expressed to Shri Chandra Shekhar and others at the Rohtak Jail that we should not appeal, and as Fundamental Rights were suspended, the courts were also under threat, and hence, under such circumstances, we should not expose our judicial system and it would take a long time for the appeal to go from court to court. After all, I said, we are dealing in politics and should not be afraid of jail. I requested Shri Tarkunde not to file the *habeas corpus* petition on behalf of Shri Jayaprakash Narayan without consulting him. This was the main reason why I wanted Shri Tarkunde to accompany me.

A Fiat car with a driver was arranged for us. In those days, I used to remain underground at night as directed by Shri Raj

Narain, as he was afraid that even I might be arrested and in that event, it would be very difficult to look after the cases. I told Shri Tarkunde that a car would be at his house at 4.30 a.m. and that he should get up early and be ready by that time. I was staying that night not at my residence but at some other place and from there I came in my car and parked it at Shri Tarkunde's place. Shri Rajeshwar Prasad, along with Shri Gulab Yadav, Shri Jayaprakash Narayan's personal attendant, also arrived there.

We started for Chandigarh soon after 4.30 a.m. and reached the residence of the DM exactly at 9 a.m. He asked me to make the necessary application. We lodged three applications with him—one by me, one by Shri Tarkunde, and one by Shri Rajeshwar Prasad. The DM asked us to meet him in his office at 2.30 p.m., at which time, he said, he would give the orders. We had to pass time until then, so we went to the house of Shri C.L. Lakhanpal,[5] the leading advocate of Chandigarh High Court and a friend of ours. We had lunch at his house and called police officers and the DM from his telephone. As a result, his name came to be in the bad books of the government. It is sad that Shri C.L. Lakhanpal was also later detained and had to die in detention.[6]

At 2.30 p.m., we reached the DM's office, which was specially opened on that day. The DM passed three orders. My application and Shri Tarkunde's application were rejected on the ground that as Fundamental Rights and the right to move the courts were suspended, the lawyers were not needed for legal advice. An interview was granted to Shri Rajeshwar Prasad for one hour between 3 and 4 p.m. We were partly happy that at least Shri Rajeshwar Prasad would get an interview and would inform us of Shri Jayaprakash Narayan's health, and partly unhappy, for obvious reasons. We stayed with the DM in his office and discussed the matter with him. I told him that it was very unfair that he had promised to me the previous afternoon that I could come there and take an interview after making the necessary applications and now he had refused the same and that it was obvious that he had taken instructions from Delhi and rejected our applications. I pointed out to him that Articles 226 and 32 of the Constitution,[7] under which writ petitions could be filed in the High Court and the Supreme Court, respectively, were not suspended, and it was up to the court to see whether in a particular case it should interfere or not. I also drew his attention to the judgement of the Delhi High Court where it was held in a smuggler's case that even after the suspension of the Fundamental Rights, the High Court had the jurisdiction to entertain writ petitions questioning the detention. The DM had got a copy of the Constitution with him and when he saw the notification of the President suspending the Fundamental Rights and when he realized that Article 226 of the Constitution was not suspended, he said that we were probably right. I told him that if he did not allow us an interview, we would file a writ petition against him impleading Smt Indira Gandhi that the rejection of our application was *mala fide* and that he had taken instructions from her and thus it was not warranted under the law.[8] I said to him that perhaps these were new provisions and it would be better if he followed the same procedure that was followed the previous day at Rohtak by the DM of that place. Then, on our suggestion, we were allowed to write letters to Shri Jayaprakash Narayan, one by me and one by Shri Tarkunde, on the same lines that were written by me at Rohtak. In our letters, we told Shri Jayaprakash Narayan that his brother Shri Rajeshwar Prasad was here and wanted us to give Shri Jayaprakash Narayan legal advice regarding the validity or invalidity of his detention order and that if he wanted to consult with us, he should express his willingness on those very letters.[9] The letters were forwarded to Shri Jayaprakash Narayan. On my letter he wrote, 'I want very much to see Mr. Goyal as a lawyer to consult him about my case.' Similarly, he wrote on Shri Tarkunde's letter, 'I do want very much to see Mr. Tarkunde as a lawyer to consult him about my case.'[10] The DM called us at his residence at 6 p.m. to decide whether he was going to give us an interview or not.

We had to pass the time until then. As mentioned earlier, Shri Rajeshwar Prasad had been given a one-hour interview between 3 p.m. and 4 p.m. in the PGI. We also went to the PGI along with him but remained in a restaurant outside the PGI while he was having his interview on the third or fourth floor. Nobody in Chandigarh knew that Shri Jayaprakash Narayan was detained there. Everybody in Delhi believed that he was in a coma, and was being treated at the G.B. Pant Hospital.[11] There were several rumours about his health. However, the real fact was that he was taken from the Gandhi Peace Foundation in the morning of 26 June 1975 to Sohna Rest House in the district of Gurgaon in Haryana, where Shri Morarji Desai was also detained. Both of them were put in adjoining rooms for three days, but were not allowed to meet each other. From there, Shri Jayaprakash Narayan was brought to the All India Institute of Medical Sciences (AIIMS) in New Delhi and kept there for three days. This information was leaked and it appeared in the *Hindustan Times* that Shri Jayaprakash Narayan had been brought to AIIMS for some ailment.

We were very happy when Shri Rajeshwar Prasad came back after having his interview with Shri Jayaprakash Narayan. Shri Rajeshwar Prasad had also been looking forward to meeting us after his interview. Shri Tarkunde and I reached the District Magistrate's residence at 6 p.m. The DM gave us two orders, giving us a half-hour interview with Shri Jayaprakash Narayan. He appointed two officers in whose presence we were to hold our interview, as the interview could be held within the presence and not within the hearing of the two officers..

Shri Tarkunde and I were taken to the PGI hospital. The floor in which Shri Jayaprakash Narayan was detained was meant for heart patients, and only patients who required intensive care were treated there. It appeared that the entire ward was vacated to put Shri Jayaprakash Narayan under detention.[12] We entered a corridor that had a police officer stationed at every corner. The corridor had glass panes that were never opened at all. Then we entered a room which contained two beds, one table, and a few chairs. These beds were also for the police officers. From that room we entered another room. There were two beds and also some chairs with police officers seated on them here as well.[13] The whole area was air-conditioned. We were asked to wait as the doctors were attending to Shri Jayaprakash Narayan in his room. We waited for about ten to fifteen minutes and after the doctors came out, we were allowed to enter his room. Shri Tarkunde was following me.

When I entered the room, Shri Jayaprakash Narayan and I shook hands and smiled at each other.[14] He was wearing a kurta and pyjama. Three chairs were arranged for us in a corner of the room. There was an air conditioner and a bed. The area of the room might be 14×12 square feet. Two officers appointed by the DM were sitting near the door and were looking at us.[15] The distance between them and us was so little that if we spoke loudly they would hear us. When we were talking in the corner sitting on the two chairs, we were fully conscious that we had only half an hour at our disposal. I put my hands on Shri Jayaprakash Narayan's shoulder so that our conversation could be at closer range. Shri Tarkunde was also very close. I requested Shri Tarkunde to start the conversation. He said that we should go to court and we should challenge the Emergency and the detention of various leaders and workers. Shri Jayaprakash Narayan asked him about the chances of winning in court. Shri Tarkunde said that nothing was certain but the chances were fifty-fifty. When my turn came, I said that I was against going to court. I gave Mahatma Gandhi's example that he never went to court for his release and insisted that political matters had to be dealt with only politically. After all, the heavens were not going to fall if we remained in jail, and if the people were with us, one day Smt Indira Gandhi would be defeated and all the detenus would have to be released. I told Shri Jayaprakash Narayan that he was a big soul, and, similarly, other political leaders who had suffered throughout their lives were above-average human beings and they should lead the people. I said that we could not do anything except for remaining in jail for the time being. I told him that I had met a number of leaders at Rohtak Jail. He asked me about their opinion on this subject. I said that they also agreed with me that we should not go to court as it was not a court fight but merely a political fight.

Shri Jayaprakash Narayan then said to Shri Tarkunde that we should not go to court, as it was also the opinion of the other incarcerated leaders in Rohtak Jail. He also said that as Shri Tarkunde and I had divergent views, we should first resolve our differing views and then come to him again. We asked for directions from him about the next course of action. He suggested that we should not move the courts till Shri Raj Narain's case was decided. I then asked him a very specific question, which I also deposed before the Alva Commission (1977–78).[16] I asked him why the government had kept him in hospitals, as we had read in newspapers that he was first taken to AIIMS and here too he was put in hospital. He said that he did not know why the government did so. He said that it was not his desire to be hospitalized and he did not want to stay in the hospital. He also said that he never asked the government to keep him in hospital.

After our interview, we came down and went to Shri C.L. Lakhanpal's place. Shri Jayaprakash Narayan also wanted to have an interview with Gulab Yadav, who was his devoted personal attendant. With great difficulty, the DM allowed an interview with him also. After the interview with Gulab Yadav, we proceeded for Delhi at about 9 p.m. by the same Fiat car in which we had come to Chandigarh. By mistake, the driver, instead of taking the car towards Delhi, took the car towards Shimla. After we had travelled about 25 kilometres, we realized that we were travelling in the wrong direction. Then we took the right path and, at about 1 a.m., reached Karnal where we could not find any food for ourselves, and ultimately came to Delhi at about 2.30 a.m. On the way, I expressed my anguish that it was indeed a sad day for the country that Shri Jayaprakash Narayan was detained at a place where he was not getting fresh air and he was asked to walk only in the air-conditioned corridor with insufficient light and no fresh air. I expressed to Shri Tarkunde and Shri Rajeshwar Prasad that in this way Shri Jayaprakash Narayan may not survive as he was put in solitary confinement without any fresh air and sunlight and without any interactions or interviews with outsiders except the police officers stationed there.[17]

Five days later, I was allowed another interview with Shri Raj Narain at Rohtak Jail. I talked to him for about two to three hours in jail and told him about Shri Jayaprakash Narayan's health and detention. He was very worried. He said he knew Shri Jayaprakash Narayan very well and that, 'He (Jayaprakash Narayan) is an emotional man and if he is put in solitary confinement we may lose this man.' He asked me as to what could be done. I told him that if we made a representation to the government, nobody was going to listen to it. I also told him that I had been informed that Shri Om Mehta and Shri H.R. Gokhale were close to Smt Indira Gandhi then, and that Shri Gokhale was known to me and I could talk to him on this subject matter.

After a few days, Shri Raj Narain was brought to Tihar Jail in New Delhi in connection with the case. I met him again in Tihar Jail and he asked, 'What have you done for Shri Jayaprakash Narayan?' I told him that I had sought an interview with Shri H.R. Gokhale and he had agreed to meet me. I met Shri Gokhale at his residence and spoke to him for about an hour. He said that whatever we talked about there should not be disclosed to anybody. I promised not to disclose it to anybody except Shri Raj Narain. I told Shri Gokhale that I had come to him not as a beggar, but as a representative of the entire Opposition in the country. I told him that preventive detention does not mean punitive detention and that the government cannot keep a detenu in solitary confinement. He apparently agreed with me, saying, 'You mean that Shri Jayaprakash Narayan should be put in confinement along with detenus of his own age, say Shri Morarji Desai, etc.' I told him there was no harm if he put persons under house arrest in Delhi or at some other place so that at least they could talk to each other and live together. He said that he would talk to Smt Indira Gandhi when she would be in a mood to talk. I urged him to talk as soon as possible, since the matter was urgent and we were worried about Shri Jayaprakash Narayan's health. He said that I should enquire during the weekend, i.e. on Saturday or Sunday. It was a Wednesday when I had met him. The second thing that I told Shri Gokhale was that we would not be participating in the case unless our client, Shri Raj Narain, was either released or at least allowed to be with us in order to prepare our case. We had taken two rooms in the India International Centre (IIC) near Lodhi Colony for the purpose of preparing the case. I told him that if Shri Raj Narain were to be put under detention in one room at the IIC and we could have the facility of talking to him, that would serve our purpose, and even if the government did not want to pay the expenses for this, we would pay them. He promised me that he would discuss this matter with Smt Indira Gandhi. When I telephoned him on Sunday he said that he had put these points to Smt Indira Gandhi but she did not reply. I communicated all this to Shri Raj Narain, to whom I was given interviews freely under an administrative order issued by the Delhi Administration. The order was that I could meet Shri Raj Narain without the presence and hearing of any officer at any time at short notice and I could take any *pairokar* also along with me. I had been laid a trap by the government. As per my information, this facility for me to interview Shri Raj Narain was arranged in such a way that we should participate in the hearing of the appeal and then lose the case, so that the judgement of Justice J.M.L. Sinha of 12 June 1975 could be overturned. The Additional District Magistrate (ADM), Ms Meenakshi Datta, (later Mrs. Meenakshi Datta Ghosh), was in charge of Shri Raj Narain's case and she was told not to refuse any interview that I wanted. I could stay in the jail for any number of hours. I told Shri Raj Narain that this was a trap and nothing else. We could not do anything for Shri Jayaprakash Narayan and he continued to remain in solitary confinement in the PGI at Chandigarh. However, his close relations, including his brother, were allowed interviews from time to time.

Shri Jayaprakash Narayan had appointed three lawyers, namely Shri V.M. Tarkunde, Shri P.N. Lekhi, and myself, as his advocates to give him advice from time to time. I could not go to Shri Jayaprakash Narayan after 6 July as I became busy with Shri Raj Narain's case. However, I saw him later in the year on 26 October in the PGI, Chandigarh. By that time, he had been taken to a bungalow in the hospital. I requested Ms. Meenakshi Datta to arrange my interview with him and also requested her that Pranab Chatterjee be allowed to accompany me for the interview to Chandigarh.[18] On 24 October, we got the order for the interview for 26 October. When we reached the DM at Chandigarh, he told me that my name was no longer on the panel of advocates. I asked him as to who got my name struck off. He could not reply. It still remains a mystery as to why and how my name was struck off from the panel of lawyers.[19] I went to the DM who could not refuse the interview as we had taken permission for the same from Delhi. Our interview was arranged for one hour from 11.15 a.m. to 12.15 p.m. on 26 October. The Assistant Superintendent of Jail was also present at the interview.[20] That day also, we were asked to wait in the adjoining room as the doctors were examining Shri Jayaprakash Narayan. A doctor there, named Dr. Khatri,[21] was known to me as the brother-in-law of a friend of mine. However, even though I greeted him twice, he did not respond. The atmosphere in the hospital was so fearful that even the doctors had no courage to show that they knew Shri Jayaprakash Narayan's advocates. We carried with us a basket of fruits and a number of books for Shri Jayaprakash Narayan that had been given by the Maharani of Patiala, Smt Mohinder Kaur. During our interview, Shri Pranab

Chatterjee started talking in Bhojpuri language. Shri Jayaprakash Narayan requested him not to talk in Bhojpuri but only in Hindi or English, as the officers who were supervising our interview did not know Bhojpuri. We conveyed everything to Shri Jayaprakash Narayan indirectly. He complained about his health and said that he was having some medicines that he did not relish. He also said that he was experiencing great pain in his stomach, which he had never had in his life before. He wanted the public outside to know about his ailment. I informed him that at present there were about 200,000 detenus in the country detained by Smt Indira Gandhi under the MISA and Defence of India Rules. He responded by saying, 'It is a very happy day for me and I am very happy to meet you.' He said that even in Mahatma Gandhi's time, such a large number of persons did not court arrest at one time. Shri Jayaprakash Narayan had never been informed by Shri Tarkunde, who would see him almost every week, that so many persons had been detained during the Emergency. In fact, it appears to me that Shri Tarkunde used to give Shri Jayaprakash Narayan a very pessimistic picture of the movement in the country against the Emergency. In his personal diary, published as *Prison Diary 1975*, Shri Jayaprakash Narayan described our interview in the following words: 'Pranav Chatterjee (Patna), Goyal (Delhi), both lawyers came to see me. It was a day of great happiness. Completed four months detention today.'[22]

After we came out of the meeting, I told Shri Pranab Chatterjee that it seemed to be a case of slow poisoning and the jail authorities would ultimately finish Shri Jayaprakash Narayan.[23] We came to Delhi and spoke to Shri Tarkunde and asked him why he had never informed us that Shri Jayaprakash Narayan was so ill. I also told him that it was a case of slow poisoning. However, he said that we should rely on the doctors and he did not suspect any foul play. I told him that something could be given to Shri Jayaprakash Narayan in his food and even if the doctor may not do so, some other persons may and could do so. I telephoned Shri Rajeshwar Prasad in Bombay about Shri Jayaprakash Narayan's health. He came to Delhi and then went to Chandigarh.

Shri Jayaprakash Narayan became extremely ill afterwards, so much so that ultimately, the government had to release him on 12 November 1975 to ensure that he did not die in jail.[24] His brother Shri Rajeshwar Prasad was in Chandigarh when he was released. He was brought to Delhi by plane from Chandigarh.[25] A number of Shri Jayaprakash Narayan's well-wishers, including Acharya J.B. Kripalani and Shri B.P. Koirala, the former prime minister of Nepal, were present at the airport to receive him. I was also present there. To our surprise, Shri Jayaprakash Narayan was whisked away from some other exit and none of us could see him at the airport. We came to know that he had been admitted in AIIMS. I went to see him there at night. He showed me the order passed by the government for his release. The order said that Shri Jayaprakash Narayan was released on parole for one month. He told me that he never asked for any parole and the order was passed by the government without his knowledge.

I saw him a number of times when he was in Delhi in AIIMS for a few days. One day, a few lawyers of the Supreme Court also accompanied me to see Shri Jayaprakash Narayan. He was lying on the bed, apparently very seriously ill. I introduced those lawyers to him. When talking about the future of the country, he said, 'Age is against me.' I said, 'We desire that you live very long for the service of the country.' We also uttered encouraging words and all of us said 'We are there'.

The atmosphere in those days was very subdued. There was a great fear complex in the country. Anybody could be arrested without any grounds or trial. Shri Jayaprakash Narayan was then taken to Bombay at his request and was admitted in the Jaslok Hospital where it was found that both his kidneys were damaged beyond repair. He was put on dialysis under the able treatment of Dr. M.K. Mani, with the Medical Director of Jaslok Hospital being Dr. Shantilal Mehta. He could live only on dialysis. A dialysis machine was purchased for him after numerous citizens of this country contributed a rupee each.[26] He preferred to live in Patna and persons very close to him were trained in operating the dialysis machine.

EDITOR'S NOTES

1. Piloo Mody was an architect–politician who had been educated at The Doon School, Dehradun and at the University of California, Berkeley. Along with Durga Shankar Bajpai, he designed and built the iconic five-star Intercontinental Hotel, now known as The Oberoi, in New Delhi. He was a founder of the Swatantra Party and was elected to the fourth Lok Sabha in 1967 representing the Godhra constituency and was re-elected to the fifth Lok Sabha in 1971, where he served as an MP till 1977. From 1978 he was a member of the Rajya Sabha till his demise in 1983. Dr. N.M. Ghatate writes that on a visit to Shri L.K. Advani in Rohtak Jail, '...the Jailor gave me an interesting news that in the morning even Piloo Mody's dogs came to interview him. And he showed me a copy of the letter written by Piloo Mody to Indira Gandhi. It read:

> "My dear I.G. (*read* Indira Gandhi),
>
> Under the conditions of Detention Order, I am allowed to meet my family members once in a fortnight. I have a wife and no children except two Irish Setter dogs. They should be treated as my family and also allowed the Interview.
>
> Thanking you,
>
> Yours faithfully
>
> Sd/-
>
> P.M. (*read* Piloo Mody)"

Indira Gandhi knew his background. Besides being a leading architect, who designed Chandigarh with the French architect Le Corbusier, he was known for his great sense of humour. Piloo Mody was a close friend of Pakistan's Prime Minister Zulfikar Ali Bhutto and after the 1971 war, during the negotiation, Indira Gandhi had invited him to Shimla. Therefore, perhaps, Indira Gandhi granted his unusual request to be interviewed by his pets. It may be mentioned that even L.K. Advani admired Piloo Mody who was used to luxuries for his adjustment to prison inconveniences.' See Dr. N.M. Ghatate, *Emergency, Constitution and Democracy: An Indian Experience*', New Delhi: Shipra Publications, 2011, pp. 47–48. Many of Piloo Mody's friends managed to get into the jail to see him by acting as minders for his dogs. See, 'Politician's Wife Recalls Emergency Times', *The Times of India*, 24 January 2016, available at https://timesofindia.indiatimes.com/city/mumbai/Politicians-wife-recalls-Emergency-times/articleshow/50701366.cms, accessed 24 June 2018.

2   In fact, many leaders also held this opinion. Dr. N.M. Ghatate quotes Atal Bihari Vajpayee as saying, 'In a situation like this, political battle cannot be won by legal means'. See, Dr. N.M. Ghatate, *Emergency, Constitution and Democracy: An Indian Experience*, New Delhi: Shipra Publications, 2011, p. 80.

3   Chand Ram was then the President of the Bharatiya Lok Dal (BLD) in Haryana.

4   This is also mentioned in M.G. Devasahayam, *JP in Jail: An Uncensored Account*, New Delhi: Roli Books Pvt Ltd, 2006, pp. 12–13.

5   C.L. Lakhanpal was the President of the Punjab and Haryana High Court Bar Association.

6   As C.L. Lakhanpal's health deteriorated while he was in jail he was kept under detention in the PGI, Chandigarh. He expired on 24 July 1976.

7   For Articles 226 and 32 of the Constitution, see Appendix III.4

and Appendix III.5, respectively.
8   Implead: To sue or prosecute or bring an action against a third party.
9   This is also mentioned in M.G. Devasahayam, *JP in Jail: An Uncensored Account*, New Delhi: Roli Books Pvt Ltd, 2006, pp. 12–16.
10 See 'JP Papers', File 4, unpublished, Cultural Informatics Lab, Indira Gandhi National Centre for Arts, New Delhi and Braj Kishore Memorial Institute, Patna.
11 Govind Ballabh Pant Institute of Postgraduate Medical Education and Research, New Delhi, formally known as Pt. Govind Ballabh Pant Hospital.
12 That the ward was meant for heart patients and was an 'Intensive Care Unit' was also deposed to the Alva Commission of Inquiry by others, including M.G Devasahayam, the DM and Inspector General of Prisons of the Union Territory of Chandigarh in 1975. However, in an e-mail communication to the editor, dated 5 May 2018, M.G. Devasahayam stated that actually the ward was a newly constructed yet-to-be-commissioned special ward that was lying vacant, which was notified temporarily as a prison under Section 541 of the CrPC. It had a big hall with corridor with two rooms—a larger one in which Shri Jayaprakash Narayan was staying, and a smaller one for the doctor-on-duty that was also used by the Deputy Superintendent, Jail.
13 The word 'police officer' has been used here in a broader sense, to include prison staff as well as policemen. In an e-mail communication with the editor, M.G. Devasahayam confirmed that all the uniformed people in the ward were prison staff who were manning the inner perimeter while the police was allowed only outside the ward. In his deposition before the Alva Commission of Inquiry, M.G. Devasahayam stated: 'An entire ward of the PGI, known as Intensive Care Unit, was placed at the disposal of Shri Jayaprakash Narayan and those attending to him. Shri Jayaprakash Narayan was lodged in one of the rooms—the

largest private room in that ward. Entry into this room as well as the personal needs of Shri Jayaprakash Narayan were looked after by a jail warden who was put on duty by rotation. The jail staff were functioning under the superintendence of Superintendent of Jail, Shri Mohinder Singh, who was directly responsible to me in my capacity also as Inspector General of Prisons. The outside security inside the ward as well as outside was the responsibility of the District Police. They were functioning under the direct control of the senior superintendent of police. ... During his strolls in the corridor of the ward, Shri Jayaprakash Narayan used to be accompanied by Shri R.D. Sharma, Astt. Suptd. (Assistant Superintendent) of Jail.' See 'JP Papers', File 2-1, unpublished, Cultural Informatics Lab, Indira Gandhi National Centre for Arts, New Delhi and Braj Kishore Memorial Institute, Patna.

14 In his deposition to the Shah Commission of Inquiry, M.G. Devasahayam stated that he met Jayaprakash Narayan at 7 p.m. on 6 July 1975, soon after Jayaprakash Narayan's meeting with J.P. Goyal and V.M. Tarkunde. Referring to Jayaprakash Narayan, he added, 'In fact, he (JP) was getting a little restless because it was for two weeks that he had not seen anyone close to him. Only when he had seen his brother, his close associates like Shri Tarkunde and Shri Goyal, he was quite composed.' See 'JP Papers', File 2-1, unpublished, Cultural Informatics Lab, Indira Gandhi National Centre for Arts, New Delhi and Braj Kishore Memorial Institute, Patna.

15 These two officers were the Deputy Superintendent of Police (DSP) and the Superintendent, Sub-Jail who also functioned as the Executive Magistrate.

16 A one-man commission headed by Dr. K. Nagappa Alva, which enquired into the nature and adequacy of treatment meted out to Jayaprakash Narayan while he was in detention in different parts of India. Prior to Dr. K. Nagappa Alva, the commission was headed by Dr. Philipose Koshy.

17 'JP said in his Open Letter, which was printed and circulated

by the Bihar Jana Sangharsh Samiti, that in this respect the behaviour of the Indira Government was worse than that of the British rulers, who had allowed him the company of Dr. Ram Manohar Lohia at least for an hour every day during his detention in the Lahore Fort in 1943. The government of Mrs. Indira Gandhi agreed only to allow him the company of his personal attendant, Gulab Yadav, on the condition that he too remain a prisoner with him. Naturally, JP declined.' See S.K. Ghose, *The Crusade and End of Indira Raj*, New Delhi: Intellectual Book Corner, 1978, p. 225. A writ petition against the solitary confinement of Jayaprakash Narayan was dismissed by the Delhi High Court on 7 August 1975, without issuing notice to the respondents, on the grounds that as Jayaprakash Narayan was in a hospital at the PGI, Chandigarh and undergoing treatment, it could not be called solitary confinement. It did not succeed in the Supreme Court too, with the case being adjourned to 15 November 1975, by which time Jayaprakash Narayan had been released on parole. See 'JP Papers', File 2-1, unpublished, Cultural Informatics Lab, Indira Gandhi National Centre for Arts, New Delhi and Braj Kishore Memorial Institute, Patna. Giving an account of the ill-treatment of Jayaprakash Narayan in detention, M.G. Devasahayam, the Inspector-General of Prisons, Chandigarh in 1975, states 'The directive from "Delhi Durbar" was that on "depositing" JP at the PGI Guest House, I should report to Mr. Bansi Lal, the then Chief Minister of Haryana and a key member of the ruling Emergency coterie. When I called him up, his instructions were terse, "*yeh salah apne aapko hero samajtha hai. Us ko wahin pade rehne do. Kisi se milne ya telephone karne nahin dena. Aap hi khatam ho jayaga*" (This damn fellow thinks he is a hero. Let him lie there. Don't allow him to meet anybody or telephone any one. He will be finished this way.) The same night the Union Territory's Home Secretary conveyed to me another "dicktat" from Bansi Lal that JP should not be allowed to take a walk in the open between sunrise and sunset. Being unaware of the actual "Emergency agenda" I did not give much importance to this. But later events were to reveal as to how ominous these remarks and these instructions turned out to be.' See M.G. Devasahayam, 'A bright light during dark hours: "Prisoner" JP in Chandigarh', *The Tribune*, Chandigarh, 18 June 2000, available at http://www.tribuneindia.com/2000/20000618/edit.htm#1, accessed 14 January 2018.

18 Pranab Chatterjee was a Socialist leader and advocate from Patna. He was the former chairman of the Bihar unit of the Samyukta Socialist Party.

19 On 13 July 1975, Jayaprakash Narayan had written to the District Commissioner, Chandigarh, nominating V.M. Tarkunde, J.P. Goyal, and P.N. Lekhi as his advocates. As mentioned earlier, there had been disagreement between V.M. Tarkunde and J.P. Goyal on whether recourse to the courts should be taken for legal redress against the detention of Jayaprakash Narayan. On 24 July 1975, Vimal Dave, advocate, met Jayaprakash Narayan at the PGI, Chandigarh. On the same day, Jayaprakash Narayan made a change in his list of nominated advocates to include Vimal Dave in place of P.N. Lekhi and J.P. Goyal. Earlier, Vimal Dave had sent a letter dated 10 July 1975 to the Lieutenant Governor of Delhi, stating that on the instructions of his client Rajeshwar Prasad, brother of Jayaprakash Narayan, he was requesting an end to solitary confinement of Jayaprakash Narayan. In a letter to Jayaprakash Narayan dated 29 July 1975, Vimal Dave stated that on his return from Chandigarh he had discussions with V.M. Tarkunde, who had advised him to prepare a petition in Jayaprakash Narayan's name for filing in the court. Perhaps Jayaprakash Narayan was influenced by V.M. Tarkunde and Vimal Dave or Rajeshwar Prasad to approach the courts. However, in their meeting with Jayaprakash Narayan on 26 October 1975, J.P. Goyal and Pranab Chatterjee made a request to Jayaprakash Narayan to add their names in the list of advocates. Jayaprakash Narayan agreed to this and said that

he would send a request to the Home Secretary, Government of India. See 'JP Papers', File 1, unpublished, Cultural Informatics Lab, Indira Gandhi National Centre for the Arts, New Delhi and Braj Kishore Memorial Institute, Patna.

20 R.D. Sharma, Assistant Superintendent Jail, filled in for the Executive Magistrate cum Superintendent Jail, as the latter was away on tour. See 'JP Papers', File 4, unpublished, Cultural Informatics Lab, Indira Gandhi National Centre for the Arts, New Delhi and Braj Kishore Memorial Institute, Patna.

21 Dr. H.N. Khatri, Senior Consultant at the PGI.

22 Jayaprakash Narayan, *Prison Diary 1975*, Bombay: Popular Prakashan, 1977, p. 96. On the same page, Jayaprakash Narayan added in footnotes the following: 'Socialist leader and advocate' (fn. 56) for 'Pranav Chatterjee' and 'J.P. Goyal, a noted advocate' (fn. 57) for 'Goyal'.

23 The slow poisoning was an impression formed by J.P. Goyal. That something was amiss in the medical treatment of Jayaprakash Narayan is also recorded in the minutes of a conversation between Allan and Wendy Scarfe and M.G. Devasahayam: 'Simultaneously JP's health deteriorated suddenly and mysteriously. He looked haggard and his doctors were providing MGD (M.G. Devasahayam) with only vague reports. Not being a medical man MGD could not question their diagnosis but he was profoundly dissatisfied. He felt there was something amiss. He suspected deliberate negligence in diagnosing his illness.' See 'Minutes of conversation between Allan and Wendy Scarfe and Shri M.G. Devasahayam—16.3.1994 in Room 419, Hilton Hotel, Melbourne, Australia', in 'JP Papers', File 9, unpublished, Cultural Informatics Lab, Indira Gandhi National Centre for Arts, New Delhi and Braj Kishore Memorial Institute, Patna.

24 Though the order for Jayaprakash Narayan's release on parole was signed on 12 November 1975, he was discharged from the PGI on 15 November 1975 and left Chandigarh on 16 November 1975. M.G. Devasahayam writes of attempts made by Bansi Lal to delay

Jayaprakash Narayan's release despite the parole order already being signed on 12 November 1975, insisting that Jayaprakash Narayan should be kept in the PGI for at least a week more. See M.G. Devasahayam, *JP in Jail: An Uncensored Account*, New Delhi: Roli Books Private Limited, 2006, pp. 278–79. It seems that the Sanjay Gandhi coterie, which included Bansi Lal, did not want Jayaprakash Narayan to be released as they were afraid that he would rally the country around himself and force elections to be held, which the Congress party was likely to lose, and thus thwart their plan of hoisting Sanjay Gandhi as prime minister of India after the possible resignation of Indira Gandhi from the post of prime minister under the pressure of the combined Opposition. The order for Jayaprakash Narayan's detention was withdrawn unconditionally on 4 December 1975, while he was undergoing treatment in Jaslok Hospital in Bombay.

25 In order to ensure that the nefarious designs, as outlined in Note 24, were thwarted, M.G. Devasahayam realized that Jayaprakash Narayan had to be taken out of Chandigarh as soon as possible. For doing this, three confirmed air tickets were needed for Jayaprakash Narayan, his brother Rajeshwar Prasad, and Jayaprakash Narayan's attendant Gulab Yadav but were not available. Devasahayam writes that he had to literally threaten Ajit Singh, the airport manager at Chandigarh Airport, that he, using his powers as DM of Chandigarh, would impound the Srinagar–Jammu–Chandigarh–Delhi aircraft on the tarmac at Chandigarh Airport unless the necessary arrangements for the required confirmed tickets were made. Within minutes of his putting the phone down, Ajit Singh called back saying that he had made the necessary arrangements for three confirmed tickets. Thus, Jayaprakash Narayan was able to leave Chandigarh by plane. See M.G. Devasahayam, *JP in Jail: An Uncensored Account*, New Delhi: Roli Books Pvt Ltd, 2006, pp. 289–92.

26 This is also mentioned in an article about Dr. M.K. Mani. To cover '....the cost of an artificial kidney so that JP could be

dialysed at home, a get-well post card was printed and sold at a rupee a piece to the public, to be posted to JP. Lakhs of people bought the postcards and mailed them. It was easy to buy the artificial kidney from the money thus collected.' See 'JP and Dr. Mani', *Madras Musings*, Vol. XXVII, No. 1, 16–30 April 2017, available at http://www.madrasmusings.com/vol-27-no-1/jp-and-dr-mani/, accessed 6 December 2017.

6

Differences among the Lawyers

After the Emergency was declared just a few minutes before the midnight of 25 June 1975, and Shri Raj Narain and other political leaders of the Opposition parties were arrested in the wee hours of 26 June 1975, the question that arose before us was whether we should argue the election appeal or not. I was definitely in favour of not arguing the appeal filed by Smt Indira Gandhi and the cross-appeal filed by us. My reasons were as follows:

1. It was a political case and Smt Indira Gandhi had put our client, who was her opponent in the election as well as in the election petition, under detention and thus our client was handicapped to prosecute the case.
2. It had become an unequal fight as Smt Indira Gandhi had manoeuvred the Constitution as well as the judiciary in her favour, and she should not be allowed to force us to argue the case shackled.
3. It being a political case, we would not gain anything by arguing the case during the Emergency, particularly when Article 14 of the Constitution was suspended during the Emergency.[1]
4. We had challenged the Representation of the People (Amendment) Act, 1974, which was made effective with retrospective effect to undo the judgement of the Supreme Court in the case of *Kanwar Lal Gupta vs Amar Nath Chawla & Ors* on 3 October 1974, 1975 AIR 308, 1975 SCR (2) 269. In that case, the Supreme Court had held that the expenses incurred by the political parties would be

treated to be the expenses incurred by the candidate. The said judgement clearly hit Smt Indira Gandhi's election case, which was, at that time, pending in the Allahabad High Court. Justice J.M.L. Sinha had held that it was not necessary to go into the validity of that Act as he found that the expenses incurred by Smt Indira Gandhi were less than the prescribed figure. However, in the Supreme Court, we had challenged the same again in our cross-appeal. Towards the end of July 1975, Smt Indira Gandhi got the Election Laws (Amendment) Act, 1975 passed, which was enacted on 6 August 1975.[2] The said Act also could be challenged on the ground of validity under Article 14 of the Constitution, which was suspended.

I was of the view that under these circumstances, we should make an application to the Supreme Court for postponement of the hearing of the case till after the Emergency was lifted and when Article 14 would be available to us. For reasons best known to Shri Shanti Bhushan, he was not agreeable to this suggestion and ridiculed it every time. A number of meetings took place on this subject matter between Shri Raj Narain and myself in Tihar Jail. Shri Raj Narain concurred with my view. However, when Shri Shanti Bhushan used to meet him, he would try to persuade Shri Raj Narain that we should argue the case and if we won from the Supreme Court, Smt Indira Gandhi would have to resign from the office of the prime minister. Shri Raj Narain and I quizzed him about our chances of victory under the present circumstances when the atmosphere was subdued and the judiciary did not seem to have the courage to decide the case independently and without fear. However, Shri Shanti Bhushan said that even if one judge, most likely Justice H.R. Khanna,[3] decided the case in our favour, that would vindicate our stand as at least one judge would have accepted our contention. He also insisted that if we did not participate in the case and applied for adjournment, the public at large would think that we were running away from the battle in the Supreme Court and our case was weak. This argument did not appeal to us as we did not believe that the public would consider our case to be weak. We had full justification for not arguing the case at a time when Shri Raj Narain and his colleagues were put behind bars, with whom even interviews were not allowed or obtained with great difficulty, and even if some interviews were allowed to close relatives after long intervals they were held under the supervision of officers appointed by the government. It was very difficult for me and Shri Raj Narain to convince Shri Shanti Bhushan that it was futile to argue the case and that it would really harm the case of the Opposition.

Shri Raj Narain was put under solitary confinement in Tihar Jail and could not meet anybody. In the beginning, he could meet Chaudhary Charan Singh only two times. However, later, he was not allowed to meet anybody except myself and the other lawyers and *pairokars* who would accompany me. I visited him almost every day, and the day I could not meet him he used to become impatient and sad. The important persons among the detenus in Tihar Jail at that time included Chaudhary Charan Singh, Shri Prakash Singh Badal, Smt Gayatri Devi (former Maharani of Jaipur), and Smt Vijayaraje Scindia (former Rajmata of Gwalior). I was told that somehow Shri Raj Narain could send messages to some of them as to what I had told him about the conditions outside the jail. One day, I asked Shri Raj Narain as to why he became sad when I or some other lawyers did not come to Tihar Jail to visit him. He said that the detenus in the Tihar Jail wanted to know as to what was happening outside, and we were the only link to give them this information.

I told Shri Raj Narain that I could contact some people who were very close to Shri A.N. Ray, the Chief Justice of India. As mentioned earlier, Shri A.N. Ray had been made Chief Justice after superseding three eminent judges, apparently with the sole purpose that whenever Smt Indira Gandhi's case would come up in the Supreme Court, he should deliver the goods to Indira Gandhi and decide the case in her favour. The Supreme Court was to reopen on 14 July. A mention was to be made about the date of hearing, as directed by Justice V.R. Krishna Iyer. I insisted that we should not agree for a date and we should make the necessary application for adjournment of the case. Shri Shanti Bhushan overruled me. Shri Raj Narain also desired that at least he should be present at the time of hearing each day in the court. When the mention was made before the Chief Justice's court, I was also present. An agreement on 11 August 1975 as the date of hearing of the appeals was made. I asked Shri Shanti Bhushan to tell the court that Shri Raj Narain would also be present at the hearing. Shri Shanti Bhushan said that he wanted his client to be present and brought to court every day from the jail. It appeared that Chief Justice A.N. Ray was not too pleased with Shri Raj Narain's presence, and said, 'Mr. Shanti Bhushan, you are such a big lawyer. Do you really require the assistance of your client?' Shri Shanti Bhushan replied, 'No, my lord.' I insisted to Shri Shanti Bhushan, 'No, no, he should know that we certainly require the presence and assistance of our client.' However, Shri Shanti Bhushan was not assertive enough. The result was that Shri Raj Narain was not permitted to be present in court at the time of hearing of the case. In fact, it appeared to me that Shri Shanti Bhushan himself did not want Shri Raj Narain to be present in court at the time of hearing of the appeal for reasons known to him. Earlier too, Shri Shanti Bhushan did not like Shri Raj Narain to be present in the court at the time when Smt Indira Gandhi was going to give her evidence at Allahabad. This is reiterated in the book *The Case That Shook India* (1978), written by Shri Prashant Bhushan, Shri Shanti Bhushan's son: 'Raj Narain himself was also present in the court. Earlier, when he had told Bhushan that he wanted to be present during the cross-examination, Bhushan had objected to it, knowing the volatile temperament of Shri Raj Narain. Bhushan, however, reluctantly agreed to Narain being present when he undertook not to utter a word during the proceedings....Mrs. Gandhi took a seat which was specially provided for her. ... She looked composed and unruffled as she sat down.'[4] Thus, Shri Raj Narain has been shown as if he is not a man of sound mind. On the same page, it has been shown that Smt Indira Gandhi was of a composed and unruffled mind. I am very sorry to say that this language should not find place in the book. It is not understood as to how Shri Prashant Bhushan knows the considered temperament of Shri Raj Narain and labelled him as 'volatile'. I have known Shri Raj Narain personally for the last more than eighteen years and regard him as my elder brother. I found Shri Raj Narain to be very sincere and devoted to the cause of the country and a very intelligent and shrewd person who knew how to behave in court. Sometimes, he pointed out mistakes of the lawyers also. Even though he is outspoken I can say that I have rarely come across a person like Shri Raj Narain who has made great sacrifices and is the most sincere man I have ever respected.[5] I may inform Shri Prashant Bhushan that during the Emergency when Shri Raj Narain was in jail at Hissar, his only son-in-law who was a lawyer at Azamgarh expired. Shri Raj Narain's son, Shri Om Prakash, was sent by us to meet Shri Raj Narain in jail. We gave Shri Om Prakash clear instructions that he should not mention to Shri Raj Narain about the death of his son-in-law. However, during the interview when Shri Raj Narain enquired about his relations, Shri Om Prakash incidentally mentioned about Shri Raj Narain's son-in-law. Shri Om Prakash could not check himself and told Shri Raj Narain that his son-in-law was dead. Shri Raj Narain was unruffled and also got himself composed at that time. I learnt this from Shri Om Prakash when he came back from visiting Shri Raj Narain. How can Shri Raj Narain be shown in a dimmer light than Smt Indira Gandhi on the same page of the book by Prashant Bhushan? I met Shri Raj Narain after a few days in the same jail. I deliberately did not remind him about the death of his son-in-law. However, even though he had been in solitary confinement for about twenty months, the man had the same love for the country and the same usual worry for his own countrymen that he had earlier.

I do not understand why Shri Shanti Bhushan should have agreed to argue the case without his client's presence. After all, the heavens were not going to fall if the hearing of the appeal had been postponed. This, in my opinion, showed great weakness and lack of boldness on the part of Shri Shanti Bhushan. It was very difficult for me to work with him on the case. However, owing to the discipline amongst us and pressure from Shri Raj Narain, I continued to work on the case anyhow.

My secret information was that the printed paper books of the appeal were scrutinized by Chief Justice A.N. Ray himself sometime in the first and second week of July. It is said that he reported to Smt Indira Gandhi and Shri H.R. Gokhale that the judgement of Justice J.M.L. Sinha was flawless and that, in fact, there were more points in our cross-appeal than their appeal. He also reportedly told them that Shri J.N. Kaushal,[6] who was the Advocate General of Haryana at that time and a Senior Advocate for Smt Indira Gandhi, could not deliver the goods and suggested that Shri Ashoke Kumar Sen be engaged as the counsel for Smt Indira Gandhi.

This piece of information was corroborated by a tip I got from the prime minister's house. I conveyed to Shri Raj Narain that my information was that Smt Indira Gandhi was going to engage Shri A.K. Sen in the case as Shri A.N. Ray had told her that Shri Jagannath Kaushal was not a match for the advocates of Shri Raj Narain and that only Shri A.K. Sen could deliver the goods for her. Shri Raj Narain told me that Shri A.K. Sen was a believer in democracy and he should not appear for Smt Indira Gandhi who was vindictive and had coined a CBI case against Shri A.K. Sen. On my way back from the jail after meeting Shri Raj Narain in the first few days of August 1975, I dropped in at Shri A.K. Sen's house. His wife was also there. I told both of them that my information was that he would be engaged in the case. Shri A.K. Sen said that it was impossible that the case would be handed over to him as Shri Siddhartha Shankar Ray, a close associate of Smt Indira Gandhi, was against him. I told Shri A.K. Sen to believe me and the case was coming to him. I advised him not to accept the case of Smt Indira Gandhi who could not be called a friend. I also told him that Smt Indira Gandhi was politically finished and it was just a question of time before we formed the government soon. I also told him that he should not think that Smt Indira Gandhi would withdraw the CBI case pending against him and it would be only our government that would do so. I advised him that if Indira Gandhi's case came to him, he should say that he is unwell and that such a big case would require health and that, hence, it would not be possible for him to argue the case. We continued talking, sitting in his veranda till 12.30 p.m. I also had dinner with him. Shri Shailendra Kumar, who later became his son-in-law, was also sitting there. We all were talking politics and other things. Shri A.K. Sen was citing Sanskrit *shlokas* that a king or a queen who becomes tyrannical, one day finishes himself or herself. A few days later, Shri Uma Shankar Dikshit, at that time a close associate of Smt Indira Gandhi, Shri D.K. Barooah, the then Congress president, and others went to Shri A.K. Sen and asked him to take on the case. He accepted it. When I came to know about it I stopped speaking to Shri A.K. Sen as the professional ethics required that I did not talk to him about the case any further. We were sitting in the Supreme Court Bar Association one day. By the way, I asked him, 'I think, now you have got the brief.' He remarked, 'Yes, those people came to me.'

After Shri A.N. Ray had conveyed to Smt Indira Gandhi and Shri H.R. Gokhale that there were more points in our cross-appeal than their appeal, as mentioned above, amendments of election laws and constitutional provisions started taking place in Parliament. The Election Laws (Amendment) Act, 1975 was passed by Parliament towards the end of July and was enacted on 6 August 1975. When the matter came up for hearing on 11 August 1975, a *Gazette* copy of the Election Laws (Amendment) Act, 1975 was given to us in the court itself. The Constitution (Thirty-ninth Amendment) Act, 1975 had also been passed by that time.[7] It got the assent of the President on the night of 10 August 1975 and its copy was also given to us in the court itself on 11 August. According to Clause (4) of Section 4 of the Constitution (Thirty-ninth Amendment) Act, 1975, the Supreme Court was, in effect, directed to allow the appeal of Smt Indira Gandhi and dismiss the election petition of Shri Raj Narain. The relevant portion of the provision is reproduced below:

> 4. Insertion of new article 329A. In Part XV of the Constitution, after Article 329, the following article shall be inserted namely:-
> 329A. Special provision as to elections to Parliament in the case of Prime Minister and Speaker ...
> (4) No law made by Parliament before the commencement of the Constitution (Thirty-ninth Amendment) Act, 1975, in so far as it relates to election petitions and matters connected therewith, shall apply or shall be deemed ever to have applied to or in relation to the election to any such person as is referred to in clause (1) to either House of Parliament and such election shall not be deemed to be void or ever to have become void on any ground on which such election could be declared to be void or has, before such commencement, been declared to be void under any such law and notwithstanding any order made by any court, before such commencement, declaring such election to be void, such election shall continue to be valid in all respects and any such order and any finding on which such order is based shall be and shall be deemed always to have been void and of no effect....[8]

TO ARGUE OR NOT TO ARGUE

On that day, to our great surprise, the Registrar of the Supreme Court, under the instructions of the Chief Justice of India, directed that the advocates who entered the courtroom would be frisked and searched. Passes were issued, and only those persons, including advocates, who could obtain passes, could enter the courtroom. Even the lawyers appearing in the case were not spared from obtaining passes. Everybody was frisked and searched before entering the courtroom, including the advocates who were appearing in the case. Even the lady advocates were searched by the police. Only six advocates, namely Shri Shanti Bhushan, myself, Shri Niren De and his junior Shri R.N. Satchety, Shri Ashoke Kumar Sen and Shri J.B. Dadachanji, were not frisked. We told the court that it was not possible for us to argue the appeal under the circumstances when so many Amendments had taken place in a short time just before the hearing and we needed time for study. The next date of hearing was fixed as 25 August 1975. I still insisted to Shri Raj Narain and Shri Shanti Bhushan that we should not argue the case. Shri Raj Narain then became helpless and said, 'What can I do? I am in prison and have no freedom. I cannot talk to my colleagues Shri Morarji Desai, Chaudhary Charan Singh, and others. I do not know what I should do.' He asked me to go to Lucknow and tell all this to Shri C.B. Gupta, who it appeared was not detained on account of his ill-health. I was required to meet him and he was expected to tell Shri Shanti Bhushan that there was no use arguing the case during the Emergency. I told Shri Raj Narain that I had no personal acquaintance with Shri C.B. Gupta and it would be better if I again requested Shri Shanti Bhushan to revise his decision. I suggested that Shri P.N. Lekhi and I go to Allahabad to meet Shri Shanti Bhushan in this connection again. Shri P.N. Lekhi at that time was underground. I was in contact with him and with many other underground workers and leaders. We would meet in the night time at different places. Shri Raj Narain said that it would not be safe to take Shri P.N. Lekhi along with me and that if the police came to know about it we both would be arrested on the way as the train made stops at a number of railway stations. I said, 'Let us take the risk and even if both of us are arrested, that does not matter because in that event we may say that if the advocates have also been arrested how can the case be argued.' Two first-class railway tickets were purchased. I, along with Shri Urmilesh Jha, then secretary to Raj Narain, went to Civil Lines, Delhi, to meet Shri P.N. Lekhi at the residence of Shri S.N. Anand, advocate. Fearing our arrest, Shri S.N. Anand said that it was not advisable to take Shri P.N. Lekhi along, as it would be of no use if both of us were arrested on the way. Under these circumstances, I proceeded to Allahabad alone.

Shri Shanti Bhushan was in Lucknow on that day and he had promised me that he would be at Allahabad by the time I arrived there. I reached there at about 11 a.m. but I found that Shri Shanti Bhushan had not come back from Lucknow. I proceeded to the residence of Shri R.C. Srivastava. He was also of the view that we should not argue the case. I telephoned Shri Shanti Bhushan at Lucknow. He asked me what I wanted. I told him that Shri Raj Narain and I had the same view that we should not argue the case and even if the court did not adjourn the matter and decided the case *ex parte* against us, the world at large would say that Smt Indira Gandhi had put Shri Raj Narain and other leaders in jail and as they had not participated in the hearing, they cannot be at fault. Shri Shanti Bhushan became angry with me and said that he did not want to hear the same thing again and again. He said that he was not going to change his views. I came back disappointed and reported this matter to Shri Raj Narain in jail. He said, 'What can I do? If I do not accept the advice of this man (Shri Shanti Bhushan), Shri Morarji Desai will say that Raj Narain has not accepted the advice of (his man) Shanti Bhushan and particularly when Shri Shanti Bhushan won the case at Allahabad.' Earlier, at one stage, during our meetings in jail, when Shri Shanti Bhushan refused to accept our suggestion for not arguing the case, Shri Raj Narain proposed that we consult Shri Jayaprakash Narayan on this issue. I said that it would be very difficult to consult Shri Jayaprakash Narayan as the officer appointed by the DM would also sit there in the meeting and make notes but nevertheless we would go there and talk to Shri Jayaprakash Narayan. I suggested that Shri Shanti Bhushan and I go to Chandigarh. Shri Shanti Bhushan insisted that he wanted to go alone. Apparently, he wanted to avoid me so that I would not influence Shri Jayaprakash Narayan regarding my view. Taking into consideration this attitude of Shri Shanti Bhushan, I did not make any arrangement for an interview with Shri Jayaprakash Narayan. Instead, I wanted to meet Shri Morarji Desai and expressed this desire to Smt Mohinder Kaur, the former Maharani of Patiala, who was one of the General Secretaries of the Congress (O) at that time. She suggested that Shri Shanti Bhushan should meet Shri Morarji Desai as I had already met other leaders. I was not counsel with Shri Morarji Desai and it was very difficult to get an interview with him in those days. Even close relatives were not allowed. Under these circumstances, I could not meet Shri Morarji Desai. It would have been better if I could have met him and expressed to him my views and those of Shri Raj Narain.

Then ultimately one afternoon, there was a final meeting in jail on the subject matter between the three of us, namely Shri Raj Narain, Shri Shanti Bhushan, and myself. Shri Shanti Bhushan became angry with Shri Raj Narain and myself when we said that it was useless to argue the case. I told him that I had definite information from a source that everything was so arranged that Chief Justice A.N. Ray would preside over the Bench and the judgement would be against us and, hence, what was the use of arguing the case. Shri Shanti Bhushan insisted that we should have faith in the judiciary. I told him that I had no faith in Shri A.N. Ray, who used to dismiss all my cases by way of vengeance because I was the Secretary of the All India Convention of Lawyers held in 1973 in the Ashoka Hotel, New Delhi, which condemned the supersession of three judges and his elevation as the Chief Justice of India. The fact is that Shri A.N. Ray used to trouble me and Shri V.M. Tarkunde in the court and, hence, we were very reluctant to argue cases before him. Shri Shanti Bhushan said that if Shri Raj Narain were to say to him that he should not appear in the case, he would not appear. On behalf of Shri Raj Narain, I immediately said, 'Why do you say all this to Shri Raj Narain? Why should Raj Narain say anything? It is not Raj Narain's case. It is the country's case and we have accepted you as our leader and we are bound to accept what you say. We have put our suggestion before you repeatedly and if you do not accept them and want to overrule our suggestion, then we shall have to follow what you say.' Shri Raj Narain also expressed in the same terms. Then Shri Shanti Bhushan said that there were advantages of arguing the case and our stand would be vindicated in the court. Under these circumstances, we were forced to argue the case and follow Shri Shanti Bhushan.

This was perhaps towards the end of August 1975. Two or three days later, my mind again became agitated on this subject matter. I was very restless. In the evening, I along with Dr. Ram Shanker Dwivedi, a leading advocate of the Allahabad High Court (who also appeared with us in the Supreme Court as well as in the Allahabad High Court in this case), and Shri M. Veerappa, an advocate of the Supreme Court, went to Shri Raj Narain. I told him, 'Of course, we have taken a decision to argue the case but I assure you that we shall lose the case. It will be a unanimous judgement against us. If we lose, Smt Indira Gandhi will crush us and will keep us in jail for an unlimited period. Many of us would die in jail and others will lose health. Therefore, let us again think over the matter and refrain from arguing the case.' I again reiterated that we could make an application under Article 359 of the Constitution and the Supreme Court would have to adjourn the case and if it did not do so, we could walk out of the Court.⁹ The court could decide the case *ex parte*. I told Shri Raj Narain that if he did not accept this then I would want to resign from his case. He became very emotional when he heard this and said that I had always been with him and at this juncture how could I leave him. I was also emotionally touched, and I almost had tears in my eyes when he expressed this confidence in me. He said, '*Tum hame chhod ke kahaan jaoge? Marenge to sab marenge.* (Where will you go after leaving me? If we die, we all die together.)' On this, I said that I was not going to reopen this subject and whatever the future brought we would face it together. I told him that if we die, then let us die together.

EDITOR'S NOTES

1   For Article 14, see Appendix III.6.
2   For the Election Laws (Amendment) Act, 1975, see Appendix III.7.
3   Justice H.R. Khanna was known to be a fearless and independent judge. His judgement in the 1973 Kesavananda Bharati case at the Supreme Court of India proved to be the deciding vote in the 7–6 majority judgement in the case, which restricted Parliament from making amendments to the Constitution of India that went against its 'Basic Structure'. *His Holiness Kesavananda Bharati Sripadagalvaru and Ors vs State of Kerala and Anr*, AIR 1973 SC 1461, 1973 (4) SCC 225.
4   Prashant Bhushan. *The Case That Shook India*, New Delhi: Bell Books, 1978, p. 24.
5   Raj Narain was born into an affluent family in Varanasi (formerly known as Benares) and was from the royal family of Benares. As a young political and social worker, he played an active role during the 1942 Quit India movement and was arrested in September 1942 and detained till 1945. He was imprisoned fifty-eight times for a period totalling about fifteen years in connection

with students' and socialist movements. After Independence, Raj Narain joined the Socialist Party. Dr. Ram Manohar Lohia described Raj Narain as 'a person who has heart of a lion and practices of Gandhi' and said that 'if in India there could be just three or four persons like him, dictatorship can never shadow the democracy'. Despite having been born in a rich Bhumihar Brahmin family, with at least 800 bighas of land, he distributed the land amongst the landless Dalits.

6   Later, Jagannath Kaushal was the Governor of Bihar from 16 June 1976 to 31 January 1979.
7   For the Constitution (Thirty-ninth Amendment) Act, 1975, see Appendix III.8.
8   'The Constitution (Thirty-ninth Amendment) Act, 1975', Ministry of Law and Justice, Government of India, available at http://legislative.gov.in/constitution-thirty-ninth-amendment-act-1975.
9   For Article 359, see Appendix III. 9.

7
Taming of the Judiciary by Indira Gandhi

The Supreme Court Bar Association was extremely agitated at the frisking of advocates that had taken place on 11 August 1975. Correspondence on this subject ensued between Shri Onkar Chand Mathur, who was the Secretary of the Supreme Court Bar Association, and the Chief Justice of India, Shri A.N. Ray. The Secretary wrote to the Chief Justice that the frisking of the advocates was improper. It so happened that one day the members of the Bar headed by its President, Shri A.K. Sen, who was also Smt Indira Gandhi's counsel, met the Chief Justice. The latter said that if Shri A.K. Sen gave an undertaking on behalf of the Bar Association that nothing untoward would happen, then the search may be withdrawn. Shri A.K. Sen put this proposal of the Chief Justice before the Bar Association. The proposal of the Chief Justice was rejected. The members of the Bar Association said, 'We are not children and the Chief Justice should not treat us like this.' Ultimately, on Thursday, 21 August, a resolution was passed by the Supreme Court Bar Association, which was proposed by me, that no member of the Bar would appear, witness or attend the cases of Smt Indira Gandhi with the restriction imposed by the Chief Justice. I conveyed this resolution of the Supreme Court Bar Association that very evening by phone to Shri Shanti Bhushan, who was in Allahabad, and told him that under these circumstances, we could not appear in the case.

Shri Shanti Bhushan came to Delhi in the morning of 23 August. I suggested that we make an application to the Court with an affidavit of Shri Raj Narain that under the circumstances, when there is a resolution of the Supreme Court Bar Association, the advocates cannot appear and argue the case. Shri Shanti Bhushan and I, along with Shri R.C. Srivastava and other advocates, went to jail to meet Shri Raj Narain in this connection. There, we got Shri Raj Narain's affidavit sworn before the Superintendent of Jail. In his application, Shri Raj Narain stated that he was exonerating his advocates and they were not bound to appear in court in this case under the circumstances when there was frisking of advocates and in view of the resolution of the Supreme Court Bar Association. It was also mentioned therein that in case the Court insisted that the arguments should take place, then in that event, Shri Raj Narain would like to appear in person. The said application, along with Shri Raj Narain's affidavit, was filed in the registry office of the Supreme Court on Saturday, 23 August 1975 itself. As per the practice of the Supreme Court, the application along with the affidavit was circulated to the members of the Bench, which could hear them on Monday, 25 August, along with the appeal.

It appears that when the papers were circulated to the judges of the Bench, namely Chief Justice A.N. Ray, Justice H.R. Khanna, Justice K.K. Mathew, Justice M.H. Beg and Justice Y.V. Chandrachud, the judges must have talked among themselves. At about 9 p.m. on Saturday, while we were having dinner in the India International Centre (IIC), I got a message that Shri Onkar Chand Mathur, the Secretary of the Supreme Court Bar Association, had telephoned to say that the Registrar had told him that there would be no frisking and searches of advocates and in that event, we should participate in the case. I telephoned Shri Onkar Chand Mathur and told him that we would not be agreeable to this assurance and we could not participate unless the General Body of the Supreme Court Bar Association, which had passed the Resolution on 21 August, allowed us to do so. I also told him that as no meeting could be held on Sunday or before 10.30 a.m. on Monday, it was not possible for us to appear in the case. The Registrar of the Supreme Court, Shri M.P. Saxena, also telephoned me while we were at the IIC. I again repeated our decision to him. I conveyed all this to Shri Shanti Bhushan who was also seated with us at the dinner table. He said that if frisking and search was not being done, then we should not have any objection to appear. I said that we could not appear unless the matter was again placed before the Supreme Court Bar Association and if it allowed us to do so, we could act accordingly. We postponed our decision for the next day.

I went to my residence at about 10.30 p.m. that night. The Registrar of the Supreme Court sent me a copy of the order passed by the Chief Justice at 8.15 p.m. on this matter. The next morning, I, along with Shri Shanti Bhushan and other lawyers, was at breakfast in the dining hall of the IIC. There was a discussion amongst us. Shri Shanti Bhushan said that now we should not have any objection to appear. I said that my views were different. It was the question of the dignity of the Bar because the restrictions still remained, the orders were not clear, and it was mentioned therein that the advocates would have to pass through a metal detector. Further, we did not know what view the General Body of the Bar Association would take of this order. Therefore, we should tell the court that the matter should be adjourned for a day, so that the Bar Association meeting may take place. Shri Shanti Bhushan was not agreeable to this procedure and he wanted that we straightaway enter the court and argue the case. On this I had a difference in view. Leaving them on the dining table, I went to the room and telephoned Shri M.H. Beg who was going to be a judge in the case.[1] Shri Shanti Bhushan used to say that Shri M.H. Beg could not be a judge in this case as he was personally connected with Smt Indira Gandhi. All norms were forgotten in the present case. Shri A.N. Ray, the Chief Justice of India, who himself had been appointed by supersession over other judges and about whom Shri Jayaprakash Narayan, in the public meeting in the Ramlila Maidan in New Delhi on the evening of 25 June

1975, had said that Shri A.N. Ray should not sit in this Bench as his appointment was under a cloud and the matter regarding his appointment was pending in court, nevertheless continued to preside over the Bench.[2]

I spoke to Shri M.H. Beg on the telephone and asked him whether he would be kind enough to meet me at his residence. He agreed to meet me at 2 p.m. He immediately asked me as to in what connection I wanted to meet him. I told him that I wanted to see him in connection with Smt Indira Gandhi's case which was coming up the following day. He said that it would be proper if I met him only after the case was over. I told him that the very purpose of my meeting would be frustrated if I did not tell him immediately all that I wanted to say. Then he said, 'Alright, you can say whatever you want to say on the telephone.' I was very angry. I told him that Shri Shanti Bhushan and I were of the view that he should not be a judge in this case as he was Smt Indira Gandhi's personal friend. He started laughing. He asked why I did not have faith in him as a judge. I told him that though we had been good friends at Allahabad, I never saw him after he became a judge of the Allahabad High Court or the Chief Justice of the Himachal Pradesh High Court or after he became a judge of the Supreme Court of India. I said, 'Today I feel it is my duty to see that justice should not only be done but also be seen to be done.' I told him that it was well known that he had been celebrating Smt Indira Gandhi's birthday publicly. I also told him that Smt Indira Gandhi was a special invitee at his daughter's marriage, and she had stayed there for quite a long time, whereas he did not invite my client, Shri Raj Narain. This showed, I told him, that he was very close to Smt Indira Gandhi. I also told him that besides having a personal friendship with the Nehru family, he was also the election agent of Shri Jawaharlal Nehru in the 1962 General Election, and that he was a witness for Smt Indira Gandhi in the transfer deed of Anand Bhavan at Allahabad.[3] He said that as regards the transfer deed of Anand

Bhavan, as he was sitting on the dais close to Smt Indira Gandhi at the meeting organized for its donation, they asked him to put his signature on the deed. I told him that his sitting so close to Smt Indira Gandhi only underlined his good relations with her. He said that he could not do anything in the matter and if I wanted to say anything, I should tell the Chief Justice. I told him that it was his duty also to tell the Chief Justice about what I had just told him. He said that he would tell the Chief Justice.

I then went to Shri Raj Narain in jail and told him all this. He said, 'What can I do under the circumstances? You do whatever you feel proper.' On my way back, I met Shri A.K. Sen, the President of the Supreme Court Bar Association, and told him that I had come to him not as a counsel for the other side but as a member of the Supreme Court Bar Association to its President and that he and I could resolve this situation. I suggested that both of us go to the Chief Justice and tell him that the matter may be adjourned for a day so that we may hold our Bar Association meeting. I also told him that I could agree even if the matter was adjourned to lunchtime so that in the meantime we could hold our Bar Association meeting. I told Shri A.K. Sen that I did not have any acquaintance with Shri A.N. Ray, who had always been against me. Shri A.K. Sen said that if he telephoned the Chief Justice and he did not respond properly then it would amount to bad relations between them throughout life.

Under these circumstances, I then telephoned Shri A.N. Ray. His private secretary took my call. I told him I wanted to speak to the Chief Justice. The private secretary told me that the Chief Justice would prefer not to talk on the phone. I then told him that the matter was urgent and it would be in the interest of justice that he talks to me. It appears that the Chief Justice was standing there and giving instructions to the private secretary. I then informed the private secretary that it was not possible for us to appear in the case the next day unless our Supreme Court Bar Association meeting was held. The Chief Justice communicated through the private secretary that whatever I wanted to say I should say in court. I did not inform Shri Shanti Bhushan about these developments. I believed he had a weak heart and could not face such situations. I did not even meet him after our breakfast owing to our vastly divergent views. In fact, I had told him that I was a regular practitioner in the Supreme Court and the advocates would abuse me and may even expel me from the Supreme Court Bar Association if I participated in the hearing of the case without the permission of the Bar Association. Since Shri Shanti Bhushan was practising in the Allahabad High Court, he would not face similar repercussions, particularly when I was the sponsor of the said resolution.

The next day, 25 August, all the twelve lawyers of our group assembled in my chamber in the Supreme Court at about 9.30 a.m. I told Shri Shanti Bhushan that it would be better if I entered the court alone without him or anyone else accompanying me. Shri Shanti Bhushan seemed angry at this suggestion, but he could not do anything because without my instructions, he could not appear in the case as I had a sanction from Shri Raj Narain who had agreed with me and had given instructions to me to act in the manner I liked. I asked Shri Shanti Bhushan to stay either in my chamber or in the Supreme Court Bar Association. I entered the court at about 10.15 a.m. I found that all the advocates of the Government of India, headed by Shri Niren De, the Attorney General of India, and Shri A.K. Sen, advocate for Smt Indira Gandhi, were present in the court. Dr. Y.S. Parmar, then chief minister of Himachal Pradesh, and Shri S.N. Mulla, an advocate of the Allahabad High Court, who was not actually appearing on Smt Indira Gandhi's behalf but who was there to supervise the case, were also present. Similarly, some other VIPs of the Congress party were there. The twelve seats allotted to Shri Raj Narain's lawyers were all empty. No advocate of the Supreme Court entered the courtroom. Some non-lawyer visitors, who had been issued passes, were in the visitors' enclosure. I sat in the court.

Shri Ashoke Sen humorously observed, 'Where are your other colleagues?' I kept mum. I simply observed, 'We have to respect our Bar Association.'

The five judges entered the court. We stood up as usual. The court sat down. When the case was called upon, I stood up. I said to the court, 'My lord, my application, which was filed on Saturday, has been listed before the court and orders may be passed first on this application. The first prayer of the application is that the appeal cannot be heard with the restrictions imposed by the Chief Justice of India, and in the alternative, Shri Raj Narain may be allowed to argue the case in person.' The Chief Justice said that he would hear the appeal then only and I would have to argue it, and that it was the order of the court. I said, 'There is no order of the court and the only order which the Chief Justice is talking about is an administrative order passed by Shri A.N. Ray, the Chief Justice of India, at 8.15 p.m. on Saturday, 23 August 1975, and no doubt the heading of that order contained the words "by the court". It is also not disclosed as to where the court sat at that time, who the judges of the court were, and where it happened. Who appeared for that? Why was I, who was the counsel for one of the parties, never called before that order was passed? I have come to know that Shri A.K. Sen, who has got a dual capacity of being both President of the Supreme Court Bar Association and the counsel for the appellant, Smt Indira Gandhi, was called, and so was the Attorney General, Shri Niren De. Neither Shri Shanti Bhushan nor I were called. Under the circumstances, it cannot be said to be the order of the court. It is only an administrative order passed by the Chief Justice of India and it cannot be an order on my application, which is listed before the Court today along with the appeals.' The Chief Justice said, 'You are talking with a raised voice. You should behave properly.' I said, 'The Chief Justice of India is talking with a raised voice and I cannot be cowed down like this.' My information was that all the search and frisking and associated drama was being enacted at the instance of

Smt Indira Gandhi and for the protection of Shri Sanjay Gandhi (the appellant's son) and for the safety of VIPs of the Congress party for whom seats had already been reserved. I said, 'I want to ask the Chief Justice of India as to why on 11 August 1975, discrimination was made in the matter of the search. According to my information, Shri Sanjay Gandhi, Dr. Y.S. Parmar, and Shri S.N. Mulla, who were the *pairokars* for Smt Indira Gandhi, were not searched while entering the court room, whereas the advocates who were appearing in the case, except six of us, were searched. Even the lady advocates were searched physically by lady police officers.' Shri Lal Narain Sinha, sitting in his chair, pointing out to me, said, 'I may warn my friend that he is committing contempt of court.' I said, 'I am not committing any contempt of court. I am saying what is true. Will the Chief Justice of India explain even now as to why this search business is being done and why the advocates are considered to be inferior to the judges? May I ask him why the judges of this Bench were not searched before they entered the court? There has always been a correlation between the Bench and the Bar, and the Bench is not higher than the Bar, and this is ridiculing us and humiliating the members of the Bar. The interesting feature is that this case is supposed to be over by 3.30 p.m. when miscellaneous matters will take place just after this case, and the security arrangements are being taken away at that time whereas during the hearing of this case they are supposed to be in force. Why this case is being given so much importance?' Shri Niren De, standing, said, 'My friend is committing contempt of court. These are all delaying tactics.' The Chief Justice said, 'We cannot delay the hearing of this case and we must hear it.' I said, 'There is no question of delaying tactics. The fact is that the advocates on the other side are not respecting the Supreme Court Bar Association resolution. I am prepared to face any punishment for contempt of court, if I am found guilty. I have come here prepared for all this. You may send me to jail, I do not mind. But I assure that the Chief Justice's Court will be boycotted not only in this case but in all other cases if he persists in the discrimination. I am speaking as a representative of the Bar of India and my learned friends do not represent it, though they pose to do so.' Justice Y.V. Chandrachud then said, 'Mr. Goyal, why are you so emotional and why cannot you say the same thing in another language?' I said, 'My lord, it is an interesting thing that I am being beaten and I am asked why I cry.' Justice H.R. Khanna said, 'After all, what do you want?' I said, 'I want that the case be adjourned for tomorrow, so that in the meantime our Bar Association may have an opportunity for considering the latest administrative order of the Chief Justice of India and unless it is done it is not possible for us to appear in the case.' Shri A.K. Sen then stood up and said, 'Yesterday, Mr. Goyal had agreed to adjournment for even up to 2 o'clock, so that our Bar Association may hold the meeting.' I said, 'Yes, I am sticking to my promise to Shri A.K. Sen. Let the case be adjourned to 2 o'clock so that we may hold our meeting.' Then the Chief Justice, Justice Khanna, and other judges talked among themselves. The Chief Justice said, 'After all, this is a difficult case for us and we hope that you will all assist us.' I said, 'We will assist, but our Bar Association should be allowed an opportunity of holding this meeting.' Then the Chief Justice adjourned the case till 2 o'clock.

The meeting of the Bar Association took place thereafter at 1 p.m., and the General Body of the Bar Association allowed the advocates to appear in the case in view of the fact that the search was not to take place. However, the Bar Association directed that we should take charge of the enclosure reserved for the advocates, where non-advocates would not be allowed to sit. Two of our advocates would remain at the gate of the Chief Justice's Court and only advocates in robes, and particularly those advocates who were known to be advocates by the two advocates at the gate, would be allowed to enter the court.

In Shri Prashant Bhushan's book, *The Case That Shook India*

(1978), in chapter 12, 'It Destroys Democracy', an attempt has been made to describe what had happened in the morning in the Chief Justice's court when I happened to have told the Chief Justice that we were not going to appear in the case unless the restrictions on advocates regarding their search etc. was withdrawn and unless the Bar Association held its meeting. I may give examples of certain inappropriate language that has been used in Shri Prashant Bhushan's book. For example, at one place the word 'violently' has been used against my name and in another place the word 'loudly' has been used (p. 143). In fact, I was not at all violent in the court nor did I use any unusual loud language. I have also practised as a lawyer for nearly twenty-eight years and I know how to address the court and how to behave in court, and whatever I want to deliver and express, I know how to do it. I very much object to the words 'violently' and 'loudly' used against my name. The main things that I had told the Chief Justice have not been mentioned there. For example, I told the Chief Justice that according to my information all this search business was being done only to protect Shri Sanjay Gandhi and for the Congress VIPs for whom a separate sitting arrangement had been made in the advocate's enclosure itself. I also told the Chief Justice that on 11 August 1975 all the advocates were searched while Shri Sanjay Gandhi, Shri Y.S. Parmar, the chief minister of Himachal Pradesh, and Shri S.N. Mulla, an advocate of the Allahabad High Court, who were the *pairokars* of Smt Indira Gandhi, were not searched. Shri Prashant Bhushan has omitted the names of Shri Y.S. Parmar and Shri Sanjay Gandhi as well as other things that I told to the court.

EDITOR'S NOTES

1. As mentioned earlier, two rooms in the IIC in New Delhi had been reserved by the legal team of Raj Narain to prepare his case against Smt Indira Gandhi.

2   See 'JP advises Ray to stay away from PM's appeal Bench', *Hindustan Times*, New Delhi, 26 June 1975, p. 1. A case was filed by the journalist P.L. Lakhanpal challenging the appointment of A.N. Ray as Chief Justice of India on 25 April 1973 with effect from 26 April 1973, by superseding three senior judges. Thus, Justice A.N. Ray's authority as Chief Justice itself was sub-judice. However, A.N. Ray did not recuse himself and continued to preside over Supreme Court Benches, giving judgements in Indira Gandhi's case and other cases, regardless of his own pending case. See *P.L. Lakhanpal vs A.N. Ray and Ors* on 15 February 1974, AIR 1975 Delhi 66, 11 (1975) DLT 1, ILR 1974 Delhi 725. In this case, a five-judge Bench of the Delhi High Court unanimously dismissed the petition on the grounds that by virtue of seniority, Justice A.N. Ray would be entitled to immediate reappointment as he had become the seniormost judge after the resignation of the three senior judges, namely Justice J.M. Shelat, Justice K.S. Hegde, and Justice A.N. Grover, and that there was no legal impediment in the way of his reappointment!

3   Anand Bhavan, a palatial bungalow in Allahabad built by Motilal Nehru in 1930, was the home of the Nehru family. Motilal Nehru and his son Jawaharlal Nehru lived there, as did Indira Gandhi in her early years. Anand Bhavan was donated by Indira Gandhi to the Government of India in 1970.

J.P. Goyal proceeding to the chamber of Justice V.R. Krishna Iyer in the Supreme Court of India, New Delhi, 24 June 1975

Photo courtesy: Virendra Prabhakar/Hindustan Times

J.P. Goyal (*third from left, in dark-coloured shirt*) with Sikander Bakht (*centre*), Nala village, Uttar Pradesh, undated

Source: J.P. Goyal's collection of photographs with the editor

J.P. Goyal (*third from right*) with Atal Bihari Vajpayee (*second from right*) and Balram Jakhar (*extreme right*) at a dinner at Viking Longhouse in Peel, Isle of Man, October 1984

Photo courtesy: Commonwealth Parliamentary Association (CPA), Isle of Man branch
Copyright: Commonwealth Parliamentary Association (CPA), Isle of Man branch

J.P. Goyal (*left*) being felicitated by Gopal Ballav Pattanaik, then Chief Justice of India, (*right*) for fifty years of service to the legal profession, New Delhi, 26 November 2002

Source: J.P. Goyal's collection of photographs with the editor

J.P. Goyal being felicitated for his contribution to the legal profession by Sushil Kumar Jain, President, Supreme Court Advocate-on-Record Association, on its behalf, New Delhi, 2 March 2008

Photo courtesy: Rama Goyal

J.P. Goyal delivering a speech at the Thirtieth Commonwealth Parliamentary Conference, Villa Marina Royal Hall, Douglas, Isle of Man, October 1984
Photo courtesy: Commonwealth Parliamentary Association (CPA), Isle of Man branch
Copyright: Commonwealth Parliamentary Association (CPA), Isle of Man branch

TOP SECRET   PRIME MINISTER,   NEW DELHI
                    INDIA   June 25, 1975.

Dear Rashtrapatiji,

  As already explained to you a little while ago, information has reached us which indicates that there is an imminent danger to the security of India being threatened by internal disturbance. The matter is extremely urgent.

  I would have liked to have taken this to Cabinet but unfortunately this is not possible tonight. I am, therefore, condoning or permitting a departure from the Government of India (Transaction of Business) Rule 1961, as amended up to date by virtue of my powers under Rule 12 thereof. I shall mention the matter to the Cabinet first thing tomorrow morning.

  In the circumstances and in case you are so satisfied, a requisite Proclamation under Article 352(1) has become necessary. I am enclosing a copy of the draft Proclamation for your consideration. As you are aware, under Article 352(3) even when there is an imminent danger of such a threat as mentioned by me, the necessary Proclamation under Article 352(1) can be issued.

  I recommend that such a Proclamation should be issued tonight, however late it may be, and all arrangements will be made to make it public as early as possible thereafter.

  With kind regards,

          Yours sincerely,
          Sd/- Indira Gandhi

Shri Fakhruddin Ali Ahmed,
Rashtrapati,
Rashtrapati Bhavan,
New Delhi.

Copy of Indira Gandhi's letter to President Fakhruddin Ali Ahmed dated 25 June 1975, obtained from President's Secretariat by Joint Secretary (IS), Ministry of Home Affairs, Government of India

Source: File No. 21/23/75-T, Ministry of Home Affairs, Section-T, in National Archives of India, New Delhi, p. 2

Photo courtesy: National Archives of India

PROCLAMATION OF EMERGENCY

In exercise of the powers conferred by Clause 1 of Article 352 of the Constitution, I, Fakhruddin Ali Ahmed, President of India, by this Proclamation declare that a grave emergency exists whereby the security of India is threatened by internal disturbance.

PRESIDENT

New Delhi - 25th June, 1975.

Draft of Proclamation of Emergency dated 25 June 1975 sent to President Fakhruddin Ali Ahmed

Source: File No. 21/23/75-T, Ministry of Home Affairs, Section-T, in National Archives of India, New Delhi, p. 3

Photo courtesy: National Archives of India

PROCLAMATION OF EMERGENCY

In exercise of the powers conferred by clause (1) of Article 352 of the Constitution, I, Fakhruddin Ali Ahmed, President of India, by this Proclamation declare that a grave emergency exists whereby the security of India is threatened by internal disturbance.

PRESIDENT

New Delhi - 25th June, 1975.

Proclamation of Emergency by President Fakhruddin Ali Ahmed, 25 June 1975
Source: File No. 21/23/75-T, Ministry of Home Affairs, Section-T, in National Archives of India, New Delhi, p. 4
Photo courtesy: National Archives of India

Ministry of Home Affairs
(Grih Mantralaya)

It is necessary in the present emergency to issue an Order by the President, in exercise of the powers under Article 359 of the Constitution, depriving the right to move the court under article 14, article 21 and article 22 of the Constitution. The Order has been prepared in consultation with the Ministry of Law and is placed below. It has also been approved by the Cabinet.

2. HM may kindly approve the proposals before it is submitted to the President.

(S.L. Khurana)
Secretary
27 June 75

H.M.

I recommend that the President may be pleased to approve the issue of the proposed order.

(K. Brahmananda Reddy)
Home Minister
27 June 75

Submitted for approval

President

Approved

PRESIDENT

1. Secy has signed the order. Issue.

Order of Ministry of Home Affairs suspending Articles 14, 21, and 22 during the Emergency, 27 June 1975

Source: File No. II/16013/1/75–S&P (D-II), Ministry of Home Affairs, Section-T, in National Archives of India, New Delhi, p. 12

Photo courtesy: National Archives of India

O R D E R

In exercise of the powers conferred by sub-clause (b) of clause (4) of article 352 of the Constitution of India as applied to the State of Jammu and Kashmir, the President, with the concurrence of the Government of that State, hereby applies to that State the Proclamation of Emergency made by him on the 25th June, 1975.

PRESIDENT

June 29, 1975

Extension of Proclamation of Emergency dated 25 June 1975 to Jammu and Kashmir by President Fakhruddin Ali Ahmed, 29 June 1975

Source: File No. II/16013/1/75–S&P (D-II), Ministry of Home Affairs, Section-T, in National Archives of India, New Delhi, p. 48

Photo courtesy: National Archives of India

Ministry of Home Affairs

The Cabinet at its meeting held today, the 29th June, 1975, has decided that the Order made by the President under clause (1) of article 359 of the Constitution suspending the right to move any court for the enforcement of the rights conferred by articles 14, 21 and 22 of the Constitution and the proceedings pending in any court for the enforcement of the above-mentioned rights, for the period during which the Proclamations of Emergency are in force, be extended to the State of Jammu & Kashmir also. The draft order placed below which has been vetted by the Ministry of Law may kindly be approved by HM before it is submitted to the President.

(P.P. Nayyar)
Joint Secretary
29.6.'75.

HM

I recommend that the President may be pleased to approve the issue of the proposed order.

(K. Brahmananda Reddi)
Home Minister
29.6.'75

President

Approved.
FAAhmed
29/6

Extension of suspension of Articles 14, 21, and 22 to Jammu and Kashmir, dated 29 June 1975

Source: File No. II/16013/1/75–S&P (D-II), Ministry of Home Affairs, Section-T, in National Archives of India, New Delhi

Photo courtesy: National Archives of India

SUMMARY

The Cabinet has decided to recommend to the President to revoke the proclamation of emergency under article 352(1) of the Constitution dated the 25th June, 1975.

President may be pleased to approve the procolamation of revocation under article 352(2) of the Constitution.

Home Minister
21 3 77

President   Approved.
21-3-77

Revocation of Emergency.
(F.16013/2/77-S&P
D-II)

Recommendation of Cabinet dated 21 March 1977 to revoke the Proclamation of Emergency dated 25 June 1975

Source: File No. 21/23/75-T, Ministry of Home Affairs, Section-T, in National Archives of India, New Delhi, p. 22

Photo courtesy: National Archives of India

PROCLAMATION

In exercise of the powers conferred by sub-clause (a) of clause (2) of article 352 of the Constitution, I, Basappa Danappa Jatti, Vice-President acting as President of India, hereby revoke the Proclamation of Emergency issued under clause (1) of that article on the 25th June, 1975, and published with the notification of the Government of India in the Ministry of Home Affairs No.GSR 353(E) dated the 26th June, 1975.

21-3-77
Vice-President acting as President

New Delhi,
the 21st March, 1977.

Proclamation dated 21 March 1977 to revoke Proclamation of Emergency dated 25 June 1975

Source: File No. 21/23/75-T, Ministry of Home Affairs, Section-T, in National Archives of India, New Delhi, p. 23

Photo courtesy: National Archives of India

8

The Historic Election Case at the Supreme Court

The hearing of the case started at 2 p.m. As I had defied Shri Shanti Bhushan, he was angry with me. First, Shri A.K. Sen, being the counsel for the appellant, Smt Indira Gandhi, started his arguments in her appeal. His simple argument was that now there was the Constitution (Thirty-ninth Amendment) Act, 1975 and in view of clause 4(4) of that Act, the appeal should be allowed. Shri Shanti Bhushan, on our side, stood up and said that we were challenging the validity of that provision in the Constitution (Thirty-ninth Amendment) Act, 1975. Thus, the arguments from our side started immediately.

VALIDITY OF THE CONSTITUTION (THIRTY-NINTH AMENDMENT) ACT

According to the judgement of the thirteen-judge Bench of the Supreme Court delivered in Kesavananda Bharati's case,[1] reported in 1973 (4) SCC 225, the constitutional validity of a Constitutional Amendment could be challenged on the grounds that the basic features of the Constitution were destroyed. Relying on that judgement, Shri Shanti Bhushan started arguments by stating that clause 4(4) of the Constitutional (Thirty-ninth Amendment) Act violated the basic features of the Constitution inasmuch as it attacked the jurisdiction of the Supreme Court, which was hearing the election appeal, and inasmuch as the Constitution makers had asked the Supreme Court to allow the appeal of an individual, even without hearing on merits.² This Amendment, he said, destroyed the jurisdiction of the Supreme Court and the very basis of our democratic system.

Since Shri Shanti Bhushan was not agreeable to the course adopted by me in the morning, and as we had had a disagreement, he wanted to have a fling at me. Apparently, for that purpose, just to show the Chief Justice and other judges that he was not responsible for what had happened in the morning regarding my dialogue with the Chief Justice in connection with the search of advocates, he said, 'If all the limbs, including the heart and brain, of my friend Shri J.P. Goyal are changed except the thumb, then when he goes to his house, it is doubtful if his wife will recognize him.' The Chief Justice remarked, 'Do you want to change his heart or brain?' Shri Shanti Bhushan replied, 'Both, my lord.' This dialogue had a double purpose. Firstly, Shri Shanti Bhushan was ironically expressing as if I had gone off my head for having the dialogue with the Chief Justice in the morning, and secondly, it served as an example for the basic features theory enunciated by the Supreme Court in the Kesavananda Bharati case. I felt that he was giving an example and his purpose was also to ridicule me. I had to bear all this as a man of discipline and to maintain unity of purpose.

PHYSICAL AND MENTAL STRAIN

Shri Shanti Bhushan had succeeded and I had failed, inasmuch as his desire to argue the case in the Supreme Court materialized and my desire not to enter the trap laid by Smt Indira Gandhi and not to argue the case during the Emergency was frustrated. I was shocked by Shri Shanti Bhushan's remarks and behaviour. The mental and bodily strain on me since the Emergency was declared was so enormous that I fell seriously ill that very day after hearing Shri Shanti Bhushan's remarks. Shri Raj Narain wanted me to see him every day, but I could not go to him that day. Dr. Ram Shanker Dwivedi, an advocate of the Allahabad High Court and a very dear friend of mine, Shri R.C. Srivastava, and other lawyers were sent to meet Shri Raj Narain in jail. The incident of that morning was narrated *inter alia* to him. I was told by these advocates that he was happy about what had happened in the morning and that we had succeeded in the sense that the insult to the advocates that Chief Justice A.N. Ray was inflicting was undone by our actions.

I remained ill for the next four to five days. Shri Shanti Bhushan and other advocates came to see me at my residence along with Dr. R.S. Dwivedi. I was very optimistic about the future of the country and mankind in the world, so much so that I remarked to Dr. Dwivedi, 'I foresee that India will be free from Smt Indira Gandhi's slavery. We in India will have the second largest population in the world and will be one of the biggest democracies in the world where people of different religions reside. One day, millions of our people will cross over the Himalayas, enter China, Russia, and other countries where democracy and freedoms cherished by us are not available. We shall be messengers, like disciples of Buddha, and the message will be of non-violence, democracy and human freedoms. We, in India, will establish a State that will be the beacon of democracy and socialism. It may take some time, but one day it will happen.' Dr. Dwivedi, a great Sanskrit scholar with a PhD in Sanskrit in addition to being an advocate, was happy about my optimism. I told him, 'You should not take whatever I say as the ramblings of "Sheikh Chilli";[3] my inner heart is speaking and I am foreseeing these visions.' He said that these ideas were a light in the darkness and we must be optimists.

Dr. Dwivedi, Shri R.C. Srivastava and other advocates were staying at the IIC where we used to prepare our case. I had shifted a part of my library there and many books that were not available with me used to be borrowed from other lawyers, friends and other libraries. Some of the books were borrowed from our Supreme Court Bar Association. Even the Judges' Library in the Supreme Court was kind enough to allow us to study the books there. Even though I was ill, I could not stay at home and visited the IIC just to see if the case was being studied properly. I recovered within a week and started participating again in the case in the Supreme Court.

A WRONG DECISION

After arguments on both the sides on the validity of the Constitution (Thirty-ninth Amendment) Act, 1975 had finished, I suggested to Shri Shanti Bhushan that we should tell the court that we would not be arguing further and that first the court should deliver the judgement on the validity of that Amendment Act. If we were to lose, we would totally lose, but if we won and the relevant clause of the Constitution (Thirty-ninth Amendment) Act, 1975 was declared *ultra vires*,[4] then the question would arise regarding the validity of the Election Laws (Amendment) Act, 1975 and the Representation of the People (Amendment) Act, 1974. I also suggested that as both these Amendments could be challenged on the grounds of non-availability of Article 14 of the Constitution, which was suspended and not available to us during the Emergency, we should tell the court that the case should be postponed till after the Emergency. In fact, I suggested to Shri Shanti Bhushan to tell the court on 25 August that we could not argue the case fully unless Article 14 became available to us. He did not value my suggestion and it seemed to me that in his heart of hearts, he used to ridicule me. I felt that I had some vision that he did not recognize. The feeling of the advocates of the Supreme Court and the Supreme Court Bar Association about Shri Shanti Bhushan was that he was continuing to argue the case for the sake of his own publicity and not for winning the case as there was no question of winning. This was my view also, but I could not express it as a matter of internal discipline.

Chief Justice A.N. Ray, who was fully siding with Smt Indira

Gandhi, which was so apparently clear during the course of the arguments, may have anticipated beforehand the possibility that we would argue for adjournment of the case. He, on his own motion, said during the arguments, 'We shall hear the full case, including the merits'. On our part, we should have told the court on 25 August itself or even earlier on 14 July and 11 August that we would not argue the case. Shri Shanti Bhushan owes an explanation to the nation about the circumstances under which he chose to argue the case overruling me and Shri Raj Narain, his own client, and others. What was he going to achieve by arguing the case during the Emergency when Article 14 of the Constitution was not available to us? He has to explain why he did not press the court that after arguing on the Constitution (Thirty-ninth Amendment) Act, 1975 we were not going to argue the case further unless judgement was given on its validity. Had the court insisted on hearing the case fully, he could have boycotted the court and walked out. The entire nation and the world was watching the proceedings of the court. It would have been a befitting response if we would have walked out of the court if the Chief Justice had insisted on full arguments. The worst that could happen was that Shanti Bhushan and I would have been arrested. Was he afraid of our arrest? The advocates on the other side were surprised as to why we were arguing the case. They expected that we would walk out of the case and would not participate in it. Politically and as a matter of tact, it was a very wrong decision on our part to argue the case.

THE CURSE OF CENSORSHIP

The foreign press represented various important news agencies in the world then. On 25 August, when we came out of the court at 4 p.m., several members of the foreign press met us in the corridor and asked us about our arguments. I told them that all this could not be discussed in the corridor of the court and it would be better if they were to come to my chamber for a briefing. After that they began visiting my chamber in the Supreme Court every day after court hours for briefings about the arguments in the case. While the Indian press was allowed inside the courts, the Chief Justice had banned the foreign press. The notes taken by the Indian press, it is authoritatively learnt, were taken and censored by Shri H.R. Gokhale, the Law Minister then, and only the censored news was printed in the newspapers. For example, my dialogue with the Chief Justice in the morning of 25 August was not published at all in any of the newspapers. The only thing that was published was that on a mention made by me, the court adjourned the case till lunch and that Shri Shanti Bhushan was not present in the court. The impression given to the public was that as Shri Shanti Bhushan was not available for arguing the case, a mention was made by me and the case was adjourned till lunch. This is how Smt Indira Gandhi and her caucus that was ruling the country at that time tried to mislead the people of India by not allowing them to be acquainted with the correct facts. The misfortune of this country has always been that the public has been fooled by its rulers in the past. Persons like me who have been critical of the Congress party after Independence cherished the formation of a united Opposition party that could replace the government of the Congress party, which Mahatma Gandhi had desired to disband after Independence in 1947 itself.

THE SUPREME COURT JUDGEMENT AND ITS EFFECT

The hearing of the two election appeals, one filed by Smt Indira Gandhi and the other cross-appeal filed by Shri Raj Narain, started at 2 p.m. on 25 August 1975, and continued till 8 October 1975. The judgement was delivered on 7 November 1975 by a Bench consisting of Chief Justice A.N. Ray and Justices H.R. Khanna, K.K. Mathew, M.H. Beg and Y.V. Chandrachud.[5] When the judgement was delivered, I was attending the court on behalf of

Shri Raj Narain. Shri Shanti Bhushan was in Allahabad on that day.

The Supreme Court held clause 4(4) of the Constitution (Thirty-ninth Amendment) Act, 1975, as *ultra vires*.[6] The judges had written separate judgements. Three judges, namely Justice H.R. Khanna, Justice K.K. Mathew and Justice Y.V. Chandrachud, wrote judgements striking down the said provisions. Chief Justice A.N. Ray and Justice M.H. Beg wrote judgements that upheld the constitutional validity of clause 4 of Article 329A. However, the Election Laws (Amendment) Act, 1975 and Representation of the People (Amendment) Act, 1974 were held to be valid. Shri Shanti Bhushan attacked the validity of these two Acts only on the ground that they violated the basic features of the Constitution. This was not acceptable to all the judges of the Bench. He did not and could not argue on the basis of violation of Article 14 as the said Article was not available during the Emergency. This was my great difference with him that he should not argue the case at all as Article 14 was not available to us and unless these two Acts were declared *ultra vires*, there was no question of our winning the case. I do not understand what the need was for giving up the most important point in the case. There was no pressure on us that we had to argue the case. It was our discretion to argue or not to argue, particularly when under Article 359 of the Constitution, we could have made an application to the effect that the proceedings of the appeal shall remain suspended till after the Emergency. The state of my mind throughout the hearing was not good, in the sense that I had to drag myself behind Shri Shanti Bhushan, fully knowing that we were going to lose the case and that Justice J.M.L. Sinha's judgement, which was in our hands, was going to be out of our hands, and when Smt Indira Gandhi's appeal would be allowed by the Supreme Court, the public at large would not question the niceties of law as to on what ground the appeal was allowed, but only say that Smt Indira Gandhi's appeal had been allowed and the High Court judgement had been set aside.

The judgement was read throughout the day by the learned judges. During the lunch hour, I telephoned Shri Shanti Bhushan and told him that we were going to lose the case as the judgement was going against us. During the lunchtime, some press people asked me my reaction about the case. I told them that this was another black day in the history of this country.

Just after the judgement was delivered on 7 November, it appeared as if Smt Indira Gandhi knew beforehand about the judgement as she had made preparations to go to Srinagar for a holiday on the morning of 8 November. She looked very cheerful, and clad in a Kashmiri dress, she left for Srinagar with her family. As she enjoyed her holiday, the rigours of Emergency were further intensified. More persons were arrested and more tortures were inflicted in the jails.[7] Interviews with the detenus were made more difficult, and even close relatives were not allowed to meet them. For example, the daughter of Shri Govind Swaminathan, the then Advocate General of Tamil Nadu, was arrested under MISA in the early hours of 26 June 1975 and put in Tihar Jail. Her father and mother were not allowed to meet her for a very long time. It was with great difficulty that Shri Swaminathan could get an interview with her after a month or so. Shri Swaminathan, who used to stay at the IIC when he came to the Supreme Court in connection with cases of Tamil Nadu, narrated the tale to us more than once. What was the fault of this young girl? It is said that she was a labour leader and used to organize the workers of Smt Indira Gandhi's family's agricultural farm near Mehrauli. Sanjay Gandhi felt she was trouble, and that is why she was considered so important as to be arrested at the first moment of imposition of the Emergency. The Maharani of Jaipur, Gayatri Devi, and Rajmata of Gwalior, Vijayaraje Scindia were both put in Tihar Jail. It so happened one day that I sent my lawyers to meet Shri Raj Narain in Tihar Jail. The relatives of these two Maharanis had also come to see them. Shri Pranab Chatterjee, one of the advocates of our side who had gone to interview Shri Raj Narain, told me that the two Maharanis were not allowed to talk to each other in confinement, and when they came to the interview rooms near the office of the Superintendent of Jail to meet their relatives, Shri Raj Narain was also on his way there, and he spoke from the corridor to the two Maharanis. Humorously, he told them, 'You are in jail on account of me, but now that you have come here, you are welcome and you should have a bold heart.'

Justice M.H. Beg, who I described earlier as a close family friend of Smt Indira Gandhi, to our great surprise, delivered the judgement on the merits of the appeal, that is to say, whether Smt Indira Gandhi had indulged in corrupt practices or not. These points were not argued at all on the other side and the arguments were restricted to the validity of the Constitution (Thirty-Ninth Amendment) Act, 1975, the Election Laws (Amendment) Act, 1975, and the Representation of the People (Amendment) Act, 1974. We discussed the matter and then filed two review applications, which came up for hearing before the same Bench on 18 December 1975. The other four judges said that they did not want to say anything on whatever their brother judge had ruled because it concerned their brother Justice M.H. Beg. On our behalf, it was said that arguments on merits did not take place and it was questionable why Justice Beg had delivered his judgement on merits. However, the review applications were dismissed by an order dated 19 December 1975. The said judgement of the Court is reported in 1977 AIR 69 and 1976 (3) SCC 321.[8] Justice Beg falsely stated that merits were also argued even though neither the judges nor the advocates on the other side corroborated this. It is an interesting feature that Justice J.M.L. Sinha's judgement, which was delivered on 12 June 1975, was not allowed to be published in any of the Law Reports,[9] whereas the order on Smt Indira Gandhi's stay application passed by Justice V.R. Krishna Iyer on 24 June 1975 and the judgement of the Supreme Court delivered on 7 November 1975 were both published in the *All India Reporter*, in the August 1975 and December 1975 issues, respectively.[10] Similarly, the judgement dated 19 December 1975 on the review application was published in the January 1977 issue of the *All India Reporter* and in the *Supreme Court Cases* (SCC) in 1976. This publicity was said to be given only to the judgements in favour of Smt Indira Gandhi while judgements against her were not allowed to be published.

Probably on 10 August 1975, we, the lawyers appearing in the case, collected in the IIC. Shri Shanti Bhushan was also there. I told my colleagues before Shri Shanti Bhushan's arrival that I would not talk to him on the subject of participation or non-participation in the case as I had already done so on a number of occasions, and therefore, they should dissuade him from arguing the case during the Emergency, particularly when amendments to the Constitution had taken place. A number of questions were put to Shri Shanti Bhushan by my colleagues, but he became angry and said, 'Can't I argue on the Amendment Acts? Am I not competent to argue on the validity of the Amendment Acts?' When he was reminded about the problem that Article 14 of the Constitution was not available to us during the Emergency, he said he knew what to argue and what not to argue. Under these circumstances, one day Shri Raj Narain told me in jail that I should consult Shri S.V. Gupte, who had once appeared in this very case at an interlocutory stage in the Supreme Court. I spoke to Shri S.V. Gupte a number of times and told him that if he appeared in the case, then Shri Raj Narain would ask Shri Shanti Bhushan to assist Shri S.V. Gupte rather than argue the case, and if Shri Shanti Bhushan did not agree to appear as a junior to Shri S.V. Gupte, then Shri S.V. Gupte and I would argue the case. However, Shri S.V. Gupte shared my view and said there was nothing to argue during the Emergency. He also told me that I should make the necessary application for adjournment of the case as Article 14 was not available to us. I reported the matter to Shri Raj Narain. The result was that Shri Shanti Bhushan could not be dispensed with. Shri Raj Narain also asked me to consult my other lawyer friends. All the people I consulted were of the same view that there was no use of arguing the case during the Emergency, particularly when the atmosphere was surcharged with fear and terror. The story would have been different had Shri Shanti Bhushan also concurred with this view.

EDITOR'S NOTES

1. *His Holiness Kesavananda Bharati Sripadagalvaru and Ors vs State of Kerala and Anr*, AIR 1973 SC 1461, 1973 (4) SCC 225.
2. Hearing on merits refers to a formal court hearing, conducted under the rules of evidence, to decide issues put forward filed in the complaint or summons.
3. In popular parlance in India and Pakistan, 'Sheikh Chilli' refers to a simpleton or fool who is an inveterate daydreamer, building castles in the air.
4. *Ultra vires:* Beyond powers (Latin), *without authority;* a decision which is beyond the powers or authority of the person or organization which took it.
5. *Indira Nehru Gandhi vs Shri Raj Narain & Anr* on 7 November 1975. Civil Appeals Nos 887 and 909 of 1975. 1975 AIR 2299, 1975 Supp SCC 1, 1976 (2) SCR 347.
6. Clauses (4) and (5) of the new Article 329A of the Constitution (Thirty-Ninth Amendment) Act, 1975 were held to be unconstitutional and, therefore, void.
7. A graphic account of the tortures is given in Michael Henderson, *Experiment with Untruth: India Under Emergency*, New Delhi: Macmillan, 1977: 'Overcrowding, insanitary conditions, inadequate medical care, illegal punishments and deprivation of sleep were the mildest of complaints....It struck people that many prisoners who went into prison healthy came out with serious ailments, and were even on the point of dying.' (p. 36) 'Around 150 detenus in Tihar Jail, including Municipal Councillors, were injured by a lathi charge on 2 October 1975,

the Mahatma's birthday' (p. 38). 'Delhi University was badly affected. Nearly two hundred teachers were arrested along with hundreds of students while files were opened on hundreds more....The President of the University Students Union, Arun Jaitley, spent nineteen months in prison' (p. 41). In the words of Hemant Kumar Vishnoi, Secretary of the Delhi University Students Union, 'They started off by abusing and threatening me. When that didn't work they handcuffed me in front and started thumping me on the back. To prevent myself screaming I kept shouting "Jayaprakash *Zindabad*". So they said, "Take him into the next room and warm him up." There they made me lie down and started beating me on the soles of my feet with "lathis". Then they made me strip and a man came and beat me for half an hour with a torn tyre. Finally they tied my hands between my knees and dangled me from a stick which they kept swinging around me to make me sick. Then they poured water with chilli powder in it down my nose and I became unconscious'. See 'Tihar Veterans' Reunion', *The Statesman*, Delhi, 21 April 1977, p. 3. For a comprehensive account of the tortures and other hardships faced by the people, see also P.G. Sahasrabuddhe and Manik Chandra Vajpayee, *The People Versus Emergency: A Saga of Struggle*, New Delhi: Suruchi Prakashan, 1991.

8   Indira Nehru Gandhi vs Shri Raj Narain and Another and Vice Versa, 1977 AIR 69, 1976 (3) SCC 321 C.A. 909 of 1975 Review Petition in Civil Appeal Nos. 887 and 909 of 1975 (An application for review of the judgement and/or for clarification and/or expunging of the observations from the judgement), decided on 19 December 1975.

9   To this date, this judgement of Justice J.M.L. Sinha on 12 June 1975 is not easily available, either as a publication or online on the website of Allahabad High Court, not even in its link to 'Important decisions that were in headlines'. An attempt by journalist Shreeja Sen to locate the judgement led her to the Allahabad High Court Museum, where the first and last two

pages of the judgement are displayed. See, Shreeja Sen, 'In search of the judgement that led to the Emergency', *Mint on Sunday*, 26 June 2015, available at https://www.livemint.com/Sundayapp/NDh93q056KDgtYecVfFkAJ/In-search-of-the-judgement-that-led-to-the-Emergency.html, accessed 24 June 2018.

10. For the judgement of the Supreme Court delivered on 24 June 1975, see *Indira Nehru Gandhi (Smt) vs Raj Narain & Anr* on 24 June 1975, 1975 AIR 1590, 1975 SCC (2) 159. For the judgement of the Supreme Court delivered on 7 November 1975, see *Indira Nehru Gandhi vs Shri Raj Narain & Anr* on 7 November 1975, 1975 AIR 2299, 1976 (2) SCR 347, 1975 Suppl. SCC 1 Civil Appeals Nos. 887 and 909 of 1975.

9

Thwarting the Ploy of the Chief Justice of 'Indi(r)a'[1]

Chief Justice A.N. Ray had arranged things in such a way that he could deliver the goods to Smt Indira Gandhi as per her desire. As mentioned earlier, the judgement was delivered on 7 November 1975. The Chief Justice had also arranged a thirteen-judge Bench to sit on 10 November 1975, clearly with the intention to overrule the judgement in the Kesavananda Bharati case, in which by a majority decision, the Supreme Court had held that the Parliament had no jurisdiction to pass a Constitution (Amendment) Act if it violated the basic structure of the Constitution. Had that judgement been set aside, then Smt Indira Gandhi would have probably got even a one-page Constitution passed, saying that she was the Empress of India and her descendants would always rule over this country. We were very worried that Chief Justice A.N. Ray would persuade the majority of the judges to overrule the judgement in the Kesavananda Bharati case. Four of the judges in that case, viz. Chief Justice A.N. Ray, Justice K.K. Mathew, Justice M.H. Beg and Justice Y.V. Chandrachud, who had given dissenting judgements, were already sitting on the Bench that was to hear the matter on 10 November. Only three more judges would be required then to overrule the judgement in the Kesavananda Bharati case.

One day, Shri C.K. Daphtary telephoned me at my residence. I was not there. When I was told by my wife that Shri Daphtary had called, I went to meet him. He said, 'What are you doing about these cases?' I told him that we were very worried. A number of cases, including some transport cases of Tamil Nadu, were going to be listed before the thirteen-judge Bench. Almost all these cases, except the first case, related to property rights and as the Supreme Court had already held in the Kesavananda Bharati case that violation of the Fundamental Right to property was not an infringement of the basic features of the Constitution, the basic feature theory was not involved in the case involving property rights. However, it was involved in the first case to be listed, namely *I. Jagadeeswara Rao vs Union of India*, in which the Constitution (Thirty-second Amendment) Act, 1973 was challenged.[2] By the said Amendment Act, the right of government servants in the state of Andhra Pradesh to file a petition for redress of their grievances in service matters was taken away and the orders of the Administrative Tribunal were made final. It was in this case that Chief Justice A.N. Ray wanted that arguments should take place regarding the basic features of the Constitution. Shri K.R. Chaudhary was the Advocate-on-Record for the petitioner in this case.

Shri C.K. Daphtary and I were of the view that it was in the interest of the petitioner himself in the *I. Jagadeeswara Rao vs Union of India* case to withdraw the writ petition in the Supreme Court and file another writ petition in the Andhra Pradesh High Court, which was bound by the judgement of the Supreme Court in the Kesavananda Bharati case. Both Shri Daphtary and I felt that if this course was adopted in this case, then the thirteen-judge Bench of the Supreme Court would have nothing before it to be argued for overruling or upsetting the judgement in the Kesavananda Bharati case, as in the other cases, which involved property rights, the question of basic features of the Constitution could not be gone into.

DIFFERENCE OF OPINION

In this case also, Shri Shanti Bhushan and I had a difference of opinion. About fifteen days before this Bench was to sit on

10 November, Shri N.A. Palkhivala sent me a message from Bombay asking me how we were dealing with these cases. I spoke to him over the phone and requested him to come to Delhi. I told him that only after he was to come to Delhi should we discuss the matter with other lawyers. I was of the opinion that we ought to discuss and decide as to who would appear in the many cases that were going to be listed. He came to Delhi and then we had a closed-door meeting in a room in the Supreme Court Bar Association. Many of the lawyers who were appearing in these cases, including Shri V.M. Tarkunde and I, attended this meeting. Shri Palkhivala addressed all of us. He was very emotional that day, saying that the country was going to be destroyed further and monarchy was going to be established in this country after the judgement in the Kesavananda Bharati case was overruled. He said that this was likely to happen because four judges who were already sitting on the Bench were minority judges in the Kesavananda Bharati case and Shri A.N. Ray could very well persuade more judges to be on his side, and, hence, the majority judgement was most likely to be against us. He suggested that we should boycott these cases and not argue them at all. It was at this meeting that I said that we should tell all our clients that this was a question not of their case only, but of the country as a whole, and if the advocates are boycotting the cases, there was no question of any professional misconduct because the whole nation was involved. At least our appeals could be dismissed for non-prosecution or default, we would not mind. We did not want to drag the jurisdiction of the court,[3] which may allow the court to overrule the judgement in the Kesavananda Bharati case. This decision was agreed upon by everyone present.

At that time, Shri Shanti Bhushan was in Bangalore, staying at Ashoka Hotel there. I told him the next morning about our decisions. He immediately became angry and said that we should respect our judiciary and have faith in it. The judgement of 7 November 1975 in the election appeal of Smt Indira Gandhi had not been delivered yet. I told him that I could assure him that we would lose the case of Smt Indira Gandhi's appeal and there was no question of faith in the judiciary when the head of the judiciary was Shri A.N. Ray, who enjoyed his position at the cost of the three senior judges who were superseded by him. On moral grounds, Shri A.N. Ray should not have accepted the office of Chief Justice offered to him after supersession. I told Shri Shanti Bhushan that I did not have any faith in such a judge. Shri Shanti Bhushan, however, insisted that we should participate. I told him that we were not going to do it because this was the decision of not just one lawyer but a number of lawyers and that this was the advice of Shri Palkhivala also. On his way back to Allahabad, Shri Shanti Bhushan met me at Delhi. I told him again about all this but he still did not agree with me. He went back to Allahabad. I continued to contact Shri Palkhivala on phone. I telephoned Shri Tarkunde, Shri Daphtary and Shri Palkhivala and informed them about the difference with Shri Shanti Bhushan regarding appearance in the case. I also told them that Shri Shanti Bhushan was our man and it would be better if we resolved our differences. I told Shri Shanti Bhushan on the phone that he may telephone Shri Palkhivala in Bombay and resolve the differences with him. He said that he was not going to telephone Shri Palkhivala as he did not have much of a personal acquaintance with him. I told Shri Shanti Bhushan that it was not a question of personal acquaintance and instead it was a question of the country, and for that we would have to talk to each other, but he said that he would not telephone Shri Palkhivala. However, on behalf of Shri Palkhivala, I promised him that Shri Palkhivala would telephone him at Allahabad. Then I telephoned Shri Palkhivala and he was kind enough to agree to make a trunk call from Bombay to Allahabad. Then I again telephoned Shri Shanti Bhushan and requested him to be in Allahabad between 11 p.m. and 12 p.m. on that particular day. He promised that he would be there. Shri Palkhivala telephoned and had a six-minute talk with Shri Shanti

Bhushan over the phone. Shri Shanti Bhushan was not agreeable to what we had decided. Under these circumstances, there was no option for us but to leave Shri Shanti Bhushan alone.

PERSUADING TO WITHDRAW

I approached Shri K.R. Chaudhary, the Advocate-on-Record for the petitioner in the *I. Jagadeeswara Rao vs Union of India* case, multiple times. He held the same view that was held by me and Shri Daphtary, viz. that it would be better to withdraw the writ petition in the Supreme Court and file it in the Andhra Pradesh High Court. I told Shri K.R. Chaudhury, 'This is a question of the entire country. This is a very crucial moment in the history of the country when about 200,000 important Opposition leaders and workers are behind bars and when Members of Parliament are also in jail. If you want to save the nation, these clients should be persuaded to withdraw the writ petition from the Supreme Court and file it in the Andhra Pradesh High Court. It is to their advantage and to the advantage of the nation.' Shri K.R. Chaudhary was very nice to me as he was also moved. He told me that he was friends with Shri H.R. Gokhale, the then law minister of India, and it would not be possible for him to appear in the *I. Jagadeeswara Rao vs. Union of India* case and that instead of him, I should appear in that case. He telephoned Shri S. Ramachandra Rao, an advocate of the Andhra Pradesh High Court, who was to appear for the petitioner in these cases, and told him that he wanted to withdraw from the case on account of his personal difficulties, and that I would be the advocate in his place. Shri Ramachandra Rao stated that he was not going to accept this proposal and that he was not going to withdraw the case. It was under these disappointing circumstances that I told Shri Daphtary that I must go to Hyderabad to tell Shri Ramachandra Rao that this was Shri Daphtary's advice also. A letter was written by Shri Daphtary addressed to Shri Ramachandra Rao. The contents of that letter were that I, a man of confidence, was being sent to him and that it was in the interest of the country as well as his clients that the writ petition from the Supreme Court should be withdrawn and be filed in the Andhra Pradesh High Court, which was bound by the judgement in the Kesavananda Bharati case and where the writ petition was bound to be allowed and his clients would get relief, whereas there was doubt whether they would get relief in the Supreme Court and that everything would be lost if the judgement in the Kesavananda Bharati case was upset.

TIMELY INTERVENTIONS

In those days, my house was under construction and I was in great financial difficulty. I conveyed the importance of I. Jagadeeswara Rao's case to Shri Raj Narain in Tihar Jail. He realized that this case was even more important than his election petition. Some arrangement was made for my going to Hyderabad. Shri Raj Narain arranged ₹1000 from the jail itself and I arranged ₹700 for my air ticket and journey to Hyderabad.

I took the morning flight on 4 November to Hyderabad and reached there at about 8.30 a.m. I went to the house of the Socialist leader Badri Vishal Pitti.[4] Fortunately, I found Shri Pitti there. His brother who looked after a factory in Bombay was also present in his house. I asked Shri Pitti as to why he had not been arrested so far. He said that his daughter was going to be married and he had written to the government that he may be arrested after the wedding. The CBI and the police remained near the gate of his house and kept an eye on all the visitors to the house. I told him that Shri Raj Narain and Shri C.K. Daphtary had sent me there and that this was an important matter. Shri Pitti said that he would talk to some lawyers and they would talk to Shri S. Ramachandra Rao. I said that this roundabout way did not suit me and I would like to talk to Shri Ramachandra Rao personally. Shri Pitti put a car at my disposal. I went to the High Court at about 10.30 a.m. A number of lawyers there were known to me. I took them into confidence. I asked them to persuade Shri Ramachandra Rao to accept the advice of Shri Daphtary. Shri Ramachandra Rao came to the Bar Association when I was sitting there. He was much younger to me. I was introduced to him by the other lawyers sitting there. I gave him Shri Daphtary's letter in the presence of those lawyers and with folded hands requested him to act according to Shri Daphtary's advice as it was the question of the entire country. There were tears in my eyes at that time when I was telling him this. He said that Shri Daphtary's letter was an order to him. I then took him into a corridor of the Bar Association and told him that it would be proper if he were to consult his clients and tell them that it was the correct position in their favour. He then promised me that he would call his client in the evening at 7 p.m. and invited me also there. At the appointed time, I reached his place where his client was also present. All of them were convinced that it was in their interest to act according to the advice of Shri Daphtary and Shri Raj Narain. They promised that they would do the needful. I was happy about all this.

I came back to Shri Badri Vishal Pitti's house in the night. Shri Pitti asked me if I was in financial trouble in Shri Raj Narain's case. I told him that certainly I was in great financial trouble and nobody was giving us a single paise. I had spent money of my own and some money came from Shri Raj Narain's house. We were prosecuting the appeal under great difficulty and we needed money for the accommodation of advocates from outside Delhi. Of course, no advocate was taking any fee. We required money for cyclostyling also, but this I was having done at my own cost and that did not matter. I told Shri Pitti that at present I would not take money from him.

From Hyderabad, I telephoned Shri N.A. Palkhivala and told him that there were certain things which I could not talk to him about over the telephone as his telephone might have been tapped and Shri Pitti's telephone was being tapped also. I informed him that I would be coming to Bombay by the morning flight. He agreed to meet me at his residence. I took the morning flight from Hyderabad to Bombay and reached there at his residence in Marine Drive. I told Shri Palkhivala about what had happened at Hyderabad and the entire situation, that Shri S. Ramachandra Rao had orally agreed to withdraw the writ petition but there was no guarantee, and in case Shri Ramachandra Rao did not withdraw the writ petition then we would have to chalk out an alternative strategy. Being fully conscious that this possibility could well arise, on the previous day, i.e. 3 November 1975, before I was to leave for Hyderabad on Wednesday, I had got five intervention applications filed in the main case of *I. Jagadeeswara Rao vs Union of India*. These intervention applications were filed by junior lawyers. One was filed by Shri Shreepal Singh, who was working with me as junior lawyer at that time, one by Shri C.K. Ratnaparkhi, two by Shri S.K. Sinha, and another was filed by Dr. N.M. Ghatate. These intervention applications were filed on behalf of political detenus who were lodged in the Ambala Jail and whose *habeas corpus* petitions were pending in the Punjab and Haryana High Court at Chandigarh, wherein the Constitution (Thirty-eighth Amendment) Act, 1975 was challenged.[5] By the Constitution (Thirty-eighth Amendment) Act, it was provided that the Emergency was not justiciable in court.[6] The said Amendment Act was challenged on the ground of infringement of the basic features of the Constitution. In these intervention applications, we said that if the judgement in the Kesavananda Bharati case was overruled by the Supreme Court, then we would lose our *habeas corpus* petitions in the Chandigarh High Court as well. Therefore, these political detenus were very interested in any decision the Supreme Court was to take in I. Jagadeeswara Rao's case, which was to come up before the thirteen-judge Bench on 10 November.

THE SUCCESSFUL PLAN

Shri Palkhivala asked me to see him again at the Bombay House (Tata Group's head office) at Churchgate in Bombay. I saw him there and then we planned that he would come to Delhi on Sunday, 9 November, and then we would prepare the case. As Shri Shanti Bhushan was in disagreement with us, he chose not to come from Allahabad for this case. I requested him to come but he said that we should start preparing the case and then he would decide. Shri S. Ramachandra Rao came to Delhi from Hyderabad on Saturday, 8 November, by the evening flight. I went to receive him at the airport. From there we went to the Lodhi Hotel. He told me that he was sorry that he could not withdraw the case as promised at Hyderabad. I asked him for his reasons for not withdrawing the case. He said he could not disclose the reasons. When I requested him to tell me in confidence, he informed me that my visit to Hyderabad came to be known by the government and there was pressure by Shri P.V. Narasimha Rao and others on him that if he withdrew the case,[7] then income tax raids and other raids would be carried out against him and he would be arrested under MISA. I was disappointed after my talk with Shri Ramachandra Rao. I then went to Shri Daphtary and told him all this. Shri Palkhivala came to Delhi the next day in the morning from Bombay and immediately telephoned me. I then contacted Shri J.B. Dadachanji. We arranged a meeting at Shri Daphtary's place at 10 a.m. Only a limited number of lawyers attended the meeting. Shri Palkhivala, Shri Dadachanji and I, apart from Shri Daphtary, were there. I had also brought Shri Ramachandra Rao to the meeting from the Lodhi Hotel. Shri Daphtary asked Shri Ramachandra Rao as to why he had not withdrawn the case as advised by Shri Daphtary earlier in his letter, which was handed over to Shri Ramachandra Rao in Hyderabad by me earlier. He said that he could not withdraw the case on account of the reasons already disclosed to me. Then Shri Daphtary asked Shri

Ramachandra Rao to allow Shri Palkhivala to lead him in the case as Shri Palkhivala had argued Kesavananda Bharati's case and he could put across the points better than any other advocate in India. Shri Ramachandra Rao said that he would not allow Shri Palkhivala or any other advocate to lead him and he would argue the case himself.

This was the difficult situation in which we were placed. In these circumstances, I requested Shri Ramachandra Rao to leave us alone and got to the hotel so that we may discuss as to what we may have to do. Then we discussed the matter. It was a masterpiece plan, which succeeded. I suggested that as five intervention applications had been filed, we divide them amongst us. One intervention application was given to Shri Daphtary, one to Shri Palkhivala, one to Dr. N.M. Ghatate, one to Shri Tarkunde, and one to me. This was to be the arrangement when the thirteen-judge Bench would sit. First, Shri Daphtary would stand up and tell the court about his intervention application and we were sure that the Chief Justice would allow the same. Then further, Shri Palkhivala and other advocates would do likewise and after all these applications were allowed, Shri Daphtary would stand again and say, 'My lord, will your lordship not mind if Shri N.A. Palkhivala opens the arguments.' I told Shri Daphtary that the Chief Justice, Shri A.N. Ray, would allow the prayer also because I knew fully well that he wanted us to be trapped just as we were in his trap in Smt Indira Gandhi's case and we should argue the case so that the judgement in the Kesavananda Bharati case may be overruled.

The Bench convened the following day. It was so arranged that in the intervention application given to Shri Palkhivala, the names of lawyers shown with him were my name, Shri Shailendra Kumar and my junior Shri Shreepal Singh, who was the Advocate-on-Record in that intervention application. It was so arranged on our side that Shri Shailendra Kumar would sit by the side of Shri Palkhivala and I would either stand or sit behind Shri Palkhivala to assist him, so that proper assistance may be given to Shri Palkhivala if there was any controversy about the facts. We were very apprehensive that if Shri S. Ramachandra Rao started the arguments, the case would flow immediately and the Chief Justice may ask Shri Niren De, then Attorney General, who would say that he was questioning the correctness of the judgement in the Kesavananda Bharati case and that the said judgement should be reviewed. In that event, Chief Justice A.N. Ray would allow Shri Niren De to argue the case against the correctness of the majority judgement in the Kesavananda Bharati case and then the arguments in the case would start and we would be nowhere. It was the good luck of this country that our plan succeeded. Shri Daphtary stood up and addressed the court.

Shri C.K. Daphtary: 'My lords, I have an intervention application, which is listed before your lordship. My client, who is a detenu lodged in Ambala Central Jail, has challenged the validity of the Constitution (Thirty-eighth Amendment) Act in the Punjab and Haryana High Court at Chandigarh. By that Act, the Emergency has been made non-justiciable and if Kesavananda Bharati's case is overruled, my client's writ petition in that High Court would be dismissed. In these circumstances, my client is very much interested in the decision which your lordship may take in this case (I. Jagadeeswara Rao's case) which is listed before your lordships. I, therefore, may be allowed to intervene in the matter.'

Chief Justice: 'Yes, we allow you to intervene.'

Then Shri Palkhivala made a similar request, which was also allowed. Shri V.M. Tarkunde, Dr. N.M. Ghatate and I made similar requests, and they were also allowed. Then Shri Daphtary stood up again and requested the court, 'Your lordships know that Shri N.A. Pakhlivala had argued Kesavananda Bharati's case. It is desired that he should be allowed to assist the court and open the arguments.'

Chief Justice: 'Yes, we can have no objection. Let Mr. Palkhivala start the arguments.'

Shri S. Ramachandra Rao, who was also sitting on the front bench, did not object to this procedure adopted by the court. We were very happy that Shri Palkhivala was allowed to argue the case. On account of paucity of time, Shri Palkhivala and we who were assisting him could not put our contentions in writing. The result was that Shri Palkhivala started his arguments orally. His contention was that the Supreme Court at this stage cannot sit to review the judgement in the Kesavananda Bharati case as there was no occasion for it.

I have heard Shri Palkhivala arguing cases in the Supreme Court before and after this case. I can say that his performance in the present case was truly superlative. For one complete day, he argued as to why the Supreme Court could not sit to decide the correctness of the judgement in the Kesavananda Bharati case. During the course of the arguments, he mentioned to the court many things that were happening during the Emergency—how the press was gagged, how Fundamental Rights were destroyed, how the atmosphere in the country was surcharged with fear and the entire country had become a 'jail' and human beings were being treated as cattle by the government of the day. Shri Palkhivala, while addressing the court, realized that an occasion was provided for him for mentioning as to what was happening in the country. He mentioned that a constitutional bill, namely the Constitution (Forty-first Amendment) Bill, which was already passed by the Rajya Sabha, provided that no case (civil or criminal) could be filed against the prime minister in the court for past, present, or future actions.[8] Representatives of the press were taking notes, but as there was press censorship, everything that Shri Palkhivala said could not be published in the newspapers.[9]

The next day, Shri Palkhivala continued his argument till lunch and thereafter Shri Niren De was asked to reply to the limited question as to whether the thirteen-judge Bench should sit for reviewing the judgement in the Kesavananda Bharati case. Shri Niren De continued his arguments till the end of the day.[10]

SHARP DIVISION IN THE BENCH

Within these two days of arguments, there was a sharp division in the Bench and it was so apparent when nine of the thirteen judges were with us and four were with the other side. Justice Khanna observed as to in what case reference to the larger Bench had been made.[11] The Chief Justice then observed that it was made in the transport cases of Tamil Nadu, which were also listed along with I. Jagadeeswara Rao's case before the thirteen-judge Bench. In fact, no reference in those cases could be made as they were property rights cases, and property cases had already been held in the Kesavananda Bharati case not to interfere with the basic features of the Constitution. The then Advocate-General of Tamil Nadu, Shri Govind Swaminathan, immediately stood up and said, 'My lords, in my cases it was not at all referred to the thirteen judges. In fact, whenever I used to appear in the Supreme Court in other cases, the Chief Justice used to remind me of my transport cases.' Then the Chief Justice said, 'Then the reference must have been made in the first case (I. Jagadeeswara Rao's case).' Luckily, Shri S. Ramachandra Rao, sitting in the first row, stood up and said, 'My lords, no such reference was made in my case also.' The Chief Justice then said that the reference was made on a mention being made by Shri J.B. Dadachanji in his case. Shri Dadachanji was not present in the court at that time.

Clearly, the Chief Justice was isolated and cornered by the judges as well as lawyers on our side. This was the state of affairs that was created within two days of arguments not on merits but on the question of whether the court should sit to review the judgement in the Kesavananda Bharati case. The court was packed from the morning till the evening and it was very difficult for the advocates as well as the visitors to find place to sit or to stand.

I had my suspicion that the Chief Justice had orally directed the Deputy Registrar of the Supreme Court or the Assistant Registrar of the Supreme Court to form a thirteen-judge Bench and list all these cases before it. The practice in the Supreme Court is that when a case is listed before a Division Bench or a Constitution Bench,[12] a reference can be made to the larger Bench only if the judges feel that some judgement of the court appears to be incorrectly decided and when they feel that it requires to be overruled. Thus, a larger Bench cannot be constituted unless such an opinion is expressed by a regular Bench order of reference. The said order of reference is also placed before the same larger Bench when it is constituted. The larger Bench is constituted by the Chief Justice on the basis of the order of reference made by the regular Bench. This procedure was not at all adopted in these cases.

At 4 o'clock, I rushed to the Court Master's room. I casually asked one of the Court Masters there who would usually sit in the Chief Justice's court, 'Can you please let me know in what case the order of reference was made and can you please give me a copy of the order of reference.' The Court Master said that they had no order of reference with them. My suspicion was thus confirmed. I came home and telephoned the Deputy Registrar. I told him that I felt that there was no order of reference and he had listed the cases only on the oral instructions of the Chief Justice.[13] The Court Master said, 'Mr. Goyal, why do you involve us in the matter?' I said, 'It is not a question of your involvement. It is a question in which the whole country is involved and our nation will be nowhere if the judgement in the Kesavananda Bharati case is upset. We are calling you in the court tomorrow to explain as to under what circumstances you have listed all these cases before the Bench of thirteen judges and you will have to reply to the questions put by us in court.'

I also contacted Shri Dadachanji over the phone and told him that he would have to be present in court the next day at 10.30 a.m. and tell the court that the Chief Justice was not right in saying that Shri Dadachanji ever made any reference for mention of the case to the thirteen-judge Bench. Shri Palkhivala was also informed of my conversation with the Deputy Registrar and of the confirmation of my suspicion that there was no order of reference by any Bench whatsoever and that the Chief Justice had gone out of the way to oblige Indira Gandhi for the ulterior motive of overruling the judgement in the Kesavananda Bharati case and thereafter enabling her to finish the Constitution of India. I suspect that after I contacted the Deputy Registrar, he must have communicated it to the Registrar, or even the Chief Justice that we would call the Deputy Registrar in the court to explain as to how the cases were listed before the thirteen-judge Bench. On the third day, 12 November 1975, when the Bench collected, the Chief Justice started talking, and said, 'We find the arguments are in the air. Therefore, this bench is dissolved.'[14] The judges then dispersed.[15]

It was a great success for us and Shri Palkhivala received thunderous applause when we came out of the courtroom. It was a great victory for the nation. During the Emergency, we had victories in court only two times. One, in the morning of 25 August 1975 when on behalf of the Bar Association of India, I protested to Chief Justice A.N. Ray about the search and frisking of the advocates before they were allowed to enter the court in Indira Gandhi's case, and second, when Shri Palkhivala delivered his most brilliant performance for two days on 10–11 November 1975 in I. Jagadeeswara Rao's case mentioned above. Shri Shanti Bhushan, as mentioned earlier, was not agreeable to the approach taken in both these cases. As he was not agreeing to our approach, he did not come from Allahabad to Delhi to participate with us in I. Jagadeeswara Rao's case. I had been telling him that I had no faith in Chief Justice A.N. Ray. Shri Shanti Bhushan was not listening to me and his attitude towards me was as if my thinking was not that of a lawyer. To the foreign press also, when we started our arguments in Shri Raj Narain's case, he said that he had full faith in the Chief Justice. He was my leader in the case and by way of discipline I could not express my views to the press.

I went to Tihar Jail after this great victory of ours to meet Shri Raj Narain. I informed him of our victory. He was also very happy and said that for the time being at least the Constitution had been saved. He cautioned, however, that it might be finished bit by bit by Smt Indira Gandhi. I also conveyed to him my views on Shri Shanti Bhushan as being a timid and arrogant lawyer who did not want to listen to others, and how Shri Shanti Bhushan had treated me and others not as close colleagues but as ignorant persons, with the result that we had lost what we had gained by the judgement of Justice J.M.L. Sinha. I further informed him that had Shri Shanti Bhushan accepted my advice not to participate in the case, then the position of the country would have been different. We would not have been languishing in jails and Smt Indira Gandhi would have been forced to remove the Emergency so that her appeal against Justice J.M.L. Sinha's judgement, which was hanging on her like a sword, might be heard. If Shri Shanti Bhushan could not understand this basic and common principle of politics and strategy, I expressed serious doubts about his ability to comprehend the larger situation. Shri Raj Narain, however, was helpless, and so was I as I could not refuse his requests, with him being my friend and client of long standing and we being together in political life. In fact, I treated Shri Raj Narain not as a client, but always as my elder brother. Sometimes, we quarrelled, but that too with love and respect for each other.

EDITOR'S NOTES

1   'Indira is India and India is Indira' was a phrase coined by Dev Kant Barooah, President of the Indian National Congress party. Many Congressmen took delight in this declaration. 'Addressing the solidarity rally at the Boat Club, the Congress President said "Mrs. Indira Gandhi's name stood for victory and he wished her victory morning and evening and victory for her actions." Reciting a couplet in chaste Urdu, Mr. Barooah said, "Indira—

tere subah ki jai, tere sham ki jai, tere kaam ki jai, tere naam ki jai.'" (Victory to your mornings, victory to your evenings, victory to your doings, victory to your name.) See 'Symbol of Victory', *The Indian Express*, New Delhi, 21 June 1975, p. 1. This led Jayaprakash Narayan to give Dev Kant Barooah the title of 'court jester'. In a letter to Mrs. Indira Gandhi dated 21 July 1975, written while he was under detention in Chandigarh, Jayaprakash Narayan wrote, 'Dear Indiraji, please do not identify yourself with the nation. You are not immortal, India is.' See 'JP Papers', File 2-2, unpublished, Cultural Informatics Lab, Indira Gandhi National Centre for Arts, New Delhi and Braj Kishore Memorial Institute, Patna.

2 For the Constitution (Thirty-second Amendment) Act, 1973, see Ministry of Law and Justice, Government of India website http://legislative.gov.in/constitution-thirty-second-amendment-act-1973.

3 Jurisdiction: Authority given by law to a court to try cases and rule on legal matters within a particular geographic area and/or over certain types of legal cases.

4 Badri Vishal Pitti was a Hyderabad-based businessman and Socialist leader who was closely associated with Ram Manohar Lohia. He was elected to the Andhra Pradesh Legislature as a Samyukta Socialist Party candidate and was a staunch supporter of a separate state of Telangana. He was also a connoisseur and patron of art, literature and music, and promoted many artists, most notably M. F. Hussain, whom he supported when the latter was a young and struggling artist.

5 For the Constitution (Thirty-eighth Amendment) Act, see Appendix III.10

6 Justiciable: Claim, issue, or matter which is appropriate for a court to review and decide by the application of legal principles; capable of being settled by law or by the action of a court.

7 P.V. Narasimha Rao hailed from Andhra Pradesh and was the General Secretary of the All India Congress Committee

(1975–76). Prior to this, he was chief minister of Andhra Pradesh (1971–73) and held many important ministerial portfolios in the state. He was prime minister of India (21 June 1991 to 16 May 1996) from the Congress (I) party.

8   Ironically, in her speech at the All India Lawyers' Conference, held at Chandigarh on 29 December 1975, Mrs. Indira Gandhi stated, '...today, there is a great deal of talk about constitutional changes.... We certainly do not want to change anything just for the sake of changing it.... If any change is required it will be not to lessen democracy but to give more meaning to democracy, to keep democracy, to make it a more living democracy.' See *Indira Gandhi: Selected Speeches and Writings 1972 to 1977*, New Delhi: Publications Division, Ministry of Information and Broadcasting, Government of India, October 1984, p. 237.

9   *The Statesman* reported an incredible exchange on 10 November 1975 between Justice M.H. Beg and N.A. Palkhivala when the latter was arguing to urge the court not to review its 1973 judgement in the Kesavananda Bharati case, in which Justice M.H. Beg was one of the judges on the Bench deciding that case then: 'Justice M.H. Beg intervened to say that the court finds it difficult to understand the 1973 decision. Mr. Palkhivala said that he could not believe that the court found its own judgement unintelligible.' 'Basic Structure of Constitution: Arguments Against Review of Decision', *The Statesman*, Delhi, 11 November 1975, p. 1.

10 That N.A. Palkhivala realized that he had been given an opportunity to comment on the happenings in the country was also reported in *The Statesman* newspaper. 'When at the close of his emotion-charged arguments on Tuesday against the Supreme Court reconsidering the Kesavananda Bharati decision Mr. N.A. Palkhivala thanked the Union Government for having given him an opportunity freely to express his views on a vital issue concerning the country Mr. Justice K.K. Mathew said: "Why you should thank the court for this"... The black-robed lawyers

who crowded the Chief Justice's court to hear the eminent lawyer build up a case against the present full Court review laughed when Mr. Palkhivala immediately said: "Yes my lordships, I do thank the court!"'. See 'Thanks to the Court', *The Statesman*, Delhi, 12 November 1975, p. 7.

11 'Reference' means an act of referring an issue by a body/court to another competent body/court.

12 'Division Bench' refers to a Bench comprising at least two judges. 'Constitution Bench' is the name given to the Benches of the Supreme Court of India which consist of at least five judges of the court which sit to decide any case 'involving a substantial question of law as to the interpretation' of the Constitution of India or 'for the purpose of hearing any reference' made by the President of India under Article 143. The Chief Justice of India has the power to constitute a Constitution Bench and refer cases to it.

13 Referring to the constitution of a five-judge Constitution Bench to hear a petition filed in the Supreme Court of India by two MPs of the Congress party challenging the decision of 23 April 2018 of the Rajya Sabha Chairman and Vice-President, Venkaiah Naidu, to reject the impeachment motion against the Chief Justice of India Dipak Misra, Prashant Bhushan stated, in a statement televised on 8 May 2018 by various news channels, including *Mirror Now* and *Republic World TV channels*, 'Mr. (Kapil) Sibal appearing for the petitioners, for the MPs, who had challenged the Vice-President's order, he said that, look, we need to know as to how this matter has come to be listed straightaway before a Constitution Bench. It has never happened before that a matter or a writ petition which is filed is listed before a Constitution Bench even without a judicial order'. (*Republic World*, https://www.youtube.com/watch?v=6JLM5H1EEaM, accessed 1 April 2019). However, contrary to the above statement, this had indeed happened earlier too. The thirteen-judge Constitution Bench to review the 1973 Kesavananda Bharati judgement was constituted

in November 1975 by Chief Justice A.N. Ray not on the basis of any judicial order of reference but on an oral direction by Chief Justice A.N. Ray. This is corroborated by Prashant Bhushan, who states, 'Therefore, the thirteen-member bench for review was not constituted in pursuance of any reference by a smaller bench, but on the oral directions of the Chief Justice.' See Prashant Bhushan, *The Case That Shook India*, New Delhi: Vikas Publishing House, 1978, Appendix 3, p. 256.

14 In his order, the Chief Justice of India also gave directions that the writ petition from Andhra Pradesh in the service matter of *I. Jagadeeswara Rao vs Union of India*, which was before the court, should be heard by a normal Constitution Bench of five judges and if that court were of the opinion that the matter should be considered by a larger Bench, it would sit later. This matter was later mentioned before a smaller Bench by S. Ramachandra Rao.

15 The importance of this case in saving democracy in India has been widely commented upon. See, for example, Arvind P. Datar, 'The Case That Saved Indian Democracy', *The Hindu*, 24 April 2013, updated 2 August 2016, available at http://www.thehindu.com/opinion/op-ed/the-case-that-saved-indian-democracy/article4647800.ece, accessed 16 December 2017. See also T.R. Andhyarujina, 'The untold story of how Kesavananda Bharati and the basic structure doctrine survived an attempt to reverse them by the Supreme Court', in Sanjay S. Jain and Sathya Narayan (eds), *Basic Structure Constitutionalism—Revisiting Kesavanada Bharati*, first edn. Eastern Book Company, 2011, p. 133. To this day, there is no official record or report of this attempt to review the Kesavananda Bharati judgement in existence.

10
'Judicial Suicide' and Other Excesses during the Emergency

The judiciary in India has always been respected and the people have had great faith in it. Even Mahatma Gandhi once said that he had high regard for the judiciary established by the British in this country.

HABEAS CORPUS CASES

After the Emergency was declared and a large number of political workers and leaders were detained without any ground or trial, the question that arose before their friends and relatives and political workers and advocates associated with the Opposition parties was whether the court should be approached for questioning the detentions. I was of the view that we should not go to the courts. My reasons were that it was a political and moral fight and it did not matter as to how many persons were arrested, and even if we were not arrested by the government, many of us should offer court-arrest in protest against the black laws of the government,[1] the various arrests made by it and against the destruction of the structure of democracy in the country. After all, Mahatma Gandhi never filed any petition for his release whenever the British arrested him.

However, a few advocates differed with me on this point. Within a few days of the imposition of the Emergency, there was a meeting of eleven lawyers of Delhi, who had associations or sympathies with the Opposition parties. I was one of them.

Shri V.M. Tarkunde, Shri P.N. Lekhi, Dr. N.M. Ghatate, Shri S.S. Khanduja and Shri K.L. Sharma were among the others who participated in that discussion. Eight of us were of the view that we should not go to the courts, our apprehension being that if we did go to the courts, then the laws would be amended in such a way that the whole fabric of democracy in the country would be finished. We were of the view that Smt Indira Gandhi was prepared to go to any length to crush any opposition against her, including the courts. However, Shri Tarkunde and Dr. Ghatate were of the view that we should file *habeas corpus* petitions. Shri P.N. Lekhi did not express any definite view. I spoke to Shri Shanti Bhushan also one day and he also appeared to be of the view that we could not prevent people from filing *habeas corpus* petitions. I told him that filing of such petitions could be prevented as we could write confidential letters to the advocates in the various High Courts who generally appeared for the leaders and workers of the Opposition and they could advise the relatives of the detenus that it was a political fight and not a court fight. I sent a few telegrams in this connection to some lawyers outside Delhi who I knew.

However, I could not succeed and *habeas corpus* petitions were filed in the Karnataka High Court on behalf of Shri Atal Bihari Vajpayee, Shri L.K. Advani and Shri Shyam Nandan Mishra. *Habeas corpus* petitions were filed in other High Courts also but most of the other important leaders refused to file *habeas corpus* petitions. In those petitions, the Emergency was also challenged. When the government thought that it could lose on this point, the Constitution (Thirty-eighth Amendment) Act was got passed by the Parliament wherein it was provided that the Emergency was not justiciable. Thus, Smt Indira Gandhi's government was bent upon frustrating all steps taken by the citizens to redress their grievances.

Shri Tarkunde tried his best to file a *habeas corpus* petition on behalf of Shri Jayaprakash Narayan, but he could not succeed, as in our first meeting with Shri Jayaprakash Narayan at the PGI,

Chandigarh on 6 July 1975, I had dissuaded Shri Jayaprakash Narayan in this regard and he had instructed that no *habeas corpus* petition should be filed for him then. Shri Jayaprakash Narayan also said that till Raj Narain's case was decided, others should also not file any *habeas corpus* petitions. I happened to meet Shri Chandra Shekhar at Rohtak Jail on 5 July 1975 along with Shri Raj Narain, Shri Asoka Mehta, Shri Biju Patnaik and Shri Piloo Mody. I advised them that even though there were certain law points in our favour regarding the proclamation of Emergency, nevertheless, political prudence required that we do not go to the courts, and for a real worker it did not matter whether he was in jail or outside it. It would be the people of India who would one day decry the conduct of Smt Indira Gandhi. Shri Tarkunde said to me once that it would be better if a *habeas corpus* petition was filed on behalf of Shri Chandra Shekhar. He said that Shri Chandra Shekhar's petition would be the best case as he was an elected member of the Congress Working Committee (CWC) and his detention would show that Smt Indira Gandhi intentions were *mala fide* and for personal gains. Shri Chandra Shekhar was transferred to Patiala Jail. I was told that some people met him in this connection, but he said that it was not a court fight but a moral fight and he was not going to file a *habeas corpus* petition. Shri Tarkunde also once asked me whether I could persuade Shri Charan Singh to agree to having a *habeas corpus* petition filed on his behalf. I told him that personally, I was against filing a *habeas corpus* petition. Shri Raj Narain was also against the filing of any *habeas corpus* petition.

The morale of the political leaders in jail was very high.[2] I must say that they were freer and clearer in their conscience[3] than many people outside jail as the latter were not allowed to utter even a single word against the government. As writ petitions had been filed in the High Courts, the High Courts had to deliver judgements. Preliminary objections were raised on behalf of the government that in view of the President's proclamation of the Emergency and in view of the fact that the right to move the court for the enforcement of Fundamental Rights under Articles 14, 19 and 21 had been suspended and in view of the fact that the Emergency was no longer justiciable, the *habeas corpus* petitions filed by the petitioners were no longer maintainable.[4] Consistently, nine High Courts declared that the petitions were maintainable. Elaborate judgements on these petitions were written by the High Courts.

The Government of India filed appeals against these orders in the Supreme Court. Chief Justice A.N. Ray formed a Constitution Bench consisting of himself, Justice H.R. Khanna, Justice M.H. Beg, Justice Y.V. Chandrachud and Justice P.N. Bhagwati for hearing these cases. The leading case was the case named *Additional District Magistrate, Jabalpur vs S.S. Shukla*. Other cases from different High Courts were connected with this leading case. The Attorney General of India, Shri Niren De, opened arguments on behalf of the government. On our behalf, Shri Shanti Bhushan was given the leading brief. Dr. N.M. Ghatate, Shri S.S. Khanduja and I were managing all these cases. The leading lawyers of the Bar on our behalf were Shri Shanti Bhushan, Shri V.M. Tarkunde, Shri Soli Sorabjee, Shri Anil Dewan, Shri Ashok Desai and Shri Ram Jethmalani. The Advocate General of Gujarat, Shri J.M. Thakore, also supported us. The arguments continued for more than a month. I wanted Shri N.A. Palkhivala also to appear in the case. I talked to him on phone a number of times in this regard. He said that this was such a simple matter and we would surely win and no court could hold that the writ petitions were not maintainable. He said that we should go on with the cases and if we found any difficulty, he would come to Delhi. The judgement was reserved.

A BLACK DAY IN THE HISTORY OF INDIA

On 28 April 1976, to our great surprise, the judgement was delivered. Four judges decided the case against us and only Justice

H.R. Khanna decided the matter in our favour.[5] This was a black day in the history of India. Shri V.M. Tarkunde aptly called it a 'judicial suicide'. The American and British press criticized this judgement. The Indian press was already gagged. The majority of the Supreme Court Bench held that during the Emergency, the government could take the lives of a number of citizens and the court was powerless in this regard. It was held that the matter was not justiciable and a citizen could not approach the court. In that view, the writ petitions were dismissed.[6] The feeling among the people of India was that the Supreme Court had not acted independently. These are the facts that nobody can forget. After this judgement of the Supreme Court, people stopped filing *habeas corpus* petitions in the courts. Though I was against filing of such petitions for political reasons, yet I, along with others, managed all these cases in the Supreme Court as it was the work of the Opposition parties.

The then Law Minister, Shri H.R. Gokhale, apparently in connivance with Smt Indira Gandhi, screened the judgement delivered by the various High Courts that the writ petitions were maintainable. All these judgements were not allowed to be published in the newspapers and *Law Reports*. Similarly, the judgement of Justice J.M.L. Sinha in the election case of Shri Raj Narain was not allowed to be published in the *Law Reports*.[7] The judges of the High Courts who delivered independent judgements were transferred by way of punishment to different High Courts in far-off places.[8] Justice H.R. Khanna, who had delivered a distinct dissenting judgement in the *habeas corpus* petition case, was superseded. He had to resign and in his place Justice M.H. Beg was appointed Chief Justice of India on 28 January 1977.[9] Shri R.N. Aggarwal, the Additional Judge of the Delhi High Court, who showed independence along with Justice S. Rangarajan in delivering the judgement in the case of Kuldeep Nayar's wife,[10] was not confirmed and he had to go back to the post of District and Sessions Judge, Delhi.[11] Later on, the Janata Party government appointed him as permanent judge of the High Court of Delhi. Shri U.R. Lalit of the Bombay High Court was similarly punished and his term as Additional Judge was not extended.[12] He is now practising in the Supreme Court of India.

This is how in Indira Gandhi's regime during the Emergency, there was a concerted attempt to tame and punish the judges. An atmosphere of terror was created and numerous speeches were made by the Law Minister and other Congress leaders that the court must behave and act according to the dictum of the ruling party.[13] Some judges submitted and those who showed independence and impartiality were punished.

OTHER EXCESSES DURING THE EMERGENCY

The Shah Commission was presented with evidence showing excesses committed during the Emergency—how people were tortured and their houses destroyed.[14] Many people were forcibly sterilized. All this was purportedly done for the benefit of the country, but in reality, it was for the sole purpose of terrorizing the people of India so that they become weak in health and have their heart subdued and do not raise their voice. During the Emergency, worse tactics than those of the British were employed by the government of Smt Indira Gandhi.[15] Her son, Shri Sanjay Gandhi, who had no political background and sacrifice to his credit, was made ruler and the real emperor of the country. He was given a red-carpet welcome by the chief ministers and other ministers at the airports. The Central ministers used to accompany him as if he was the emperor of India and they were ministers-in-waiting with him. His word was law in the country. Wherever he went, people were allegedly forced to collect money and give purses. In this way, millions of rupees were given to him.[16] Wherever he went, industrialists and others were pressured to collect money and send workers and other people to receive him and in this way crowds were collected by different officers, who had their quota fixed.[17] At one stage, it appeared that the officers and the ministers were even more obedient to him than to Smt Indira Gandhi.

Arranging interviews with detenus during the Emergency was almost impossible. Though I was granted an interview with Shri Raj Narain in the beginning with other leaders, later I could have interviews with Shri Jayaprakash Narayan only twice and with other leaders only once. With Shri Raj Narain, however, I had several interviews—twice at Rohtak Jail, several times at Tihar Jail and two times in Hissar Jail. After the case was over, the authorities did not allow me an interview with Shri Raj Narain. However, at his great insistence, I was granted interview with him at Hissar Jail. Even that was to be within the presence and hearing of the CID officer and the Deputy Superintendent of Jail.[18] The interview was held in the office of the Deputy Superintendent. The officers were sitting on one side of the small table. Shri Raj Narain sat on one chair. I wanted to sit with Shri Raj Narain on his side of the table, but the officers did not allow me to sit with him and insisted that I sit only across the table. I told Shri Raj Narain that there was no use of my talking to him when every word of our conversation was being noted by the Crime Investigation Department (CID) officer. The CID officer insisted that we do not talk politics. I could not talk about politics, but what else was there to be talked about? Of course, we could talk about the health of each other. Shri Raj Narain was infuriated and asked me as to why should we not move the United Nations as our basic human freedoms were being destroyed in the country. The CID officer rebuked Shri Raj Narain, saying that he could not talk politics. I was also enraged. Both of us felt trapped, but we continued talking. The CID officer continued rebuking us and said that he would take action if our further talks were held on political lines.[19] Shri Raj Narain and I felt insulted with that interview. I told Shri Raj Narain, 'Please don't call me again. You may die here in jail and we shall die outside, but we shall not meet with this insult at the hands of the officers of the government.' This was the situation of interviews with the other detenus too. The letters written by the detenus to their friends and relatives were also censored. Similarly, letters sent to the detenus were also censored.

A number of people died in the country in connection with the programme of forcible sterilization.[20] Police resorted to firing in Muzaffarnagar, Sultanpur, and several places in Haryana when people revolted against forcible sterilization. There was a reign of terror everywhere in the country. Everybody felt insecure, in shackles, and as helpless as caged birds. The whole nation was demoralized.

A number of workers who could not be arrested on the night of 25-26 June 1975 went underground and continued their activities of keeping up the morale of the people by writing underground leaflets. However, many of them were arrested during the Emergency when the police conducted raids at different houses and cyclostyle machines and underground presses were seized. Many of these workers used to meet me and I was kept fully acquainted with the activities of somehow communicating the correct news to the public.

We could not do anything for the families of the detenus, and many families in this country went through hardships during the Emergency. One of the important leaders who remained underground almost throughout was Shri Karpoori Thakur, who later became the chief minister of Bihar. Throughout the Emergency, he did not rest and remained active in various parts of the country. I was taken to him one night when he was in Delhi at Dr. Rajendra Prasad Road, sitting with Shri Digvijay Narain Singh, an MP. I and Shri Pranab Chatterjee (later a member of the Rajya Sabha) went to see him at about 10 p.m. and spent more than an hour with him. Shri Tridib Chaudhary, who fought the presidential election against the former President, Shri Fakhruddin Ali Ahmed, was also present. Shri Satya Deo Tripathy, who became minister of state in the UP state government, took Shri Karpoori Thakur incognito to Lucknow, where he met Shri C.B. Gupta, who later became the Treasurer of the Janata Party.

EDITOR'S NOTES

1. 'Court-arrest' refers to when a person voluntarily surrenders before a magistrate, who then orders his arrest, and the person is sent in the custody of magistrate.
2. In a letter to Prime Minister Indira Gandhi on 21 July 1975, while he was under detention at the PGI, Chandigarh, Jayaprakash Narayan wrote: 'I have given all my life, after finishing education, to the country and asked for nothing in return. So I shall be content to die a prisoner under your regime. ...Would you listen to the advice of such a man? Please do not destroy the foundations that the Fathers of the Nation, including your noble father, had laid down. There is nothing but strife and suffering along the path that you have taken. You inherited a great tradition, noble values and a working democracy. Do not leave behind a miserable wreck of all that. It would take a long time to put all that together again. For it would be put together again, I have no doubt. A people who fought British imperialism and humbled it cannot accept indefinitely the indignity and shame of totalitarianism. The spirit of man can never be vanquished, no matter how deeply suppressed. In establishing your personal dictatorship you have buried it deep. But it will rise from the grave.' See 'JP Papers', File 2-2, unpublished, Cultural Informatics Lab, Indira Gandhi National Centre for Arts, New Delhi and Braj Kishore Memorial Institute, Patna. Speaking in the Lok Sabha on 21 July 1975 during the discussion on the resolution moved by the then Minister of Agriculture Jagjivan Ram to approve the Proclamation of Emergency dated 25 June 1975, A.K. Gopalan, an MP of the CPI (M), stated that he had been arrested and kept in jail for one week and described the 'inhuman treatment' meted

out to him over two days. He added, 'Had not my comrades prevented the policemen my head would have been broken. But I got only injuries because my comrades saved me. I wanted that my comrades should not have prevented that and that I should have died. It would be a glory for me that by fighting the cause of working class in this country, and for saving democracy in this country, I died. Unfortunately I did not die and I am here to express my feelings.' See 'Lok Sabha Debates' No. 1, 21 July 1975, p. 88 in *Lok Sabha Debates* (Fifth Series), Vol. LIII, 21 July to 1 August 1975.

3   For example, see the poem '*Toot sakte hain hum magar hum jhuk nahin sakte* (Though we may break, we will never bend)', written by Atal Bihari Vajpayee in Hindi in prison in 1976, available at http://www.geeta-kavita.com/hindi_sahitya.asp?id= 755, accessed 3 April 2018. Translated in English by the editor, it reads:

Though we may break, we will never bend
Truth struggles against power
Rules fight against unruliness
Darkness itself challenges us
The last ray of light is invisible

Our lamp of conviction is unwavering
Whether there be lightning or an earthquake
This battle is not amongst equals
We are unarmed, the enemy is endowed
With every form of weaponry it is adorned

And the beastly power has become shameless
Yet still we vow to fight
As the mythical Angad planted his foot
Our life pledged to undertake resistance
The call for surrender is unacceptable

Everything is at stake, we cannot halt
Though we may break, we will never bend.

4   For Articles 19 and 21, see Appendix III.11 and Appendix III.12, respectively.
5   *Additional District Magistrate, Jabalpur vs S.S. Shukla etc. etc.* on 28 April 1976, 1976 AIR 1207, 1976 SCR 172.
6   In August 2017, the judgement in the ADM Jabalpur *habeas corpus* case was overruled by the Supreme Court by a nine-judge Bench, presided over by the Chief Justice of India and including, ironically, Justice D.Y. Chandrachud, the son of Justice Y.V. Chandrachud, who gave the majority judgement in the 1976 ADM Jabalpur case. Justice D.Y. Chandrachud held that 'the judgments rendered by all the four judges constituting the majority in ADM Jabalpur are seriously flawed. Life and personal liberty are inalienable to human existence.' He further held: 'When histories of nations are written and critiqued, there are judicial decisions at the forefront of liberty. Yet others have to be consigned to the archives, reflective of what was, but should never have been.' *Justice K.S. Puttaswamy (Retd) and Anr vs Union of India and Ors* on 24 August, 2017, Writ Petition (Civil) No. 494 of 2012, Supreme Court of India.
7   *The Tribune* newspaper of 14–15 June 1975 managed to publish the text of the Allahabad High Court judgement of Justice J.M.L. Sinha of 12 June 1975.
8   Dr. N.M. Ghatate writes, 'The fear of Government's revengeful attitude even affected judges except very few. For instance Justice O. Chinappa Reddy who was transferred from Chief Justice of Andhra Pradesh High Court to the Punjab and Haryana High Court for giving judgment against the Government.' Dr. Ghatate writes that when C.L. Lakhanpal, President of the Punjab and Haryana High Court Bar Association, died in jail, 'The Bar as usual represented to Chief Justice Reddy for Full Court Reference to which he readily agreed for the next day at 10.30 A.M. The Chief Justice's court was crowded by the members of the Bar but no judge came for one hour. At about 11.30, Chief Justice O. Chinappa Reddy came alone and said "My colleagues have

declined to join the Reference, I will take the Reference."' See Dr. N.M. Ghatate, *Emergency, Constitution and Democracy: An Indian Experience*, New Delhi: Shipra Publications, 2011, pp. 60–61.

9 Speaking on Justice H.R. Khanna's supersession, 'Soli Sorabjee commented, "He might have been superseded by the Government but he has superseded all the Judges in our heart."' See Dr. N.M. Ghatate, *Emergency, Constitution and Democracy: An Indian Experience*, New Delhi: Shipra Publications, 2011, p. 79. See also the editorial 'Fading Hope in India', *New York Times*, 30 April 1976, which stated that 'If India ever finds its way back to the freedom and democracy that were proud hallmarks of its first eighteen years as an independent nation, someone will surely erect a monument to Justice H.R. Khanna of the Supreme Court.'

10 *Bharti Nayyar vs Union of India and Ors* on 15 September 1975, ILR 1977 Delhi 23, 1977 RLR 312. Kuldip Nayar, Editor of the Express News Service, was arrested on 25 July 1975 under the Emergency laws and was released on 12 September 1975. No reason for his arrest was given but ostensibly it was because he had organized a protest by journalists in Delhi.

11 Justice R.N. Aggarwal was demoted after four years in the Delhi High Court. Justice S. Rangarajan was transferred to Gauhati as punishment.

12 Justice U.R. Lalit's term was not extended because he granted bail to some students during the Emergency.

13 Replying to the debate on the Constitutional (Forty-second) Amendment in the Lok Sabha on 28 October 1976, Law Minister H.R. Gokhale had threatened the judiciary by stating that, 'If the Supreme Court were to strike down a Constitution Amendment hereafter, it would be a bad day for the judiciary'. Earlier, in a speech in the Lok Sabha on 12 May 1973, Mohan Kumaramangalam, Minister of Steel and Mines, defending the appointment of Chief Justice A.N. Ray, stated: 'We had to take into account what was a judge's basic outlook on life....Was it

not right to take all these aspects into consideration? Was it not right to think in terms of more suitable relationship between the court and the government? ...In appointing a person as Chief Justice, I think we have to take into consideration his basic outlook, his attitude to life and his politics.'

14   The Shah Commission of Inquiry was set up under Section 3 of the Commissions of Inquiry Act, 1952 by the Government of India on 28 May 1977 to inquire into all excesses committed during the Emergency. It was headed by Justice J. C. Shah, former Chief Justice of India. The Commission published its report in three volumes, totalling 525 pages. When Indira Gandhi came back to power in January 1980 she attempted to erase the presence of this report and withdrew copies of the report wherever possible, from libraries and government institutions. However, she was not entirely successful in doing so as the report was republished by Era Sezhiyan. See Era Sezhiyan, (compiled and edited), *Shah Commission Report: Lost, and Regained*, Chennai: Aazhi, 2011. A copy of the report of the Shah Commission is held in the National Library of Australia. The report is also available on http://www.countercurrents.org/cc280615.htm.

15   Coomi Kapoor writes that under the censorship rules imposed after the proclamation of the Emergency in 1975, 'No names were to be given of the people arrested under MISA and DIR. Communist leader E.M.S. Namboodiripad, in a letter to Indira Gandhi, said her regime had outdone the British colonizers, because even in the crucial years 1920–21, 1930–31, and 1942 the newspapers had been free to publish the names of those arrested.' See Coomi Kapoor, *The Emergency: A Personal History*, New Delhi: Penguin Books India, 2015, p. 54. See also Jayaprakash Narayan's comments in Editor's Note 17 in Chapter 5.

16   That vast sums of money were collected by Sanjay Gandhi and his supporters is alluded to by many writers. For example, in his autobiography *Nice Guys Finish Second: An Autobiography* (New Delhi: Penguin Books India (P) Ltd, 1997), B.K. Nehru, a

cousin of Indira Gandhi and uncle to Rajiv and Sanjay Gandhi, writes: 'The horror stories that I heard were not only about the incredibly childish, hamhanded and tyrannical way in which he (Sanjay Gandhi) had decided to solve the Indian population problem. They were also about the manner in which money was extorted from all kinds of businessmen for the grant of all kinds of permissions...' (p. 560) He goes on to state that the day after Sanjay Gandhi's funeral, 'I asked Rajiv whether the money Sanjay had collected allegedly for the Congress was safe. He said all they found in the almirahs of the Congress office was Rs 20 lacs. I asked how much Sanjay had. He held his head in his hands and said, "Crores and uncounted crores."' (p. 582).

17. This is well-documented by other writers too. For example, Anand Sarup, Secretary of the Transport, Public Works, Tourism and Estate Departments in Uttar Pradesh during the Emergency, states '...my boss, Transport Minister Shiv Prasad Singh, tried to force me to commandeer trucks and buses for bringing crowds to Lucknow, with a view to impressing Sanjay Gandhi, Indira Gandhi's son, on his first visit to Lucknow after the declaration of Emergency.' Sarup recalls that Sanjay Gandhi telephoned him one day, and asked him to buy at least twenty road rollers from his car company Maruti. When Sarup expressed his inability to do so since the PWD already had many more roadrollers than it needed, 'Shiv Prasad Singh tried to pressurise me. This time, in sheer desperation, he resorted to much cruder tactics....He asked me what I would do if some boys from a nearby village came and roughed me up. I did not react to this immediately and went back to my office wondering what I should do after this obvious attempt to intimidate me....Later, one Sunday, while I was at home, some odd-looking youngsters came calling. They told me that they needed a donation for carrying out some programme to be organised for inviting and feting their leader, Sanjay Gandhi. At this time, many school and college dropouts, and a ragtag of roughnecks had declared

themselves as Sanjay's followers. Apart from those who somehow got anointed by Sanjay Gandhi personally, many enterprising young men, unknown to Sanjay, wore Sanjay-style clothes, and started browbeating ordinary citizens. They would extract money from government functionaries, small time traders and street vendors for "furthering Sanjay Gandhi's programmes."' See, Anand Sarup, 'Defying Sanjay Gandhi: A Civil Servant Remembers the Emergency', in 'India of the Past: Preserving Memories of India and Indians', available at https://www.indiaofthepast.org/contribute-memories/read-contributions/the-unforgettable/147-defying-sanjay-gandhi-by-anand-sarup, accessed 28 March 2019. Pankaj Mishra writes, 'Lumpen young men gathered around Sanjay. They extorted money from small and big businessmen....' Pankaj Mishra, *Temptations of the West: How to be Modern in India, Pakistan and Beyond*, New Delhi: Pan Macmillan, 2006, p. 60. Kuldip Nayar states, 'The Directorate and the Income-Tax Department came in handy to raid business and the homes of leading industrialists. One purpose was to instill fear and to ensure that they would not support, financially or otherwise, her opponents and critics. The other was to extort money, which her son, Sanjay Gandhi, needed to run a parallel force of roughnecks and goons. Many Congressmen too acquired wealth arranging the release of 'economic offenders.' See, Kuldip Nayar, 'Emergency: Thuggery in Disguise', *Hindu Business Line*, 23 June 2000, available at https://www.thehindubusinessline.com/2000/06/23/stories/042355ku.htm, accessed 28 March 2019.

18   CID officer refers here generically to a police officer deputed for the interview.

19   Indeed, the CID officer was empowered to stop the interview if the talk turned to party or political matters. Rule 14(8) of the Haryana Detenus (Conditions of Detention) Order, 1971, stipulated that 'The Superintendent or the Officer deputed by the Superintendent of Police of the District may stop the interview if the conversation turns on any undesirable subject such as

party and political matters.' Haryana Detenus (Conditions of Detention) Order, 1971, Haryana Government, Home (Jails) Department, *Haryana Government Gazette (extra.), Part-III,* dated 11 December 1971.

20 These forced sterilizations were done under the guise of family planning as a part of Sanjay Gandhi's Five Point Programme. During the two years 1975–76 and 1976–77, 10,756,964 sterilisations were performed, according to the Shah Commission of Inquiry (*Third and Final Report*, August 1978, p. 207, available at http://www.countercurrents.org/Shah-commission-of-Inquiry-3rd-Final-Report.pdf, accessed 9 December 2017). Marika Vicziany writes: 'Between June 25, 1975 and March 1977, an estimated 11 million men and women were sterilized using such tactics. Another 1 million women were inserted with IUDs … The sterilizations were performed in assembly-line fashion, in great haste, and in unhygienic conditions. There was no "follow-up care" offered whatsoever. Many men and women died from subsequent infections. Some 1,800 families filed wrongful death lawsuits on behalf of deceased relatives, but the actual death toll was much higher. … It did not take long, given these horrific tactics, for public anger over the forced sterilization campaign to result in riots. Over 20 people died, and many more were injured, in violent "anti-family-planning" protests. Prime Minister Gandhi called a halt to the campaign in March 1977, and was quickly voted out of office as soon as "the emergency" ended.' See Marika Vicziany, 'Coercion in a Soft State: The Family-Planning Program of India: Part I: The Myth of Voluntarism', *Pacific Affairs*, Vol. 55, No. 3, Autumn, 1982, pp. 373–402.

11

The People Versus Indira Gandhi: Democracy Restored At Last

At a meeting attended by Shri Sanjay Gandhi at Jaipur, the then chief minister of Rajasthan, Shri Harideo Joshi, is said to have collected about 500,000 people for his meeting. According to my information, these were all hired and forced gatherings. It is said that Shri Sanjay Gandhi told his mother, Smt Indira Gandhi, when he reached Delhi that he was now so popular that a vast crowd collected everywhere, and, therefore, if elections were to be held then the Congress party would win. The mother-son duo never realized that Smt Indira Gandhi was isolated from the public, who hated her, and the people were trying to find an opportunity to throw her out.

It was under this misconception that the atmosphere was congenial for her and she would win the elections if they were to take place then that Smt Indira Gandhi dissolved the existing Lok Sabha on 18 January 1977, paving the way for the general elections of 1977.[1] Shri Morarji Desai, who was then detained in Karnal Rest House at Tarao in the district of Gurgaon, was released that very day. It was the great luck of the country that four erstwhile Opposition parties, namely the Bharatiya Lok Dal, Jana Sangh, Congress (O) and the Socialist Party of India, came together and merged themselves into one party, namely the Janata Party. Within a few days of the declaration of the elections, Shri Morarji Desai was made the chairman of the Janata Party and a Working Committee was formed. Bit by bit, the Opposition leaders and workers were released from various jails.[2] Shri Raj

Narain, however, was released only on 7 February 1977. Elections took place in the month of March 1977.

People were enthusiastic about the election, which saw lawyers play a very important role. In a conference held in Delhi, the legal fraternity resolved to defeat the Congress party and the Communist Party of India (CPI) at the polls.[3] Five constituencies were considered to be prestigious, those of Smt Indira Gandhi, Shri Sanjay Gandhi, Shri Bansi Lal, Shri H.R. Gokhale and Shri V.C. Shukla, all of whom were considered by the legal community as the main architects of the tyrannical regime during the Emergency. All of them were defeated at the polls by huge margins. Lawyers from Delhi and other places went to campaign and canvass votes in these constituencies particularly, and also to other constituencies in general. I, along with others, happened to be in the constituency from which the Janata Party candidate Shri Ram Jethmalani was contesting against Shri H.R. Gokhale. There was great enthusiasm and the Janata Party meetings were attended by large numbers of people, whereas the meetings of the Congress party had very thin attendance. The best lot of lawyers also went to Rae Bareli and Amethi from where Shri Raj Narain was contesting against Smt Indira Gandhi and Shri Ravindra Pratap Singh was contesting against Shri Sanjay Gandhi, respectively. I happened to be in both these constituencies for two days along with other lawyers.

On 13 March, Smt Indira Gandhi addressed ten meetings in her constituency. Shri Raj Narain and I went together to Rae Bareli and addressed fourteen meetings. We used to get information from our workers about the meetings addressed by Smt Indira Gandhi and were told that her election meeting in Unchahar was attended by only fifty-five persons, most of whom were her security personnel. It is said that at the last meeting addressed by her at Lalganj, she was so disappointed that she had tears in her eyes. She must have realized that she would lose. Candidates set up by the Janata Party, even if they were considered weak at the beginning of the election campaign, became so strong by the time of the close of the election campaign that everybody felt that success would be with the Janata Party.

THE CONGRESS IS DECIMATED

When the Janata Party workers and leaders came out of jail they were penniless. There were no funds with the party. There was no organization. It was a people's election and people arranged everything for themselves. The response was tremendous. In UP, all the eighty-five seats were won by the Janata Party. Similarly, in Bihar, Haryana, Himachal Pradesh and Punjab, no seats went to the Congress party. In Rajasthan and Madhya Pradesh, the Congress party got one seat each. In Orissa and Bengal, it got four and three seats, respectively. Thus, in nine states, the Congress party could secure a total of only nine seats in the Lok Sabha. In South India, the Congress party succeeded in getting a vast majority, possibly because the rigours of the Emergency were not fully felt in that region. On the night of 20 March 1977, the result of the election in the Rae Bareli constituency was declared by the Returning Officer, who was the DM of Rae Bareli. Various attempts were made on Smt Indira Gandhi's behalf to delay and torpedo the results. An application was filed for recounting and the same was rejected by the Returning Officer. This was followed by yet another application, which was rejected too. I stayed awake throughout that night when the Rae Bareli result was to be announced. To know about and discuss the election results, I contacted people in various cities, including Rae Bareli, where Shri Raj Narain was stationed, to know and discuss the election results.

When the All India Radio declared the result of the election early next morning, there was great rejoicing all over the country. Smt Indira Gandhi had acted like Bhasmasur[4] and got herself burnt in the elections. She lost personally to Shri Raj Narain in Rae Bareli by 55,250 votes. Shri Raj Narain was later appointed

India's Health Minister in the Janata Party government.

Even after the election results were declared, Smt Indira Gandhi did not lift the Emergency. It was obvious that her plan was that in case the election results were to go against her, she would put the leaders and workers behind bars again.[5] However, the atmosphere in the country became so much against her, fuelled by the fervour of the election campaigns, that she could not have the courage thereafter to execute her plan. There was great apprehension that she might declare martial law after her defeat. But it appears that she could not do so as perhaps she felt that the army would not side with her in these changed circumstances.

In spite of the fact that she and her party had lost the election, Smt Indira Gandhi did not resign immediately. She resigned only two days later on 22 March 1977, and it is alleged that during this period she destroyed important files and made some other arrangements of her own.[6] The rules of democracy require that she should have submitted her resignation immediately after she was defeated at the polls but she did not do so. This clearly shows that she did not believe in democracy. After the formation of the Janata Party at the Centre, the state governments, which were mostly of the Congress party, were extremely uncooperative and indulged in anti-people activities in their respective states. Then, a President's Order was promulgated under Article 356 of the Constitution, dissolving the Assemblies in the nine states[7] where people had expressed their lack of faith in the Congress party by electing Janata Party candidates with overwhelming majority. Six state governments, including that of Rajasthan and Punjab, filed petitions in the Supreme Court challenging the dissolving of their state Assemblies. However, these petitions were dismissed by the Supreme Court. Nine Assemblies were dissolved and then elections took place in these states. The Congress was badly defeated again in all these states. In West Bengal, the Communist Party of India (Marxist) [CPI (M)] won with a majority, leading to the formation of a CPI (M) government there. The Janata

Party formed governments in Bihar, Haryana, Himachal Pradesh, Madhya Pradesh, Orissa, Rajasthan and UP. In Punjab, a coalition of the Akali Dal and the Janata Party formed the government. The Janata Party withdrew the Emergency imposed in 1975 on account of 'internal disturbance' as well as the Emergency imposed in 1971 on account of external aggression and restored to the people all freedoms, including the valuable Fundamental Rights. The party also formed its economic policy and began work with sincere earnestness. There were high hopes that the country would make great progress. It was rather unfortunate that before realising their dream, the Janata Party government crumbled like a house of cards. Various factors, including divisions and differing ambitions within the party, were responsible for this. Morarji Desai resigned from the office of prime minister on 19 July 1979. Charan Singh succeeded him as the prime minister but had to resign after only three weeks. The then President of India, Neelam Sanjeeva Reddy, called fresh elections to the Lok Sabha for January 1980.

EDITOR'S NOTES

1   In a broadcast to the nation on 18 January 1977, Prime Minister Indira Gandhi announced the holding of elections in March 1977.
2   Initially, the leaders were released, and then slowly, bit by bit, the party workers were also released. 'Since all leading political leaders were released, Prime Minister Mrs. Gandhi invited them for discussion. In that meeting, Atalji told her that all the opposition political workers should be released immediately in order to fight the elections. She replied it would take some time. Atalji countered, "*Jis Chaturai se aapne do din mey hazaron ko giraftar kiya, aap unko chhod bi sakti hai*" (The shrewdness you showed in arresting thousands of people in two days, can also be used to release them).' See N.M. Ghatate, *Emergency,*

Constitution and Democracy: An Indian Experience, New Delhi: Shipra Publications, 2011, pp. 94–95.

3   The CPI wholeheartedly supported the Emergency imposed by Smt Indira Gandhi in June 1975. Speaking in the Lok Sabha on 21 July 1975, A.K. Gopalan, veteran leader of the CPI (M), stated, 'The CPI, the wretched traitors to the working class and the toiling people, continues to function as Her Majesty's loyal opposition.' See Lok Sabha Debates No. 1, 21 July 1975, p. 102 in *Lok Sabha Debates* (Fifth Series), Vol. LIII, 21 July to 1 August 1975.

4   In Hindu mythology, Bhasmasura Praveen or Bhasmasur Praveen (Sanskrit: भस्मासुर, Bhasmāsura Praveen) was an *asura* or demon who was granted the power to burn up and immediately turn into ashes (*bhasma*) anyone whose head he touched with his hand. The *asura* was tricked by the god Vishnu's only female *avatar*, the enchantress Mohini, to turn himself into ashes.

5   The General Election was held under the shadow of the Emergency, as both the Emergency of 1971 and the Emergency of 1975 continued to be in force and were revoked only on 21 March 1977 after the announcement of the election results. From information sourced from the Ministry of Home Affairs files at the National Archives of India, it seems that there was considerable discussion in the government on the pros and cons of revoking the Emergency and lifting press censorship. It was deemed by the government that not removing the Emergency even though elections had been announced would be seen unfavourably by the press, particularly the foreign press, foreign governments, and also Opposition parties in India who could try to embarrass the government by making it an election campaign issue. At the same time, it was felt that the 'gains of the Emergency' would be lost if the Emergency were to be revoked. In her broadcast to the nation on 18 January 1977, Mrs. Indira Gandhi stated that the 'rules of Emergency are being further relaxed to permit all legitimate activities necessary for the recognised parties to put

forth their points of view.' (See *Indira Gandhi: Selected Speeches and Writings 1972 to 1977*, New Delhi: Publications Division, Ministry of Information and Broadcasting, Government of India, October 1984, pp. 303–304.) A few measures were taken to relax the Emergency, such as lifting of prohibitory orders on public meetings and the release of political detenus held under MISA, except for members of banned organizations and economic offenders, amongst others. A document titled 'Note on Emergency', dated 15 February 1977, prepared by R.L. Misra, Joint Secretary (IS) and sent to the Home Secretary for use by the Home Minister, stated, 'The continuance of emergency has a healthy psychological effect in the maintenance of discipline and order which is an essential perquisite for a fair and orderly poll. ... the emergency is in no way coming in the way of normal electioneering process nor does it create any impediment in the conduct of a free and fair poll. ... the revocation of emergency would lead to certain very undesirable consequences which may not only cause incalculable harm to the nation but may create a situation in which the conduct of a peaceful and orderly poll may become impossible.' The government thus came 'to the conclusion that the time is not yet ripe for the lifting of the emergency'. See File No. 21/92/77-T (Vol. I), Ministry of Home Affairs, Section-T, National Archives of India, New Delhi, p. 77. The main focus seems to have been to avoid criticism of Mrs. Indira Gandhi's government by the Opposition and press, both foreign and Indian, being turned into an electoral advantage for the Opposition. A 'Top Secret/Most Immediate' Note by R.L. Mishra, Joint Secretary (IS) dated 20 January 1977, stated that the review of existing detenus detained under Section 16A of MISA be expedited, and added, '... it appears desirable that certain restraints be placed on the use of Section 16A on the State Governments *at least till the elections are over* in order to avoid criticism of the misuse of these provisions for political purposes. ...the provisions of DISIR (Defence and Internal Security of

India Rules) are very wide and the possibility of some of the provisions being misused by local authorities under political pressure cannot be ruled out. This would generate unnecessary criticism and give a handle to the opposition to propagate that the elections are not free and fair' (emphasis added). See File No. 21/92/77-T (Vol. I), Ministry of Home Affairs, Section-T, National Archives of India, New Delhi, pp. 17–19.

6   For example, the original signed letter of Prime Minister Indira Gandhi dated 25 June 1975 to President Fakhruddin Ali Ahmed has still not been traced.

7   These nine states were Bihar, Haryana, Punjab, Orissa, Rajasthan, Uttar Pradesh, West Bengal, Himachal Pradesh and Madhya Pradesh.

APPENDICES

Appendix I
Proclamation of Emergency and Press Censorship

The proclamation of the Emergency was made by the President under clause (1) of Article 352 of the Constitution of India around midnight on 25 June 1975. The 'Interim Report I' of the Shah Commission of Inquiry provides a detailed account of the events leading up to the Proclamation of Emergency on 25 June 1975, including the stratagem adopted by Smt Indira Gandhi to get the Proclamation signed by President Fakhruddin Ali Ahmed without informing the Cabinet (See Appendix II). Important officials such as the Home Secretary to the Government of India, the Cabinet Secretary, the Director of the Intelligence Bureau, and the Minister of Law and Justice came to know of the Proclamation of Emergency only on 26 June 1975 after it had already been proclaimed on 25 June 1975. The next day after the Proclamation of Emergency, i.e. 26 June 1975, the Cabinet met at 6 a.m. and approved the Promulgation of Emergency under Article 352 of the Constitution on the ground of the existence of a grave emergency threatening the security of India through internal disturbances. Prime Minister Indira Gandhi informed the Cabinet after the *fait accompli* of the Proclamation of Emergency and not before. The approval of the Proclamation of Emergency by the Cabinet was thus *ex post facto*.

The Cabinet met at 8.30 p.m. on 26 June 1975 and agreed with the recommendation of the Ministry of Home Affairs to impose press censorship. Press censorship was imposed by promulgating the Central Censorship Order, dated 26 June 1975, under Rule 48 of the Defence of India Rules, 1971, and Guidelines for the Press in the

Emergency period. The Central Censorship Order, 1975 addressed all printers, publishers and editors and prohibited the publication of news, comments, rumours or other reports relating to actions taken by the government without their first being submitted for scrutiny to an authorized officer and the publication being authorized in writing by the officer. The Prevention of Publication of Objectionable Matters Act, dated 11 February 1976, further defined objectionable matter to include words '(a) which are likely to bring into hatred or contempt, or excite disaffection towards the government established by law in India or in any State thereof and thereby cause or tend to cause public disorder'.

On 27 June 1975, on the recommendation of Home Minister K. Brahmananda Reddy, an Order of the President was issued, in exercise of the powers under Article 359 of the Constitution of India, depriving the right of any person (including foreigners) to move the court under Article 14, Article 21 and Article 22 of the Constitution. On 29 June 1975, the Proclamation of Emergency of 25 June 1975 was made applicable to the state of Jammu and Kashmir by an Order of the President of India, after suitable enabling amendment had been made by an Order of the President of India in clause (4) of Article 352 of the Constitution of India as pertaining to that state on the basis of a recommendation by the Cabinet in its meeting at 8 p.m. on 28 June 1975 and the concurrence of Sheikh Abdullah, the chief minister of the state of Jammu and Kashmir to the application of the Emergency in the state had been obtained.[1] It was also clarified that restrictions imposed on the legislative and executive powers of the State by Article 19 of the Constitution of India did not operate while a Proclamation of Emergency made under Article 352 was in operation by virtue of Article 358 of the Constitution of India. On 29 June 1975, the Cabinet met at 8.30 p.m. and decided that the Presidential Order of 27 June 1975 issued under Article 359 of the Constitution of India suspending the right to move any court for the

---

[1] See Appendix III.13 for the enabling amendment.

enforcement of Articles 14, 21 and 22 be extended to the state of Jammu and Kashmir also. On 11 July 1975, nearly sixteen days after the Proclamation of Emergency on 25 June 1975, the Intelligence Bureau (IB) submitted to the Ministry of Home Affairs a thirty-four-page (single-space) report titled 'The Threat of Grave Internal Disturbance: The Need for the Proclamation of an Emergency'. In this manner, justification for the Proclamation of Emergency was sought to be provided *ex post facto*, when in fact such a report should have preceded the Proclamation of the President. A publication titled 'Why Emergency' was tabled in the Lok Sabha on 21 July 1975. Resolutions for the approval of the Proclamation of Emergency were moved on 21 July 1975 in the Rajya Sabha and Lok Sabha by Home Minister K. Brahmananda Reddy and Minister of Agriculture and Irrigation Jagjivan Ram, respectively, which were passed by majority votes on 22 July 1975 by the Rajya Sabha and on 23 July 1975 by the Lok Sabha.[2]

---

[2]Source: (i) File Nos. 21/23/75-T, II/16013/1/75–S&P (D-II), and II/16013/10/75–S&P (D-II), Ministry of Home Affairs, Section-T, National Archives of India, New Delhi; (ii) 'Some of the important events between June 23 and June 25, 1975', Shah Commission of Inquiry, Interim Report I, 11 March 1978, available at https://www.countercurrents.org/shah-commission-interimreport%201.pdf, pp. 21–25, accessed 1 June 2018; (iii) Lok Sabha Debates No. 1, 21 July 1975, p. 73 and No. 3, 23 July 1975, pp. 32–42 in *Lok Sabha Debates* (Fifth Series), Vol. LIII, 21 July to 1 August 1975, Lok Sabha Secretariat, New Delhi; (iv) Parliamentary Debates Rajya Sabha, Official Report, No. 1, 21 July 1975, pp. 44–45, and 22 July 1975, pp. 120–124 in Rajya Sabha Debates, Vol. 93, Nos. 1–16, 1975, Rajya Sabha Secretariat, New Delhi; (v) 'Prevention of Publication of Objectionable Matter Act, 1976', available at http://www.indianlegislation.in/BA/BaActToc.aspx?actid=16081, accessed 20 May 2018; (vi) Soli J. Sorabjee, *The Emergency, Censorship and the Press in India, 1975-77*, New Delhi: Central News Agency (Pvt) Ltd, 1977, p. 43.

Appendix II

Excerpt from 'Interim Report I' of the Shah Commission of Inquiry

Planning and preparation for the Emergency began many days before the day the Emergency was proclaimed on 25 June 1975. A handful of people enjoying the trust of Smt. Indira Gandhi oversaw the logistical preparations for the Emergency—informing chief ministers of some states of impending 'drastic action', informing police and security agencies of possible arrests, checking that there was enough vacant capacity in the jails for the political leaders and other persons to be arrested, preparing lists of persons to be arrested, cutting off the electricity supply to newspapers to ensure that no newspapers appeared the next day on 26 June 1975, drafting a letter to the President of India and a draft Proclamation for him to sign, getting the President to sign the Proclamation of Emergency in, what some would call, a somewhat devious fashion, drafting Mrs. Indira Gandhi's broadcast to the nation about the proclamation of the Emergency on All India Radio on 26 June 1975, etc. The Cabinet and many senior ministers and government officials were unaware of the proclamation of the Emergency on 25 June 1975 and were informed about the Emergency only after its proclamation.

Details of the above-mentioned preparations are to be found in the 'Interim Report I' of the Shah Commission of Inquiry, which provides an account of the actual preparation and logistics of the proclamation and promulgation of the Emergency. The Shah Commission of Inquiry (Appointed under Section 3 of the Commissions of Inquiry Act, 1952), headed by former Chief Justice of India, Justice J.C. Shah, was appointed by the Government of India in 1977 to inquire into the Emergency and the excesses committed therein. The Commission gave its report in three volumes.[1] Relevant excerpts[2] from 'Interim Report I' are given below:

'5.29 The decision to take certain drastic steps including even the declaration of Emergency was, apparently, in contemplation even as early as June 22, 1975. On June 22, 1975, Shri R.K. Dhawan rang up Andhra Pradesh Chief Minister Shri J. Vengala Rao, and told him to be available at Delhi on June 24, 1975, when the judgment of the Supreme Court relating to the stay order applied for by Smt. Gandhi pending decision of the appeal filed by her was expected to be announced. Presumably, the order which the Supreme Court would make was to be the deciding factor on whether the drastic action contemplated to be taken should in effect be instituted. If the judgement had been in the nature of a categorical and an unconditional stay, probably no action of the nature, which was ultimately taken, would have followed. But the Supreme Court gave only a conditional order. On June 24, 1975, Shri Justice Krishna Iyer delivered his judgment on the appeal of Smt. Indira Gandhi. The operative portions of the judgment are as follows:

"(i) Subject to paragraph (iii) below there will be a stay of the operation of the judgment and order of the High Court under appeal.

(ii) Consequently, the disqualification imposed upon the appellant as a statutory sequal under section 8A of the Act and as forming part of the judgment and order impugned will also stand suspended. That is to say, the petitioner will remain a Member of the Lok Sabha for all purposes except

---

[1]The reports of the Shah Commission of Inquiry were compiled into a book by Era Sezhiyan. See Era Sezhiyan (compiled and edited), *Shah Commission Report: Lost, and Regained*, Chennai: Aazhi Publishers, 2011; also available at https://www.countercurrents.org/shah-commission-interimreport%201.pdf.

[2]'Interim Report I', Shah Commission of Inquiry (Appointed under Section 3 of the Commissions of Inquiry Act, 1952), 11 March 1978, pp. 21–26.

to the extent restricted by para (iii) so long as the stay lasts.

(iii) The appellant petitioner, a Lok Sabha Member, will be entitled to sign the register kept in the House for the purpose and attend the Session of the Lok Sabha. But she will neither take part in the proceedings in the Lok Sabha nor vote, nor draw a remuneration in her capacity as a Member of the Lok Sabha.

(iv) Independently of the restrictions under para (iii) on her Membership of the Lok Sabha, her right as Prime Minister or Minister so long as she fills that office, to speak in and otherwise to take part in the proceedings of either House of Parliament or attend sitting of the Houses (without the right to vote) and to discharge other functions such as are laid down in the Article 74, 75, 78, 88 etc. or under any other law, and to draw salary as Prime Minister, shall not be affected or detracted from on account of the conditions contained in the stay order."

5.30 Since the judgment was conditional, it appears to have been decided that the plan of taking drastic action was to be gone through with expedition and despatch.

5.31 According to Shri Krishan Chand, the Lt. Governor, Delhi, even as early as the evening of 23rd, a decision had been taken to take the Opposition leaders into custody soon after the Opposition rally, scheduled for June 24, was held. Lists of the Opposition leaders, which were to be arrested were also under preparation.

5.32 It appears from the report dated June 18, 1975, of the Director of the Intelligence Bureau, Shri Atma Jaya Ram that considerable political activity took place between June 15 and 18. The important aspects of the political activity were that Shri Krishan Kant, Shri Chandra Shekhar and Shri Mohan Dharia were active in putting forth the view that Smt. Indira Gandhi should step down and that the party should elect a new leader. Smt. Lakshmi Kanthamma was also of this view. Shri Krishan Kant pointedly expressed the view that so long as Smt. Gandhi remained in office the Opposition would get "a one-line programme" and it could snowball into a revolution. Shri Mohan Dharia was advised by Shri Y. B. Chavan in the afternoon of June 17 not to raise any dissent in the Parliamentary Party meeting on June 18. S/Shri Chandra Shekhar and Krishan Kant met Shri Bahugana on June 17, 1975 at U.P. Nivas. Substantial portions of his report have not been verified to be correct and some of them have been denied by Shri Jagjiwan Ram, who made his statement before the Commission.

Some of the important events between June 23 and 25, 1975

5.33 It was expected that a rally would take place, headed by Shri Jaya Prakash Narayan on June 24, 1975. In the evening of June 23 an indication was given to Shri Krishan Chand, Lt. Governor by Shri R.K. Dhawan that the Opposition Leaders may have to be taken into custody after the rally on June 24 and lists of prominent political leaders to be arrested were prepared by S.P. (CID) at P.M.'s House. Shri Krishan Chand stated that he was shown the lists and that changes were made in the lists and continued to be made from time to time as a result of continued discussions at P.M.'s House, but that he did not see the final list. He also stated that the Opposition rally did not take place on June 24 as announced to take place on that day, and so the action proposed to be taken on June 24 was stayed.

5.34 On June 24, Shri Justice Krishna Iyer announced the judgment. The Hindi version of the judgment broadcast over the All India Radio gave the complete story. This gave rise to certain angry reactions and the Minister spoke to the Director of News. Within a short time a revised Hindi version was broadcast which was intended to be favourable to Smt. Indira Gandhi, as broadcast in the English bulletin at 4 p.m. In the meanwhile, the authentic copies of the judgment were obtained. According to Shri Krishan Chand, after the import of the judgment was fully realized, it was decided to take drastic action against the Opposition leaders as soon as there were tangible signs of any effort on their part to dislodge the Prime Minister from her office and it was decided by the Prime Minister that action would be taken on June 25 after the Opposition rally.

5.35 On June 24, 1975, Shri J. Vengala Rao received a telephonic message from Shri R.K. Dhawan requesting him to meet the Prime Minister on June 25. Shri Vengala Rao has stated that Smt. Indira Gandhi informed him that having regard to the prevailing conditions and the contemplated country-wide agitation, it had been decided to take strong and deterrent action; and as this was sure to cause resentment and there was a possibility of some violent action, it would be necessary to take all preventive actions including arrests of persons who were likely to cause disturbance. He further stated that he was requested to pass on the message to the Chief Minister of Karnataka, who could not be present and that both the Chief Minister of Karnataka and Shri Vengala Rao were asked to be available on the telephone on June 25 when the final decision of the Government of India would be communicated to them by Shri Dhawan. Shri Vengala Rao left by an IAF plane, which was specially arranged for him for making a trip to Bangalore. He stated that he met the Chief Minister of Karnataka at Bangalore, apprised him of what the Prime Minister wanted him to tell him and in the evening he reached Hyderabad by the same plane.

5.36 Shri P.C. Sethi, Chief Minister of Madhya Pradesh, was told at the residence of the Prime Minister on the morning of June 25 by Shri Om Mehta, Minister of State for Home Affairs, about the guidelines that he would have to observe in taking into custody certain persons, who were capable of creating disturbances. According to Shri P.C. Sethi, it took place in the presence of the Prime Minister.

5.37 The Prime Minister tried to get in touch with Shri Harideo Joshi, Chief Minister of Rajasthan, but she was unsuccessful in conveying that message to Shri Harideo Joshi on telephone. Shri Sethi was then asked to contact Shri Harideo Joshi at Banswara on his way to Bhopal and convey the same message to him. Accordingly,

Shri Sethi went to Bhopal via Banswara by an IAF aircraft. At Bhopal Shri Sethi took steps in pursuance of the instructions that had been given to him by the Prime Minister. Shri Harideo Joshi returned to Jaipur by the same aircraft, which after leaving Shri Sethi at Bhopal, had come to Banswara for this purpose.

5.38 The records maintained at the Air Headquarters of the IAF confirm the flights of Shri Vengala Rao, Shri P.C. Sethi and Shri Harideo Joshi by the IAF aircrafts on June 25, 1975. No payments were apparently made by anyone for the use of the IAF aircrafts.

5.39 Shri S. K. Mishra, who was the Principal Secretary to the Chief Minister, Haryana, has in his statement before the Commission, stated that between 12 noon and 2 p.m. on June 25, 1975, he received from Delhi a telephonic information from Shri Bansi Lal, the then Chief Minister of Haryana, asking him to alert the Deputy Commissioners to remain at their Headquarters and be available on telephones and also to reserve huts at Sohna Tourist Complex for two VIPs, who were to reach there on the night of June 25/26, 1975. Lists of persons to be taken into custody were to be prepared by A.D.I.G., C.I.D. Shri Misra met Shri Bansi Lal at about 10 p.m. on his return from Delhi. At that time the latter told him that Emergency was expected to be declared that night. This statement of Shri S. K. Misra is corroborated by the statement of Shri N.K. Garg, the then Deputy Commissioner, Rohtak, who had also met Shri Bansi Lal at Rohtak at about 4.30 p.m.

5.40 Shri M. K. Miglani, who was the Deputy Commissioner at Gurgaon, had taken steps to reserve two huts in Sohna Tourist Complex on June 25 in pursuant to the message received from Shri S. K. Misra. He also contacted the Lt. Governor of Delhi and in response to his directions detailed one of his officers to reach Haryana Bhawan, New Delhi, at about 10 p.m. on the night of June 25, 1975, where the Delhi Administration authorities were to contact him.

5.41 The District Magistrate, Darbhanga (Bihar) had conveyed to the then Chief Minister of Bihar a message, which he had received from Patna, to the effect that the Chief Minister of Bihar was to contact the Prime Minister's House at about 9 p.m. on the night of June 25. Accordingly, the Chief Minister contacted the Prime Minister's House and after the telephonic talk that the Chief Minister had with the Prime Minister, the Chief Minister is reported to have told the District Magistrate that he wanted to get back to Patna the same night by road and he wanted to know the provisions under the Defence of India Rules with regard to the Press. The Chief Minister told the District Magistrate to convey to the Home Secretary and IGP the desire of the Chief Minister that they should meet him at his residence at about 2.30 a.m. on the night between June 25/26, 1975.

5.42 According to the statement of Shri Krishan Chand, all arrangements in connection with the impending arrests were discussed at a meeting in the afternoon of June 25 in the room of Shri R.K. Dhawan in the presence of Shri Om Mehta, the then Minister of State for Home Affairs, Shri Bansi Lal and Shri Bajwa, S.P. (CID), Delhi Administration. Shri Krishan Chand then called a meeting at about 7.30 p.m. at Raj Niwas at which the Chief Secretary, I.G. Police, Deputy Commissioner, DIG (Range) and others were present. The Chief Secretary of Delhi Administration, Shri J.K. Kohli had been instructed to visit the Tihar Jail to arrange necessary accommodation in the jail for those who would be rounded up in the course of the night between June 25/26, 1975 and taken to Tihar Jail. Accordingly, Shri Kohli had visited the Tihar Jail at about 8.15 p.m. in the night, checked up the availability of accommodation there and had tipped off the superintendent of the jail that he should be prepared to receive about 200 "Naga Political Prisoners", by the next morning.

5.43 Efforts were also made to ensure that some important newspapers were prevented from bringing out the morning editions on June 26, 1975. Shri B.N. Mehrotra, Ex-General Manager, Delhi Electric Supply Undertaking has stated that he was called to Raj Niwas by the Lt. Governor at about 10 p.m. and told that the electricity connections to the Press were to be disconnected from 2 a.m. that night and Shri Krishan Chand said that these were the orders from the Prime Minister's House and had got to be carried out. Shri

Mehrotra carried out the orders and reported compliance thereof at about 2 a.m. to Shri Navin Chawla, Secretary to the Lt. Governor.

5.44 Efforts were also made to prevent publication of newspapers in Chandigarh and Bhopal. Shri N.P. Mathur, who was the Chief Commissioner at Chandigarh, had not received any direct instructions either from the Home Secretary or from any other responsible quarters in Delhi. Shri N.P. Mathur had contacted over the phone on June 25, 1975 the Home Secretary, Shri S.L. Khurana to obtain confirmation of the instructions of the Chief Minister of Punjab. Shri Khurana disclaimed any knowledge on the subject. He, therefore, did not act on the verbal instructions received by him from Shri Zail Singh, Chief Minister of Punjab, to lock up "The Tribune" and its Editor, Shri Madhavan Nair at Chandigarh.

5.45 Initially instructions were issued by the Chief Minister of Madhya Pradesh at about 9 or 10 p.m. on June 25, 1975 to the effect that news about the arrests should not appear in the newspapers of Bhopal and other important places. The same instructions were subsequently countermanded as testified by Shri Narendra Prasad, the then S.P., Bhopal.

5.46 It would, therefore, appear clear that in varying degrees the Chief Ministers of several States were taken into confidence as early as the morning of June 25, and they had been instructed to take steps to take action on receipt of the advice from the Prime Minister's House that night. Those who had information to this effect were the Chief Ministers of Andhra Pradesh, Karnataka, Madhya Pradesh, Rajasthan, Haryana, Punjab, Bihar and West Bengal. The Lt. Governor of Delhi was fully in the picture even before June 25, 1975.

5.47 Shri Siddhartha Shankar Ray, Chief Minister of West Bengal, has stated that he received a message from the Prime Minister's Secretariat on the morning of June 25, and accordingly, he went to her house. When she came to the room where he was waiting, she had some reports in her hand and she stated that the country was in great difficulty; and that in view of the all-round indiscipline and lawlessness, she wanted that something should be done. According to Shri Ray, she had told him on two or three occasions prior to this that India required a shock treatment and something had to be done and some sort of emergent power or drastic power was necessary. Shri Ray remembered that one such occasion when she had mentioned about the shock treatment was sometime before the announcement of Allahabad judgment on June 12, 1975. On this occasion he had told her that they could manage with the laws, which were already on the statute books. In this context he had also mentioned the success with which they had tackled the law and order problems of West Bengal within the framework of the laws then in force. According to Mr. Ray, the reports that read out indicated that there was lawlessness or threats of lawlessness in many parts of the Northern India; that while they were discussing, a bearer came in with a piece of paper from which she read out and said that this was a report giving advance information about what Shri Jaya Prakash Narayan was going to say at a public meeting scheduled for that day in Delhi; that Shri Jaya Prakash Narayan would be calling for a mass movement within two or three days all over India and that the usual things would be said by him; such as, parallel administration, parallel courts, students not to join Universities, Schools and Colleges; appeal to policemen and to armed forces not to obey what were supposed to be illegal orders etc. Shri Ray said that he did not know from where this report originated. According to Shri Ray, there were certain things, which when they came from the Prime Minister, he could not say that they were totally wrong, particularly if they were factual; but, according to him, she was firm on the factual aspect that those reports indicated that India was drifting towards chaos and anarchy. Shri Ray then stated that he told her that he would like to consider the steps that had to be taken, after consulting the relevant literature on the subject; that she gave him the impression that she was seriously and sincerely disturbed with the conditions prevailing in the country; and that he asked for some time to consult the relevant law and left the Prime Minister's House; that he came back at about 4.30 or 5 p.m. and told her that she could consider if she so desired, Article 352 of the Constitution for the purpose of imposing internal Emergency; and thereupon she asked Shri Ray to go along with her to the President immediately. The President was then contacted and an appointment was taken and she went to the President along with Shri Ray. She gave to the President a summary of what she had told Shri Ray with regard to the facts; that the President heard her for about 20 minutes to half an hour and then asked Shri Ray as to what were the exact words in the Constitution; that the President then told the Prime Minister to make her recommendation; and when she was returning with him from the President's house, he told her that she should involve the other leaders also in that decision; that though he did not name anyone in particular, except the name of Shri Dev Kant Barooah, who was the President of the Indian National Congress, he wanted that she should involve the other leaders and talk to them about this matter; that she wanted to know the answers to three questions, which she had raised:

"Firstly, she wants to take a decision without going to the Cabinet. Is it possible? Can it be done?
Secondly, what should be the language of the letter to be addressed to the President?
Thirdly, what should be the text of the Proclamation?"

Shri Ray thereafter consulted the Business Rules and a notification pertaining to proclamation of Emergency in 1971. According to Shri Ray the first category dealt with matters, which must go to the Cabinet; the second category dealt with matters, which need not go at all to the Cabinet; and the third category dealt with matters which could be dealt with by the Prime Minister, but had to be ratified by the Cabinet. Smt. Gandhi said that she wanted to take the decision herself and that she would call a meeting of the Cabinet early next morning. Shri Ray then told her that if she wanted to take the decision herself, she should write recommending to the President the proclamation of Internal Emergency and avail herself of the relevant

Rules, as provided in the third category of the Business Rules. Shri Ray prepared two drafts. According to him, the letter, which Smt. Gandhi had written to the President recommending the proclamation of the Emergency and which was published subsequently in the proceedings of the Commission, was not the draft which he had made on the subject and given to the Prime Minister. According to Shri Ray, Shri Barooah was also called in later in the evening and his advice was sought by Smt. Gandhi as to the kind of speech she should make on the radio announcing the proclamation of Emergency. Smt. Gandhi, Shri Barooah and Shri Ray worked over the speech and this exercise took a long time—perhaps about three hours. This was because Shri Sanjay Gandhi used to come into the room and ask his mother to come out. Smt. Gandhi would then go out and not return for 5 to 10 minutes, and what she did when she went out, Shri Ray did not know. After finishing the speech writing, when he was going out through the door of the room, Shri Ray heard to his surprise from Shri Om Mehta that orders had been passed to lock-up the High Courts, the next day and to cut off the electricity connections to all newspapers. Shri Ray was surprised because he had told her that under the Emergency one could not take any action unless rules were framed. Shri Ray said that the locking up of the High Courts and cutting off of electricity connections could not just happen and he told that to those who were present there. He stayed on and wanted to see Smt. Gandhi and convey to her his reactions. He said that he would not leave unless and until she saw him because what was happening was important. Smt. Gandhi was late in coming and while he was waiting Shri Sanjay Gandhi met him in a highly excited and infuriated state of mind and told him quite rudely and offensively that he did not know how to rule the country. Shri Ray did not lose his temper but made him understand that he should mind his own business and should not try to interfere with what was not his sphere. Later Smt. Gandhi came and he told her about the impending closure of the High Courts and cutting off of electricity connections to newspapers. Smt. Gandhi immediately said that this should be stopped.

5.48 Shri Om Mehta in his deposition before the Commission has stated that he had given information to Shri Ray in the Prime Minister's house that night regarding the intended closure of the courts and cutting off of electricity, which had come to his knowledge while he was waiting in one of the rooms of the Prime Minister's house on that night.

5.49 Shri Brahmananda Reddy, the then Home Minister, has said in his statement that he was called to the house of the Prime Minister at about 10.30 p.m. and was told that on account of the deteriorating law and order situation it was felt necessary to impose Internal Emergency. He told Smt. Gandhi that there was already an Emergency on and that the powers already available under the existing Emergency could be availed of to deal with the situation. Thereafter, he left, but he was sent for again a little later and he was told by Smt. Gandhi that his earlier suggestion had been examined and it was found that the declaration of Internal Emergency was considered necessary. Shri Brahmananda Reddy thereupon told her to do what she thought was best. He has stated that on this occasion he also signed a letter to the President of the Republic making reference to the telephonic conversation which the then Prime Minister had with the President and appended the draft proclamation of Emergency for the President's assent along with his letter. The letter signed by Shri Brahmananda Reddy was on a plain sheet of paper and was not on a sheet with the letter-head of the Home Minister of India.

5.50 Shri Akhtar Alam, who functioned as the Special Assistant to the President of India, has stated that an important letter from the Prime Minister's house was delivered to him at about 10.30 p.m. on June 25, 1975, and that he delivered it to the President, who sent for his Secretary, Shri K. Balachandran and also Shri Neelkanthan, Deputy Secretary, who dealt with such letters. Some discussion ensued between the President and the Secretary about the wording of the letter about which Shri Balachandran raised certain doubts.

At about 11.20 p.m., Shri Dhawan came and he brought with him some papers. He says that he did not know what the papers were and he did not know whether the President signed those papers. The next morning at about 10.30 or 11 a.m. Shri Akhtar Alam was given by the President the letter from the Prime Minister and he kept it in his custody till he handed it over to Shri Balachandran when Shri Akhtar Alam left the post in February, 1977.

5.51 Shri K. Balachandran in his deposition has referred to the top secret letter received from the Prime Minister Smt. Indira Gandhi to the President. This letter referred to the discussion which the Prime Minister had with the President earlier in the day. She had stated that the President was satisfied on the score of the imminent danger to the security of India due to internal disturbances. She had also stated that if the President was satisfied on this score, a proclamation under Article 352(1) of the Constitution had become necessary; and that she was enclosing a copy of the draft proclamation for the President's consideration. Shri Balachandran has stated that there was no draft proclamation enclosed with the letter. According to Shri Balachandran the Prime Minister had also stated that she was not consulting the Cabinet due to shortage of time and the matter was urgent; and that she was, therefore, permitting a departure from the Transaction of Business Rules in exercise of her powers under Rule 12 thereof. According to Shri Balachandran he had advised the President that it would be Constitutionally impermissible for him to act in the manner suggested in that letter; and that he had to act on the advice of his Council of Ministers; and, therefore, his personal satisfaction in this matter would not arise. The letter from the Prime Minister indicated that the Cabinet had not considered the matter. Moreover, it was worded in such a manner as would make it appear that the decision to declare Emergency was that of the President based on his personal satisfaction. The President, apparently, saw the force of this argument and contacted the Prime Minister on the telephone immediately thereafter. Afterwards, he left the President's room, and came back after about 10 minutes. In the intervening brief period, Shri Dhawan had visited the President and had delivered the draft of the proclamation of Emergency for his signature. The President told him that he had signed the proclamation and given the same to Shri Dhawan, who had taken it back with him along with the Prime Minister's letter. The next day Shri Akhtar Alam had told Shri Balachandran over the telephone that a revised letter had been received from the Prime Minister, which was subsequently passed on to him by Shri Akhtar Alam in February 1977, and he kept it in his file.

5.52 The Prime Minister's letter and the proclamation of Emergency which are available in the President's office file are reproduced below:

"TOP SECRET
PRIME MINISTER
INDIA
NEW DELHI June 25, 1975

"Dear Rashtrapati ji,

As already explained to you, a little while ago, information has reached us which indicates that there is an imminent danger to the security of India being threatened by internal disturbance. The matter is extremely urgent.

I would have liked to have taken this to the Cabinet but unfortunately this is not possible tonight. I am, therefore, condoning or permitting a departure from the Government of India (Transaction of Business) Rule 1961, as amended up-to-date by virtue of my powers under Rule 12 thereof. I shall mention the matter to the Cabinet first thing tomorrow morning.

"In the circumstances and in case you are so satisfied, a requisite Proclamation under Article 352(1) has become necessary. I am enclosing a copy of the draft Proclamation for your consideration. As you are aware, under Article 352(3) even when there in an imminent danger of such a threat as mentioned by me, the necessary

Proclamation under Article 352(1) can be issued.

"I recommend that such a Proclamation should be issued tonight, however, late it may be, and all arrangements will be made to make it public as early as possible thereafter.

With kind regards,

Yours sincerely
Sd/- Indira Gandhi"

"PROCLAMATION OF EMERGENCY

In exercise of the powers conferred by Clause 1 of Article 352 of the Constitution, I, Fakhruddin Ali Ahmed, President of India, by this Proclamation declare that a grave emergency exists whereby the security of India is threatened by internal disturbance.

New Delhi—25th June, 1975.

PRESIDENT"

5.53 On the basis of the evidence it is clear that some of the important functionaries in the Home Ministry, Cabinet Secretariat and the Prime Minister's Secretariat, who should have been consulted before such an important decision was taken, did not know anything about the proclamation of Emergency till very late and some of them learnt about it only on the morning of June 26, 1975.

5.54 Shri P.N. Dhar, Secretary to the Prime Minister, in his statement has said that he knew about it only when he was called to the Prime Minister's House around 11.30 p.m. on June 25, when he was given for perusal the draft of the speech that the Prime Minister was going to make over the All India Radio.

5.55 Shri B.D. Pande, the Cabinet Secretary, received a phone-call from the Prime Minister's House at about 4.30 a.m. on June 26, and was told that a Cabinet meeting was scheduled to take place at 6 a.m. that morning. He knew about the proclamation of Emergency for the first time that morning only. He was surprised as to how and who functioned to bring about the large number of arrests which had taken place between 25th and 26th June. Normally, all instructions for such expeditious actions were routed through the Ministry of Home Affairs which used their own channels of communications.

5.56 According to Shri B.D Pande, the need for the declaration of emergency or the situation in the country warranting any such declaration had not figured in any of the Cabinet meetings preceding June 26, 1975.

5.57 Shri Atma Jayaram, Director, Intelligence Bureau, has stated that he learnt about the proclamation of Emergency only after he went to the office on June 26th.

5.58 Shri S.L. Khurana, who was the Home Secretary to the Government of India, had known about it only when he attended the Cabinet meeting on 26th morning for which he received intimation past 6 a.m. Accordingly, he arrived at the Cabinet meeting only around 6.30 a.m. when the meeting was already on.

5.59 Shri H.R. Gokhale, former Minister of Law and Justice, came to know about the proclamation of Emergency for the first time at the Cabinet meeting held on the morning of June 26, 1975. Neither he nor his Ministry was consulted with regard to the proclamation of Emergency at any time before, nor was the proclamation vetted by him or by his Ministry.

5.60 Some of the special features of the proclamation of Emergency, as gathered from the official records, are as follows:-

(a) on the economic front there was nothing alarming. On the contrary, the whole-sale price index had declined by 7.4 per cent between December 3, 1974 and the last week of March 1975 as per the Economic Survey 1975–76, a Government of India Publication;

(b) on the law and order front, the fortnightly reports sent by the Governors of various States to the President of India and by the Chief Secretaries of the States to the Union Home Secretary indicated that the law and order situation was under complete control all over the country;

(c) the Home Ministry had received no reports from the State Governments indicating any significant deterioration in the law and order situation in the period immediately preceding the proclamation of Emergency;
(d) the Home Ministry had not prepared any contingency plans prior to June 25, 1975, with regards to the imposition of internal Emergency;
(e) the Intelligence Bureau had not submitted any report to the Home Ministry any time between 12th of June and 25th of June, 1975, suggesting that the internal situation in the country warranted the imposition of internal Emergency;
(f) the Home Ministry had not submitted any report to the Prime Minister expressing its concern or anxiety about the internal situation in the country. Till after the Emergency was lifted, the Home Ministry did not have on its file the copy of the communication which was sent by the Prime Minister to the President recommending imposition of the Emergency;
(g) while the Director of Intelligence Bureau, the Home Secretary, the Cabinet Secretary and the Secretary to the Prime Minister had not been taken into confidence, Shri R.K. Dhawan, the then Additional Private Secretary to the Prime Minister had been associated with the preparation and promulgation of the Emergency right from the early stage;
(h) Shri Om Mehta, the then Minister of State in the Ministry of Home Affairs, appears to have been taken into confidence much earlier than the Home Minister, Shri K. Brahmananda Reddy, who came into the picture only when the draft proclamation was forwarded to the President;
(i) while the Lt. Governor of Delhi and the Chief Ministers of Haryana, Punjab, Madhya Pradesh, Rajasthan, Karnataka, Andhra Pradesh, Bihar and West Bengal had been given advance intimation by the Prime Minister about the

contemplated action, no such advance information was given to the Governments of U.P., Maharashtra, Gujarat, Tamil Nadu, J&K, Tripura, Orissa, Kerala, Meghalaya and other Union Territories. In fact, Shri H.N. Bahugana, the then Chief Minister of Uttar Pradesh has stated in his affidavit that he came to know about the proclamation of Emergency on the morning of June 26, when he was having breakfast along with Shri Uma Shankar Dikshit and Shri Keshav Deo Malaviya, the Central Ministers, and they were as surprised as he was about the promulgation of Emergency.'

Appendix III

Statutes and Amendments

APPENDIX III.1: REPRESENTATION OF THE PEOPLE (AMENDMENT) ACT, 1974

INTRODUCTION

An Act further to amend the Representation of the People Act, 1951.

BE it enacted by Parliament in the Twenty-fifth Year of the Republic of India as follows:

1. Short title and commencement.

(1) This Act may be called the Representation of the People (Amendment) Act, 1974.

(2) It shall be deemed to have come into force on the 19th day of October, 1974.

2. Amendment of Act 43 of 1951.-

In section 77 of the Representation of the People Act, 1951, in sub-section (1), the following Explanations shall be inserted at the end, namely:-

'Explanation 1.-Notwithstanding any judgment, order or decision of any court to the contrary, any expenditure incurred or authorized in connection with the election of a candidate by a political party or by any other association or body of persons or by any individual (other than the candidate or his election agent) shall not be deemed to be, and shall not ever be deemed to have been, expenditure in connection with the election incurred or authorized by the candidate or by his election agent for the

purposes of this sub-section:
Provided that nothing contained in this Explanation shall affect-
(a) any judgment, order or decision of the Supreme Court whereby the election of a candidate to the House of the People or to the Legislative Assembly of a State has been declared void or set aside before the commencement of the Representation of the People (Amendment) Ordinance, 1974; (13 of 1974)
(b) any judgment, order or decision of a High Court where-by the election of any such candidate has been declared void or set aside before the commencement of the said Ordinance if no appeal has been preferred to the Supreme Court against such judgment, order or decision of the High Court before such commencement and the period of limitation for filing such appeal has expired before such commencement.

Explanation 2.-For the purposes of Explanation 1, "political party" shall have the same meaning as in the Election Symbols (Reservation and Allotment) Order, 1968, as for the time being in force.'

3. Repeal.-
The Representation of the People (Amendment) Ordinance, 1974, (13 of 1974) is hereby repealed.

APPENDIX III.2:
THE MAINTENANCE OF INTERNAL SECURITY ACT, 1971

A. MAINTENANCE OF INTERNAL SECURITY ACT, 1971, AS AMENDED UPTO 5 AUGUST 1975

Year: 1971

[Act No. 26 of 1971]
[2nd July, 1971]

PREAMBLE

An Act to provide for detention in certain cases for the purpose of maintenance of internal security and matters connected therewith.

BE it enacted by Parliament in the Twenty-second Year of the Republic of India as follows:

1. Short title and extent.-
   (1) This Act may be called the Maintenance of Internal Security Act, 1971.
   (2) It extends to the whole of India.[1]
   [2][Provided that every person in respect of whom an order of detention made under the Jammu and Kashmir Prevention Detention Act, 1964 (J.&K Act XIII of 1964) is in force immediately before the commencement of the [3]{Defence of India Act, 1971}, shall continue to be governed by the provisions of that Act in respect of such detention as if this Act had not been extended to the State of Jammu and Kashmir.]

2. Definitions.-In this Act, unless the context otherwise requires,—
   (a) "appropriate Government" means as respects a detention order made by the Central Government or a person detained under such order, the Central Government, and as respects a detention order made by a State Government or by an officer subordinate to State Government or as respects a person detained under such order, the State Government;
   (b) "detention order" means an order made under Section 3;
   (c) "foreigner" has the same meaning as in the Foreigners Act, 1946;

---

[1]The words 'except the State of Jammu and Kashmir' after the words '...whole of India' deleted by Defence of India Act (42 of 1971), w.e.f. 4 December 1971.
[2]Ins. by Defence of India Act (42 of 1971), w.e.f. 4 December 1971.
[3]Subs. by the words 'Defence and Internal Security of India Act' by the Defence of India (Amendment) Act, 1975 (No. 32 of 1975) dated 31 July 1975 for the period of operation of the Proclamation of Emergency issued on 25 June 1975 and for a period of six months thereafter.

(d) "State Government", in relation to Union Territory, means the administrator thereof.

[4][(e) any reference in this Act to a law which is not in force in the State of Jammu and Kashmir shall, in relation to that State, be construed as a reference to the corresponding law, if any, in force in that State.]

3. Power to make orders detaining certain persons.-

(1) The Central Government or the State Government may,—

(a) if satisfied with respect to any person (including a foreigner) that with a view to preventing him from acting in any manner prejudicial to:

(i) the defence of India, the relations of India with foreign powers, or the security of India, or

(ii) the security of the State or the maintenance of public order, or

(iii) the maintenance of supplies and services essential to the community, or

(b) if satisfied with respect to any foreigner that with a view to regulating his continued presence in India or with a view to making arrangements for his expulsion from India, it is necessary so to do, make an order directing that such person be detained.

(2) Any of the following officers, namely:

(a) district magistrates,

(b) additional district magistrates specially empowered in this behalf by the State Government,

(c) Commissioners of Police, wherever they have been appointed,

[5][may also, if satisfied as provided in sub-section (1)] exercise the power conferred by the said sub-section.

---

[4]Ins. by the Defence of India Act (42 of 1971), w.e.f. 4 December 1971.
[5]Subs. for 'may, if satisfied as provided in sub-clauses (ii) and (iii) of clause (a) of sub-section (1)' by the Defence of India Act (42 of 1971), w.e.f. 4 December 1971.

(3) When any order is made under this section by an officer mentioned in sub-section (2), he shall forthwith report the fact to the State Government to which he is subordinate together with the grounds on which the order has been made and such other particulars as in his opinion have a bearing on the matter, and no such order shall remain in force for more than twelve days after the making thereof unless in the meantime it has been approved by the State Government:

Provided that where under section 8 the grounds of detention are communicated by the authority making the order after five days but not later than fifteen days from the date of detention, this sub-section shall apply subject to the modification that for the words "twelve days", the words "twenty-two days" shall be substituted.

(4) When any order is made or approved by the State Government under this section, the State Government shall, within seven days, report the fact to the Central Government together with the grounds on which the order has been made and such other particulars as in the opinion of the State Government have a bearing on the necessity for the order.

4. Execution of detention orders.- A detention order may be executed at any place in India in the manner provided for the execution of warrants of arrest under the [6][Code of Criminal Procedure, 1973].

5. Power to regulate place and conditions of detention.- Every person in respect of whom a detention order has been made shall be liable—

---

[6]Subs. for 'Code of Criminal Procedure, 1898' by the Maintenance of Internal Security Act (Second Amendment) Ordinance, 1975 (No. 7 of 1975) dated 15 July 1975 w.e.f. 29 June 1975 and the Maintenance of Internal Security (Amendment) Act, 1975 (No. 39 of 1975) dated 5 August 1975 w.e.f. 29 June 1975.

(a) to be detained in such place and under such conditions, including conditions as to maintenance, discipline and punishment for breaches of discipline, as the appropriate Government may, by general or special order, specify; and
(b) to be removed from one place of detention to another place of detention, whether within the same State or in another State, by order of the appropriate Government:
Provided that no order shall be made by a State Government under clause (b) for the removal of a person from one State to another except with the consent of the Government of that other State.

6. Detention orders not to be invalid or inoperative on certain grounds.- No detention order shall be invalid or inoperative merely by reason—
(a) that the person to be detained hereunder is outside the limits of the territorial jurisdiction of the Government or officer making the order, or
(b) that the place of detention of such person is outside the said limits.

7. Powers in relation to absconding persons.-
(1) If the Central Government or the State Government or an officer specified in sub-section (2) of Section 3, as the case may be, has reason to believe that a person in respect of whom a detention order has been made has absconded or is concealing himself so that the order cannot be executed, that Government or officer may—
(a) make a report in writing of the fact to a [7][Metropolitan Magistrate or a Judicial Magistrate of the first class having

---

[7]Subs. for 'Presidency Magistrate or a Magistrate of the first class having jurisdiction in the place where the said person ordinarily resides, and thereupon the provisions of sections 87, 88 and 89 of the Code of Criminal Procedure, 1898' by the Maintenance of Internal Security Act (Second Amendment) Ordinance, 1975 (No. 7 of 1975) dated 15 July 1975 w.e.f. 29 June 1975 and the Maintenance of Internal Security (Amendment) Act, 1975 (No. 39 of 1975) dated 5 August 1975 w.e.f. 29 June 1975.

jurisdiction in the place where the said person ordinarily resides, and thereupon the provisions of sections 82 to 86 (both inclusive) of the Code of Criminal Procedure, 1973], shall apply in respect of the said person and his property as if the order directing that he be detained were a warrant issued by the Magistrate;

(b) by order notified in the official Gazette direct the said person to appear before such officer, at such place and within such period as may be specified in the order; and if the said person fails to comply with such direction he shall, unless he proves that it was not possible for him to comply therewith and that he had, within the period specified in the order, informed the officer mentioned in the order of the reason which rendered compliance therewith impossible and of his whereabouts, be punishable with imprisonment for a term which may extend to one year or with fine or with both.

(2) Notwithstanding anything contained in the [8][Code of Criminal Procedure, 1973], every offence under clause (b) of sub-section (1) shall be cognizable.

8. Grounds of order of detention to be disclosed to persons affected by the order.-

(1) When a person is detained in pursuance of a detention order, the authority making the order shall, as soon as may be, but ordinarily not later than five days and in exceptional circumstances and for reasons to be recorded in writing, not later than fifteen days, from the date of detention communicate to him the grounds on which the order has been made and shall afford him the earliest opportunity of

---

[8]Subs. for 'Code of Criminal Procedure, 1898' by the Maintenance of Internal Security Act (Second Amendment) Ordinance, 1975 (No. 7 of 1975) dated 15 July 1975 w.e.f. 29 June 1975 and the Maintenance of Internal Security (Amendment) Act, 1975 (No. 39 of 1975) dated 5 August 1975 w.e.f. 29 June 1975.

making a representation against the order to the appropriate Government.

(2) Nothing in sub-section (1) shall require the authority to disclose facts which it considers to be against the public interest to disclose.

9. Constitution of Advisory Boards.-
   (1) The Central Government and each State Government shall, whenever necessary, constitute one or more Advisory Boards for the purposes of this Act.
   (2) Every such Board shall consist of three persons who are or have been, or are qualified to be appointed as, Judges of a High Court, and such persons shall be appointed by the Central Government or the State Government, as the case may be.
   (3) The appropriate Governments shall appoint one of the members of the Advisory Board, who is, or has been, a Judge of a High Court to be its chairman, and in the case of a Union territory the appointment to the Advisory Board of any person who is a Judge of the High Court of a State shall be with the previous approval of the State Government concerned.

10. Reference to Advisory Boards.- Save as otherwise expressly provided in this Act, in every case where a detention order has been made under this Act, the appropriate Government shall, within thirty days from the date of detention under the order, place before the Advisory Board constituted by it under section 9 the ground on which the order has been made and the representation, if any, made by the person affected by the order, and in case where the order has been made by an officer, also the report by such officer under sub-section (3) of Section 3.

11. Procedure of Advisory Boards.-
    (1) The advisory Board shall, after considering the materials placed before it and, after calling for such further information

as it may deem necessary from the appropriate Government or from any person called for the purpose through the appropriate Government or from the person concerned, and if, in any particular case, it considers it essential so to do or if the person concerned desires to be heard, after hearing him in person, submit its report to the appropriate Government within ten weeks from the date of detention.

(2) The report of the Advisory Board shall specify in a separate part thereof the opinion of the Advisory Board as to whether or not there is sufficient cause for the detention of the person concerned.

(3) When there is a difference of opinion among the members forming the Advisory Board, the opinion of the majority of such members shall be deemed to be the opinion of the Board.

(4) Nothing in this section shall entitle any person against whom a detention order has been made to appear by any legal practitioner in any matter connected with the reference to the Advisory Board, and the proceedings of the Advisory Board and its report, excepting that part of the report in which the opinion of the Advisory Board is specified shall be confidential.

12. Action upon the report of Advisory Board.-

(1) In any case where the Advisory Board has reported that there is in its opinion sufficient cause for the detention of a person, the appropriate Government may confirm the detention order and can continue the detention of the person concerned for such period as it thinks fit.

(2) In any case where the Advisory Board has reported that there is in its opinion no sufficient cause for the detention of the person concerned, the appropriate Government shall revoke the detention order and case the person be released forthwith.

13. Maximum period of detention.- The maximum period for which

any person may be detained in pursuance of any detention order which has been confirmed under section 12 shall be twelve months from the date of detention[9] [or until the expiry of the [10]{Defence of India Act}, 1971, whichever is later].

Provided that nothing contained in this section shall affect the power of the appropriate Government to revoke or modify the detention order at any earlier time.

14. Revocation of detention orders.-

(1) Without prejudice to the provisions of section 21 of the General Clauses Act, 1897, a detention order may, at any time, be revoked or modified—

(a) notwithstanding that the order has been made by an officer mentioned in sub-section (2) of Section 3, by the State Government to which that officer is subordinate or by the Central Government;

(b) notwithstanding that the order has been made by the State Government or by the Central Government.

[11][(2) The revocation of a detention order shall not bar the making of another detention order under Section 3 against the same person.]

15. Temporary relates of persons detained.-

(1) The appropriate Government may, at any time, direct that

---

[9]Ins. by the Defence of India Act (42 of 1971), w.e.f. 4 December 1971.

[10]Subs. by the words 'Defence and Internal Security of India Act' by the Defence of India (Amendment) Act, 1975 (No. 32 of 1975) dated 31 July 1975 for the period of operation of the Proclamation of Emergency issued on 25 June 1975 and for a period of six months thereafter.

[11]Subs. for '(2) The revocation or expiry of a detention order shall not bar the making of a fresh detention order under section 3 against the same person in any case where fresh facts have arisen after the date of revocation or expiry on which the Central Government or a State Government or an officer, as the case may be, is satisfied that such an order should be made.' by the Maintenance of Internal Security (Amendment) Ordinance, 1975, w.e.f. 29 June 1975 and the Maintenance of Internal Security (Amendment) Act, 1975 (No. 39 of 1975) dated 5 August 1975 w.e.f. 29 June 1975.

any person detained in pursuance of a detention order may be released for any specified period either without conditions or upon such conditions specified in the direction as that person accepts, and may at any time, cancel his release.

(2) In directing the release of any person under sub-section (1), the appropriate Government may require him to enter into a bond with or without sureties for the due observance of the conditions specified in the direction.

(3) Any person released under sub-section (1) shall surrender himself at the time and place, and to the authority, specified in the order directing his release, or cancelling his release, as the case may be.

[12][(3A) If the appropriate Government has reason to believe that any person who has failed to surrender himself in the manner specified in sub-section (3) has absconded or is concealing himself, that Government may make a report in writing of the fact to a Metropolitan Magistrate or a Judicial Magistrate of the first class having jurisdiction in the place where the said person ordinarily resides and thereupon the provisions of Sections 82 to 86 (both inclusive) of the Code of Criminal Procedure, 1973, shall apply in relation to such person as they apply in relation to a person who has absconded or is concealing himself so that a warrant issued by a magistrate cannot be executed.]

(4) If any person fails without sufficient cause to surrender himself in the manner specified in sub-section (3), he shall be punishable with imprisonment for a term which may extend to two years, or with fine, or with both.

(5) If any person released under sub-section (1) fails to fulfil

---

[12]Ins. by the Maintenance of Internal Security Act (Second Amendment) Ordinance, 1975 (No. 7 of 1975) dated 15 July 1975 w.e.f. 29 June 1975 and the Maintenance of Internal Security (Amendment) Act, 1975 (No. 39 of 1975) dated 5 August 1975 w.e.f. 29 June 1975.

any of the conditions imposed upon him under the said subsection or in the bond entered into by him, the bond shall be declared to be forfeited and any person bound thereby shall be liable to pay the penalty thereof.

[13][(6) Notwithstanding anything contained in any other law and save as otherwise provided in this section, no person against whom a detention order made under this Act is in force shall be released whether on bail or bail bond or otherwise.]

16. Protection of action taken in good faith.- No suit or other legal proceeding shall lie against the Central Government or a State Government, and no suit, prosecution or other legal proceedings, shall lie against any person, for anything in good faith done or intended to be done in pursuance of this Act.

[14][16A. (1) Notwithstanding anything contained in this Act or any rules of natural justice, the provisions of this section shall have effect during the period of operation of the proclamation of emergency issued under Clause (1) of Article 352 of the Constitution on the 3rd day of December, 1971, or the Proclamation of Emergency issued under that clause on the 25th day of June, 1975, or a period of twelve months from the 25th day of June, 1975, whichever period is the shortest.

(2) The case of [15]{every person (including a foreigner) against whom an order of detention was made under this Act} on or after the 25th day of June, 1975, but before the commencement

---

[13]Ins. by the Maintenance of Internal Security (Amendment) Ordinance, 1975, w.e.f. 29 June 1975 and the Maintenance of Internal Security (Amendment) Act, 1975 (No. 39 of 1975) dated 5 August 1975 w.e.f. 29 June 1975.

[14]Ins. by the Maintenance of Internal Security (Amendment) Ordinance, 1975, w.e.f. 29 June 1975 and the Maintenance of Internal Security (Amendment) Act, 1975 (No. 39 of 1975) dated 5 August 1975 w.e.f. 29 June 1975.

[15]Sub. for 'every person against whom an order of detention was made' by the Maintenance of Internal Security Act (Second Amendment) Ordinance, 1975 (No. 7 of 1975) dated 15 July 1975 w.e.f. 29 June 1975 and the Maintenance of Internal Security (Amendment) Act, 1975 (No. 39 of 1975) dated 5 August 1975 w.e.f. 29 June 1975.

of ¹⁶{this section} shall, unless, such person be sooner released from detention, be reviewed within 15 days from the such commencement by the appropriate Government for the purpose of determining whether the detention of such person under this Act is necessary for dealing effectively with the emergency in respect of which the Proclamations referred to in sub-section (1) have been issued (hereafter in this section referred to as the emergency), and if, on such review, the appropriate Government is satisfied that it is necessary to detain such person for effectively dealing with the emergency, that Government or officer may make a declaration to that effect and communicate a copy of that declaration to the person concerned.

(3) When making an order of detention under this Act ¹⁷{(including a foreigner)} against any person after the commencement of the Maintenance of Internal Security (Amendment) Ordinance, 1976, the Central Government or the State Government or, as the case may be, the officer making the order of detention shall consider whether the detention of such person under this Act is necessary for dealing effectively with the emergency and if, on such consideration, the Central Government or, as the case may be, the State Government or the officer is satisfied that it is necessary to detain such person for effectively dealing with the emergency, that Government or officer may make a declaration to that effect and communicate a copy of the declaration tote person concerned.

Provided that where such declaration is made by an officer,

---

¹⁶Subs. by the Maintenance of Internal Security (Amendment) Act, 1975 (No. 39 of 1975) dated 5 August 1975 w.e.f. 29 June 1975 for 'the Maintenance of Internal Security (Amendment) Ordinance, 1975' inserted by the Maintenance of Internal Security (Amendment) Ordinance, 1975, w.e.f. 29 June 1975.

¹⁷Ins. by the Maintenance of Internal Security Act (Second Amendment) Ordinance, 1975 (No. 7 of 1975) dated 15 July 1975 w.e.f. 29 June 1975.

it shall be reviewed by the State Government to which such officer is subordinate within 15 days from the date of making of the declaration and such declaration shall cease to have effect unless it is confirmed by the State Government, after such review, within the said period of 15 days.

(4) The question whether the detention of any person in respect of whom a declaration has been made under Sub-Section (2) or Sub-Section (3) continues to be necessary for effectively dealing with the emergency shall be reconsidered by the appropriate Government within four months from the date of such declaration and thereafter at intervals not exceeding four months and if, on such reconsideration, it appears to the appropriate Government that the detention of the person is no longer necessary for effectively dealing with the emergency, that Government may revoke the declaration.

(5) In making any review, consideration or reconsideration under sub-sections (2), (3) or (4), the appropriate Government or officer may, if such Government or officer considers it to be against the public interest to do otherwise, act on the basis of the information and materials in its or his possession without disclosing the facts or giving an opportunity of making a representation to the person concerned.

[18]{(6) In the case of every person detained under a detention

---

[18]Subs. by the Maintenance of Internal Security Act (Second Amendment) Ordinance, 1975 (No. 7 of 1975) dated 15 July 1975 w.e.f. 29 June 1975 and the Maintenance of Internal Security (Amendment) Act, 1975 (No. 39 of 1975) dated 5 August 1975 w.e.f. 29 June 1975 for:

6. It shall not be necessary:

(A) to disclose to any person detained under a detention order to which the provisions of Sub-Section (2) apply, the grounds on which the order has been made during the period within which his case may be reviewed under that sub-section and where, on such review, a declaration has been made in respect of such person under the sub-section, also during the period when such declaration is in force.

(B) to disclose to any person detained under a detention order to which the provisions of Sub-Section (3) apply, the grounds on which the order has been made during order to which the provisions of Sub-section (2) apply, being a person the review of whose case is pending under that sub-section or in respect of whom a declaration has been made under that sub-section,—

(i) sections 8 to 12 shall not apply; and

(ii) section 13 shall apply subject to the modification that the words and figures "which has been confirmed under section 12" shall be omitted.

(7) In the case of every person detained under a detention order to which the provisions of sub-section (3) apply, being a person in respect of whom a declaration has been made under that sub-section,—

(i) section 3 shall apply subject to the modification that for sub-sections (3) and (4) thereof, the following sub-section shall be substituted, namely:—

"(3) When any order of detention is made by a State Government or by an officer subordinate to it, the State Government shall, within twenty days, forward to the Central Government a report in respect of the order.";

(ii) sections 8 to 12 shall not apply; and

(iii) Section 13 shall apply subject to the modification that the words and figures "which has been confirmed under section 12" shall be omitted.'}

17. Duration of detention in certain cases of foreigners.-

---

the period the declaration made in respect of such person under that sub-section is in force, and, accordingly, such periods shall not be taken into account for the purposes of Section 8.

7. In the case of every person detained under a detention order to which the provisions of Sub-Section (2) or Sub-Section (3) apply, and in respect of whom a declaration has been made thereunder, the period during which such declaration is in force shall not be taken into account for the purpose of computing the periods mentioned in Section 10 or Section 11.] inserted by the Maintenance of Internal Security (Amendment) Ordinance, 1975.

(1) Notwithstanding anything contained in this Act, any foreigner in respect of whom an order of detention has been made under this Act may be detained without obtaining the opinion of the Advisory Board for a period longer than three months, but not exceeding two years from the date of his detention, in any of the following classes of cases or under any of the following circumstances, namely:—
   (a) where such foreigner enters or attempts to enter the territory of India or found therein with arms, ammunition or explosives, or
   (b) where such foreigner enters or attempts to enter a notified area or is found therein in contravention of section 3 of the Criminal Law Amendment Act, 1961, or
   (c) where such foreigner enters or attempts to enter the local limits or is found within the local limits of such area adjoining the borders of India as may be specified in an order made under Section 139 of the Border Security Force Act, 1968, without a valid travel document, or
   (d) where the Central Government has reason to believe that such foreigner commits or is likely to commit any offence under the Official Secrets Act, 1923.
(2) In the case of foreigner to whom sub-section (1) applies, Sections 10 to 13 shall have effect subject to the following modifications, namely—
   (a) In section 10, for the words "shall, within thirty days", the words "may, at any time prior to but in no case later than three months before the expiration of two years" shall be substituted;
   (b) In section 11—
       (i) in sub-section (1), for the words "from the date of detention" the words "from the date on which reference is made to it" shall be substituted;
       (ii) in sub-section (2), for the words "the detention of

the person concerned" the words "the continued detention of the person concerned" shall be substituted;

(c) In section 12, for the words "for the detention" in both the places where they occur, the words "for the continued detention" shall be substituted;

(d) in section 12, for the words "twelve months" the words "three years" shall be substituted.

¹⁹[17A. Duration of detention in cases of detention on certain grounds.-

(1) Notwithstanding anything contained in the foregoing provisions of this Act, during the period of operation of the Proclamation of Emergency issued on the 3rd day of December, 1971, any person (including a foreigner) in respect of whom an order of detention has been made under this Act, may be detained without obtaining the opinion of the Advisory Board for a period longer than three months, but not exceeding two years from the date of his detention in any of the following classes of cases or under any of the following circumstances, namely:—

(a) where such person had been detained with a view to preventing him from acting in any manner prejudicial to the defence of India, relations of India with foreign powers or the security of India; or

(b) where such person had been detained with a view to preventing him from acting in any manner prejudicial to the security of the State or the maintenance of public order.

(2) In the case of any person to whom sub-section (1) applies, sections 10 to 13 shall have effect subject to the following modifications, namely:

(a) in section 10, for the words "shall, within thirty days",

---

¹⁹Ins. by the Defence of India Act (42 of 1971), w.e.f. 4 December 1971.

the words "may, at any time prior to but in no case later than three months before the expiration of two years" shall be substituted;
(b) in section 11,—
  (i) in sub-section (1), for the words "from the date of detention", the words "from the date on which reference is made to it" shall be substituted;
  (ii) in sub-section (2), for the words "the detention of the person concerned", the words "the continued detention of the person concerned" shall be substituted;
(c) in section 12, for the words "for the detention", in both the places where they occur, the words "for the continued detention" shall be substituted;
(d) in section 13, for the words "twelve months", the words "three years" shall be substituted.]

[20][**18.** Exclusion of common law or natural law rights, if any.- No person (including a foreigner) detained under this Act shall have any right to personal liberty by virtue of natural law or common law, if any.]

[21][**19**]. Repeal and saving.-
(1) The Maintenance of Internal Security Ordinance, 1971, is hereby repealed.
(2) Notwithstanding such repeal, anything done or any action taken under the said Ordinance shall be deemed to have been done or taken under the corresponding provisions of

---

[20]Ins. by the Maintenance of Internal Security Act (Second Amendment) Ordinance, 1975 (No. 7 of 1975) dated 15 July 1975 w.e.f. 25 June 1975 and the Maintenance of Internal Security (Amendment) Act, 1975 (No. 39 of 1975) dated 5 August 1975 w.e.f. 25 June 1975.
[21]Subs. for '18' by the Maintenance of Internal Security Act (Second Amendment) Ordinance, 1975 (No. 7 of 1975) dated 15 July 1975 w.e.f. 25 June 1975 and the Maintenance of Internal Security (Amendment) Act, 1975 (No. 39 of 1975) dated 5 August 1975 w.e.f. 25 June 1975.

this Act as if this Act had come into force on the 7th day at May, 1971

B. THE MAINTENANCE OF INTERNAL SECURITY (SECOND AMENDMENT) ACT, 1976

No. 78 of 1976

[25th August, 1976]

An Act further to amend the Maintenance of Internal Security Act, 1971.

BE it enacted by Parliament in the Twenty-seventh Year of the Republic of India as follows:—

1. Short title and commencement.-
   (1) This Act may be called the Maintenance of Internal Security (Second Amendment) Act, 1976.
   (2) It shall be deemed to have come into force on the 16th day of June, 1976.
2. Amendment of Act 26 of 1971.- In section 16A of the Maintenance of Internal Security Act, 1971 (hereinafter referred to as the principal Act), in sub-section (1), for the words "twelve months", the words "twenty-four months" shall be substituted.
3. Removal of doubts.- For the removal of doubts, it is hereby declared that every declaration made under section 16A of the principal Act before the commencement of this Act and in force immediately before such commencement shall have effect as if the amendment made in that section by this Act had been in force on and from the 29th day of June, 1975.
4. Repeal and Saving.-
   (1) The Maintenance of Internal Security (Amendment) Ordinance, 1976 is hereby repealed.
   (2) Notwithstanding such repeal, anything done or any action taken under the principal Act as amended by the said Ordinance shall be deemed to have been done or taken under the principal Act as amended by this Act.

C. THE MAINTENANCE OF INTERNAL SECURITY (REPEAL) ACT, 1978

No. 27 of 1978
[3rd August, 1978]

An Act to repeal the Maintenance of Internal Security Act, 1971
BE it enacted by Parliament in the Twenty-ninth Year of the Republic of India as follows:—

1. Short title.- This Act may be called the Maintenance of Internal Security (Repeal) Act, 1978.
2. Repeal of Act 26 of 1971.- The Maintenance of Internal Security Act, 1971, is hereby repealed.

APPENDIX III.3: ARTICLE 352 IN THE CONSTITUTION OF INDIA

ARTICLE 352 IN THE CONSTITUTION OF INDIA, ADOPTED ON 26 NOVEMBER 1949

352. Proclamation of Emergency.-
   (1) If the President is satisfied that a grave emergency exists whereby the security of India or of any part of the territory thereof is threatened, whether by war or external aggression or internal disturbance, he may, by Proclamation, make a declaration to that effect.
   (2) A Proclamation issued under clause (1)-
      (a) may be revoked by a subsequent Proclamation;
      (b) shall be laid before each House of Parliament;
      (c) shall cease to operate at the expiration of two months unless before the expiration of that period it has been approved by resolutions of both Houses of Parliament: Provided that if any such Proclamation is issued at a time when the House of the People has been dissolved or the

dissolution of the House of the People takes place during the period of two months referred to in sub-clause (c), and if a resolution approving the Proclamation has been passed by the Council of States but no resolution with respect to such Proclamation has been passed by the House of the People before the expiration of that period, the Proclamation shall cease to operate at the expiration of thirty days from the date on which the House of the People first sits after its reconstitution unless before the expiration of the said period of thirty days a resolution approving the Proclamation has also been passed by the House of the People.

(3) A Proclamation of Emergency declaring that the security of India or any part of the territory thereof is threatened by war or by external aggression or by internal disturbance may be made before the actual occurrence of war or of any such aggression or disturbance if the President is satisfied that there is imminent danger thereof.

AMENDMENTS PERTAINING TO ARTICLE 352

38th Amendment (with effect from 1 August 1975)

5. Amendment of article 352.- In article 352 of the Constitution, after clause (3), the following clauses shall be inserted, and shall be deemed always to have been inserted, namely:-

"(4) The power conferred on the President by this article shall include the power to issue different Proclamations on different grounds, being war or external aggression or internal disturbance or imminent danger of war or external aggression or internal disturbance, whether or not there is a Proclamation already issued by the President under clause (1) and such Proclamation is in operation.

(5) Notwithstanding anything in this Constitution,-

(a) the satisfaction of the President mentioned in clause (1) and clause (3) shall be final and conclusive and shall not be questioned in any court on any ground;
(b) subject to the provisions of clause (2), neither the Supreme Court nor any other court shall have jurisdiction to entertain any question, on any ground, regarding the validity of-
   (i) a declaration made by Proclamation by the President to the effect stated in clause (1); or
   (ii) the continued operation of such Proclamation."

42nd Amendment (with effect from 3 January 1977)

48. Amendment of article 352.- In article 352 of the Constitution,-
   (a) in clause (1), after the words "make a declaration to that effect", the following shall be inserted, namely:
   "in respect of the whole of India or of such part of the territory thereof as may be specified in the Proclamation";
   (b) in clause (2), in sub-clause (a), after the word "revoked", the words "or varied" shall be inserted;
   (c) after clause (2), the following clause shall be inserted, namely:-
   "(2A) Where a Proclamation issued under clause (1) is varied by a subsequent Proclamation, the provisions of clause (2) shall, so far as may be, apply in relation to such subsequent Proclamation as they apply in relation to a Proclamation issued under clause (1)."

44th Amendment (with effect from 20 June 1979)

37. Amendment of article 352. In article 352 of the Constitution,-
   (a) in clause (1),
      (i) for the words "internal disturbance", the words "armed rebellion" shall be substituted;
      (ii) the following Explanation shall be inserted at the end, namely:-
   "Explanation. A Proclamation of Emergency declaring that

the security of India or any part of the territory thereof is threatened by war or by external aggression or by armed rebellion may be made before the actual occurrence of war or of any such aggression or rebellion, if the President is satisfied that there is imminent danger thereof.";

(b) for clauses (2), (2A) and (3), the following clauses shall be substituted, namely:

"(2) A Proclamation issued under clause (1) may be varied or revoked by a subsequent Proclamation.

(3) The President shall not issue a Proclamation under clause (1) or a Proclamation varying such Proclamation unless the decision of the Union Cabinet (that is to say, the Council consisting of the Prime Minister and other Ministers of Cabinet rank appointed under article 75) that such a Proclamation may be issued has been communicated to him in writing.

(4) Every Proclamation issued under this article shall be laid before each House of Parliament and shall, except where it is a Proclamation revoking a previous Proclamation, cease to operate at the expiration of one month unless before the expiration of that period it has been approved by resolutions of both Houses of Parliament:

Provided that if any such Proclamation (not being a Proclamation revoking a previous Proclamation) is issued at a time when the House of the People has been dissolved, or the dissolution of the House of the People takes place during the period of one month referred to in this clause, and if a resolution approving the Proclamation has been passed by the Council of States, but no resolution with respect to such Proclamation has been passed by the House of the People before the expiration of that period, the Proclamation shall cease to operate at the expiration of thirty days from the date on which the House of the People first sits after its reconstitution, unless before the expiration of the said period of thirty days a resolution approving the Proclamation has been also passed by the House of the People.

(5) A Proclamation so approved shall, unless revoked, cease

to operate on the expiration of a period of six months from the date of the passing of the second of the resolutions approving the Proclamation under clause (4):

Provided that if and so often as a resolution approving the continuance in force of such a Proclamation is passed by both Houses of Parliament the Proclamation shall, unless revoked, continue in force for a further period of six months from the date on which it would otherwise have ceased to operate under this clause:

Provided further that if the dissolution of the House of the People takes place during any such period of six months and a resolution approving the continuance in force of such Proclamation has been passed by the Council of States but no resolution with respect to the continuance in force of such Proclamation has been passed by the House of the People during the said period, the Proclamation shall cease to operate at the expiration of thirty days from the date on which the House of the People first sits after its reconstitution unless before the expiration of the said period of thirty days, a resolution approving the continuance in force of the Proclamation has been also passed by the House of the People.

(6) For the purposes of clauses (4) and (5), a resolution may be passed by either House of Parliament only by a majority of the total membership of that House and by a majority of not less than two-thirds of the members of that House present and voting.

(7) Notwithstanding anything contained in the foregoing clauses, the President shall revoke a Proclamation issued under clause (1) or a Proclamation varying such Proclamation if the House of the People passes a resolution disapproving, or, as the case may be, disapproving the continuance in force of, such Proclamation.

(8) Where a notice in writing signed by not less than one-tenth of the total number of members of the House of the People has been given, of their intention to move a resolution for disapproving, or, as the case may be, for disapproving the continuance in force of, a Proclamation issued under clause (1) or a Proclamation varying such Proclamation,-

(a) to the Speaker, if the House is in session; or
(b) to the President, if the House is not in session,
a special sitting of the House shall be held within fourteen days from the date on which such notice is received by the Speaker, or, as the case may be, by the President, for the purpose of considering such resolution.";
(c) clause (4) shall be renumbered as clause (9) and in the clause as so renumbered, for the words "internal disturbance" in both the places where they occur, the words "armed rebellion" shall be substituted;
(d) clause (5) shall be omitted.

APPENDIX III.4: ARTICLE 226 IN THE CONSTITUTION OF INDIA

ARTICLE 226 IN THE CONSTITUTION OF INDIA, ADOPTED ON 26 NOVEMBER 1949

226. Power of High Courts to issue certain writs.- (1) Notwithstanding anything in Article 32, every High Court shall have power, throughout the territories in relation to which it exercises jurisdiction, to issue to any person or authority, including in appropriate cases any Government, within those territories directions, orders or writs, including writs in the nature of habeas corpus, mandamus, prohibitions, quo warranto and certiorari, or any of them, for the enforcement of any of the rights conferred by Part III and for any other purpose.

(2) The power conferred on a High Court by clause (1) shall not be in derogation of the power conferred on the Supreme Court by clause (2) of article 32.

AMENDMENTS PERTAINING TO ARTICLE 226

42nd Amendment (with effect from 1 February 1977)

38. Substitution of new article for article 226.- For article 226 of the Constitution, the following article shall be substituted, namely:-
"**226. Power of High Courts to issue certain writs.-**

(1) Notwithstanding anything in article 32 but subject to the provisions of article 131A and article 226A, every High Court shall have power, throughout the territories in relation to which it exercises jurisdiction, to issue to any person or authority, including in appropriate cases, any Government, within those territories directions, orders or writs, including writs in the nature of habeas corpus, mandamus, prohibition, quo warranto and certiorari, or any of them,-
  (a) for the enforcement of any of the rights conferred by the provisions of Part III; or
  (b) for the redress of any injury of a substantial nature by reason of the contravention of any other provision of this Constitution or any provision of any enactment or Ordinance or any order, rule, regulation, bye-law or other instrument made thereunder; or
  (c) for the redress of any injury by reason of any illegality in any proceedings by or before any authority under any provision referred to in sub-clause (b) where such illegality has resulted in substantial failure of justice.

(2) The power conferred by clause (1) to issue directions, orders or writs to any Government, authority or person may also be exercised by any High Court exercising jurisdiction in relation to the territories within which the cause of action, wholly or in part, arises for the exercise of such power, notwithstanding that the seat of such Government or authority or the residence of such person is not within those territories.

(3) No petition for the redress of any injury referred to in sub-clause (b) or sub-clause (c) of clause (1) shall be entertained if any other remedy for such redress is provided for by or under any other law for the time being in force.

(4) No interim order (whether by way of injunction or stay or in any other manner) shall be made on, or in any proceedings relating to, a petition under clause (1) unless-
  (a) copies of such petition and of all documents in support of the plea for such interim order are furnished to the party against whom such petition is filed or proposed to be filed; and
  (b) opportunity is given to such party to be heard in the matter.

(5) The High Court may dispense with the requirements of sub-clauses (a) and (b) of clause (4) and make an interim order as an exceptional measure if it is satisfied for reasons to be record in writing that it is necessary so to do for preventing any loss being caused to the petitioner which cannot be adequately compensated in money but any such interim order shall, if it is not vacated earlier, cease to have effect on the expiry of a period of fourteen days from the date on which it is made unless the said requirements have been complied with before the expiry of that period and the High Court has continued the operation of the interim order.

(6) Notwithstanding anything in clause (4) or clause (5), no interim order (whether by way of injunction or stay or in any other manner) shall be made on, or in any proceedings relating to, a petition under clause (1) where such order will have the effect of delaying any inquiry into a matter of public importance or any investigation or inquiry into an offence punishable with imprisonment or any action for the execution of any work or project of public utility, or the acquisition of any property for such execution, by the Government or any corporation owned or controlled by the Government.

(7) The power conferred on a High Court by this article shall not

be in derogation of the power conferred on the Supreme Court by clause (2) of article 32."

39. Insertion of new article 226A.-After article 226 of the Constitution, the following article shall be inserted, namely:-
"226A. Constitutional validity of Central laws not to be considered in proceedings under article 226.- Notwithstanding anything in article 226, the High Court shall not consider the constitutional validity of any Central law in any proceedings under that article."

43rd Amendment (with effect from 13 April 1978)

7. Amendment of article 226.- In article 226 of the Constitution, in clause (1), the words, figures and letters "but subject to the provisions of article 131A and article 226A" shall be omitted.

8. Omission of article 226A.- (1) Article 226A of the Constitution shall be omitted.

(2) Any proceedings pending before a High Court under article 226 of the Constitution immediately before the commencement of this Act may be dealt with by the High Court as if the said article 226A had been omitted with effect on and from the 1st day of February, 1977.

44th Amendment (with effect from 20 June 1979)

30. Amendment of article 226.- In article 226 of the Constitution,-
  (a) in clause (1), for the portion beginning with the words "writs in the nature of habeas corpus, mandamus, prohibition, quo warranto and certiorari, or any of them" and ending with the words "such illegality has resulted in substantial failure of justice.", the following shall be substituted, namely:-
  "writs in the nature of habeas corpus, mandamus, prohibition, quo warranto and certiorari, or any of them, for the enforcement of any of the rights conferred by Part III and for any other purpose.";
  (b) for clauses (3), (4), (5) and (6), the following clause shall be substituted, namely:-

"(3) Where any party against whom an interim order, whether by way of injunction or stay or in any other manner, is made on, or in any way proceedings relating to, a petition under clause (1), without-
    (a) furnishing to such party copies of such petition and all documents in support of the plea for such interim order; and
    (b) giving such party an opportunity of being heard,
makes an application to the High Court for the vacation of such order and furnishes a copy of such application to the party in whose favour such order has been made or the counsel of such party, the High Court shall dispose of the application within a period of two weeks from the date on which it is received or from the date on which the copy of such application is so furnished, whichever is later, or where the High Court is closed on the last day of that period, before the expiry of the next day afterwards on which the High Court is open; and if the application is not so disposed of, the interim order shall, on the expiry of that period, or, as the case may be, the expiry of the said next day, stand vacated.";
    (c) clause (7) shall be renumbered as clause (4).

APPENDIX III.5: ARTICLE 32 IN THE CONSTITUTION OF INDIA

ARTICLE 32 IN THE CONSTITUTION OF INDIA ADOPTED ON 26 NOVEMBER 1949

32. Remedies for enforcement of rights conferred by this Part.-
    (1) The right to move the Supreme Court by appropriate proceedings for the enforcement of the rights conferred by this Part is guaranteed.
    (2) The Supreme Court shall have power to issue directions or orders or writs, including writs in the nature of *habeas corpus*, *mandamus*, prohibition, *quo warranto* and *certiorari*,

whichever may be appropriate, for the enforcement of any of the rights conferred by this Part.

(3) Without prejudice to the powers conferred on the Supreme Court by clauses (1) and (2), Parliament may by law empower any other court to exercise within the local limits of its jurisdiction all or any of the powers exercisable by the Supreme Court under clause (2).

(4) The right guaranteed by this article shall not be suspended except as otherwise provided for by this Constitution.

AMENDMENTS

42nd Amendment (with effect from 1 February 1977)

6. Insertion of new article 32A.-After article 32 of the Constitution, the following article shall be inserted, namely:-

"32A. Constitutional validity of State laws not to be considered in proceedings under article 32.-Notwithstanding anything in article 32, the Supreme Court shall not consider the constitutional validity of any State law in any proceedings under that article unless the constitutional validity of any Central law is also in issue in such proceedings."

43rd Amendment (Date of assent: 13 April 1978; with effect from 1 February 1977)

3. Omission of article 32A.-(1) Article 32A of the Constitution shall be omitted.

(2) Any proceedings pending before the Supreme Court under article 32 of the Constitution immediately before the commencement of this Act may be dealt with by the Supreme Court as if the said article 32A had been omitted with effect on and from the 1st day of February, 1977.

APPENDIX III.6: ARTICLE 14 IN THE CONSTITUTION OF INDIA

ARTICLE 14 IN THE CONSTITUTION OF INDIA ADOPTED ON 26 NOVEMBER 1949

14. Equality before law.- The State shall not deny to any person equality before the law or the equal protection of the laws within the territory of India.

APPENDIX III.7: THE ELECTION LAWS (AMENDMENT) ACT, 1975 (NO. 40 OF 1975)

[6th August, 1975]

An Act further to amend the Representation of the People Act, 1951 and the Indian Penal Code.

BE it enacted by Parliament in the Twenty-sixth Year of the Republic of India as follows:

1. Short title.- This Act may be called the Election Laws (Amendment) Act, 1975.
2. Substitution for new section for section 8A.- In the Representation of People Act, 1951 (hereinafter referred to as the principal Act), for Section 8A, the following section shall be substituted, namely:—

> "Disqualification on ground of corrupt practices-8A. (1) The case of every person found guilty of a corrupt practice by an order under section 99 shall be submitted, as soon as may be, after such order takes effect, by such authority as the Central Government may specify in this behalf, to the President for determination of the question as to whether such person shall be disqualified and if so, for what period: Provided that the period for which any person may be disqualified under this sub-section shall in no case exceed

six years from the date on which the order made in relation to him under Section 99 takes effect.

(2) Any person who stands disqualified under section 8A of this Act as it stood immediately before the commencement of the Election Laws (Amendment) Act, 1975, may, if the period of such disqualification has not expired, submit a petition to the President for the removal of such disqualification for the unexpired portion of the said period.

(3) Before giving his decision on any question mentioned in sub-section (1) or on any petition submitted under sub-section (2), the President shall obtain the opinion of the Election Commission on such question or petition and shall act according to such opinion."

3. Amendment of Section 11.- In section 11 of the principal Act, after the words "under this Chapter", the brackets, words, figure and letter "(except under Section 8A)" shall be inserted.

4. Amendment of Section 11A.- Section 11A of the principal Act shall be re-numbered as sub-section (1) thereof and—

(a) in the sub-section as so re-numbered, clause (b) shall be omitted; and

(b) after the sub-section as so re-numbered, the following sub-sections shall be inserted, namely:

"(2) Any person disqualified by a decision of the President under sub-section (1) of Section 8A for any period shall be disqualified for the same period for voting at any election.

(3) The decision of the President on a petition submitted by any person under sub-section (2) of Section 8A in respect of any disqualification for being chosen as, and for being, a member of either House of Parliament or of the Legislative Assembly or Legislative Council of a State shall, so far as may be, apply in respect of the disqualification for voting at any election incurred by him under clause (b) of sub-section (1) of section 11A of this Act as it stood immediately before the commencement of the Election Laws (Amendment) Act,

1975, as if such decision were a decision in respect of the said disqualification for voting also."

5. Amendment of Section 11B.- In Section 11B of the principal Act, for the words "any disqualification under this Chapter", the words, brackets, figures, and letter "any disqualification under sub-section (1) of Section 11A" shall be substituted.

6. Amendment of Section 77.- In Section 77 of the principal Act, in sub-section (1),—
   (a) for the words "the date of publication of the notification calling the election", the words "the date on which he has been nominated" shall be substituted;
   (b) after Explanation 2, the following Explanation shall be inserted, namely:
   "Explanation 3.—For the removal of doubt, it is hereby declared that any expenditure incurred in respect of any arrangement made, facilities provided or any other act or thing done by any person in the service of the Government and belonging to any of the classes mentioned in clause (7) of section 123 in the discharge or purported discharge of his official duty as mentioned in the proviso to that clause shall not be deemed to be expenditure in connection with the election incurred or authorized by a candidate or by his election agent for the purposes of this sub-section.".

7. Amendment of Section 79- In Section 79 of the principal Act, for clause (b), the following clause shall be substituted, namely:—
   '(b) "candidate" means a person who has been or claims to have been duly nominated as a candidate at any election;'.

8. Amendment of Section 123.-In Section 123 of the principal Act,—
   (a) in clause (3), the following proviso shall be inserted at the end, namely:—
   "Provided that no symbol allotted under this Act to a candidate shall be deemed to be a religious symbol or a national symbol for the purposes of this clause.";

(b) in clause (7), the following proviso shall be inserted at the end, namely:—

"Provided that where any person, in the service of the Government and belonging to any of the classes aforesaid, in the discharge or purported discharge of his official duty, makes any arrangements or provides any facilities or does any other act or thing, for, to, or in relation to any candidate or his agent or any other person acting with the consent of the candidate or his election agent, (whether by reason of the office held by the candidate or for any other reason), such arrangements, facilities or act or thing shall not be deemed to be assistance for the furtherance of the prospects of that candidate's election.";

(c) in the Explanation at the end, the following shall be added, namely:-

"(3) For the purposes of clause (7), notwithstanding anything contained in any other law, the publication in the Official Gazette of the appointment, resignation, termination of service, dismissal or removal from service of a person in the service of the Central Government (including a person serving in connection with the administration of a Union Territory) or of a State Government shall be conclusive proof—

  (i) of such appointment, resignation, termination of service, dismissal or removal from service, as the case may be, and

  (ii) where the date of taking effect of such appointment, resignation, termination of service, dismissal or removal from service, as the case may be, is stated in such publication, also of the fact that such person was appointed with effect from the said date, or in the case of resignation, termination of service, dismissal or removal from service, such person ceased to be in such service with effect from the said date.".

9. Amendment of Section 171A of Act 45 of 1860.- In the Indian Penal Code, in Section 171A, for clause (a), the following clause shall be substituted, namely:—
'(a) "candidate" means a person who has been nominated as a candidate at any election;'.

10. Amendments to have retrospective effect.-The amendments made by sections 6, 7, and 8 of this Act in the principal Act shall also have retrospective operation so as to apply to and in relation to any election held before the commencement of this Act to either House of Parliament or to either House of the Legislature of a State—
    (i) in respect of which any election petition may be prescribed after the commencement of this Act; or
    (ii) in respect of which any election petition is in any High Court immediately before such commencement; or
    (iii) in respect of which any election petition has been decided by any High Court before such commencement but no appeal has been preferred to the Supreme Court against the decision of the High Court before such commencement and the period of limitation for filing such appeal has not expired before such commencement; or
    (iv) in respect of which appeal from any order of any High Court made in any election petition under section 98 or section 99 of the principal Act is pending before the Supreme Court immediately before such commencement.

APPENDIX III.8: THE CONSTITUTION (THIRTY-NINTH AMENDMENT) ACT, 1975

Statement of Objects and Reasons appended to the Constitution (Fortieth Amendment) Bill, 1975 which was enacted as the Constitution (Thirty-ninth Amendment) Act, 1975

STATEMENT OF OBJECTS AND REASONS

Article 71 of the Constitution provides that disputes arising out of the election of the President or Vice-President shall be decided by the Supreme Court. The same article provides that matters relating to their election shall be regulated by a parliamentary law. So far as the Prime Minister and the Speaker are concerned, matters relating to their election are regulated by the provisions of the Representation of the People Act, 1951. Under this Act the High Court has jurisdiction to try an election petition presented against either of them.

2. The President, the Vice-President, the Prime Minister and the Speaker are holders of high offices. The President is not answerable to a court of law for anything done, while in office, in the exercise of his powers. A fortiori matters relating to his election should not be brought before a court of law but should be entrusted to a forum other than a court. The same reasoning applies equally to the incumbents of the offices of Vice-President, Prime Minister and Speaker. It is accordingly proposed to provide that disputes relating to the election of the President and Vice-President shall be determined by a forum as may be determined by a parliamentary law. Similar provision is proposed to be made in the case of the election to either House of Parliament or, as the case may be, to the House of the People of a person holding the office of Prime Minister or the Speaker. It is further proposed to render pending proceedings in respect of such election under the existing law null and void. The Bill also provides that the parliamentary law creating a new forum for trial of election matters relating to the incumbents of the high offices abovementioned shall not be called in question in any court.

3. Recourse was had in the past to the Ninth Schedule whenever it was found that progressive legislation conceived in the interests of the public was imperilled by litigation. It has become necessary to have recourse to this device once again now. Between 1971 and 1973 legislation was enacted for nationalising coking coal and coal

mines for conserving these resources in the interests of steel industry. These enactments have been brought before courts on the ground that they are unconstitutional. So is the case of sick textile undertakings which were nationalised in 1974. To prevent smuggling of goods and diversion of foreign exchange which affected national economy Parliament enacted legislation which again has been challenged in the Supreme Court and in High Courts. These and other important and special enactments which it is considered necessary should have the constitutional protection under article 31B, are proposed to be included in the Ninth Schedule. Certain State legislations relating to land reform and ceiling on agricultural land holdings have already been included in the Ninth Schedule. Certain amendments made to these legislations also require protection of the provisions of article 31B.

4. The Bill seeks to give effect to the above objects.

NEW DELHI; H.R. GOKHALE.

6th August, 1975.

THE CONSTITUTION (THIRTY-NINTH AMENDMENT) ACT, 1975

[10th August, 1975.]

An Act further to amend the Constitution of India.

BE it enacted by Parliament in the Twenty-sixth Year of the Republic of India as follows:-

1. Short title.- This Act may be called the Constitution (Thirty-ninth Amendment) Act, 1975.
2. Substitution of new article for article 71.- For article 71 of the Constitution, the following article shall be substituted, namely: "71. Matters relating to or connected with the election of a President or Vice-President.-

    (1) Subject of the provisions of this Constitution, Parliament may by law regulate any matter relating to or connected

with the election of a President or Vice-President, including the grounds on which such election may be questioned: Provided that the election of a person as President or Vice-President shall not be called in question on the ground of the existence of any vacancy for whatever reason among the members of the electoral college electing him.

(2) All doubts and disputes arising out of or in connection with the election of a President or Vice-President shall be inquired into and decided by such authority or body and in such manner as may be provided for by or under any law referred to in clause (1).

(3) The validity of any such law as is referred to in clause (1) and the decision of any authority or body under such law shall not be called in question in any court.

(4) If the election of a person as President or Vice-President is declared void under any such law as is referred to in clause (1), acts done by him in the exercise and performance of the powers and duties of the office of President or Vice-President, as the case may be, on or before the date of such declaration shall not be invalidated by reason of that declaration.".

3. Amendment of article 329.-In article 329 of the Constitution, for the words "Notwithstanding any thing in this Constitution", the words, figures and letter "Notwithstanding anything in this Constitution but subject to the provisions of article 329A" shall be substituted.

4. Insertion of new article 329A.-In Part XV of the Constitution, after article 329, the following article shall be inserted, namely:- "329A. Special provision as to elections to Parliament in the case of Prime Minister and Speaker.-

(1) Subject to the provisions of Chapter II of Part V [except sub-clause (e) of clause (1) of article 102], no election-

(a) to either House of Parliament of a person who holds the office of Prime Minister at the time of such election

or is appointed as Prime Minister after such election;
(b) to the House of the People of a person who holds the office of Speaker of that House at the time of such election or who is chosen as the Speaker for that House after such election, shall be called in question, except before such authority [not being any such authority as is referred to in clause (b) of article 329] or body and in such manner as may be provided for by or under any law made by Parliament and any such law may provide for all other matters relating to doubts and disputes in relation to such election including the grounds on which such election may be questioned.
(2) The validity of any such law as is referred to in clause (1) and the decision of any authority or body under such law shall not be called in question in any court.
(3) Where any person is appointed as Prime Minister or, as the case may be, chosen to the office of the Speaker of the House of the People, while an election petition referred to in clause (b) of article 329 in respect of his election to either House of Parliament or, as the case may be, to the House of the People is pending, such election petition shall abate upon such person being appointed as Prime Minister or, as the case may be, being chosen to the office of the Speaker of the House of the People, but such election may be called in question under any such law as is referred to in clause (1).
(4) No law made by Parliament before the commencement of the Constitution (Thirty-ninth Amendment) Act, 1975, in so far as it relates to election petitions and matters connected therewith, shall apply or shall be deemed ever to have applied to or in relation to the election to any such person as is referred to in clause (1) to either House of Parliament and such election shall not be deemed to be void or ever to have become void on any ground on which

such election could be declared to be void or has, before such commencement, been declared to be void under any such law and notwithstanding any order made by any court, before such commencement, declaring such election to be void, such election shall continue to be valid in all respects and any such order and any finding on which such order is based shall be and shall be deemed always to have been void and of no effect.

(5) Any appeal or cross appeal against any such order of any court as is referred to in clause (4) pending immediately before the commencement of the Constitution (Thirty-ninth Amendment) Act, 1975, before the Supreme Court shall be disposed of in conformity with the provisions of clause (4).

(6) The provisions of this article shall have effect notwithstanding anything contained in this Constitution.".

5. Amendment of the Ninth Schedule.-In the Ninth Schedule to the Constitution, after entry 86 and before the Explanation, the following entries shall be inserted, namely:-

"87. The Representation of the People Act, 1951 (Central Act 43 of 1951), the Representation of the People (Amendment) Act, 1974 (Central Act 58 of 1974) and the Election Laws (Amendment) Act, 1975 (Central Act 40 of 1975).

88. The Industries (Development and Regulation) Act, 1951 (Central Act 65 of 1951).

89. The Requisitioning and Acquisition of Immovable Property Act, 1952 (Central Act 30 of 1952).

90. The Mines and Minerals (Regulation and Development) Act, 1957 (Central Act 67 of 1957).

91. The Monopolies and Restrictive Trade Practices Act, 1969 (Central Act 54 of 1969).

92. The Maintenance of Internal Security Act, 1971 (Central Act 26 of 1971).

93. The Coking Coal Mines (Emergency Provisions) Act, 1971 (Central Act 64 of 1971).

94. The Coking Coal Mines (Nationalisation) Act, 1972 (Central Act 36 of 1972).
95. The General Insurance Business (Nationalisation) Act, 1972 (Central Act 57 of 1972).
96. The Indian Copper Corporation (Acquisition of Undertaking) Act, 1972 (Central Act 58 of 1972).
97. The Sick Textile Undertakings (Taking Over of Management) Act, 1972 (Central Act 72 of 1972).
98. The Coal Mines (Taking Over of Management) Act, 1973 (Central Act 15 of 1973).
99. The Coal Mines (Nationalisation) Act, 1973 (Central Act 26 of 1973).
100. The Foreign Exchange Regulation Act, 1973 (Central Act 46 of 1973).
101. The Alcock Ashdown Company Limited (Acquisition of Under-takings) Act, 1973 (Central Act 56 of 1973).
102. The Coal Mines (Conservation and Development) Act, 1974 (Central Act 28 of 1974).
103. The Additional Emoluments (Compulsory Deposit) Act, 1974 (Central Act 37 of 1974).
104. The Conservation of Foreign Exchange and Prevention of Smuggling Activities Act, 1974 (Central Act 52 of 1974).
105. The Sick Textile Undertakings (Nationalisation) Act, 1974 (Central Act 57 of 1974).
106. The Maharashtra Agricultural Lands (Ceiling on Holdings) (Amendment) Act, 1964 (Maharashtra Act XVI of 1965).
107. The Maharashtra Agricultural Lands (Ceiling on Holdings) (Amendment) Act, 1965 (Maharashtra Act XXXII of 1965.
108. The Maharashtra Agricultural Lands (Ceiling on Holdings) (Amendment) Act, 1968 (Maharashtra Act XVI of 1968).
109. The Maharashtra Agricultural Lands (Ceiling on Holdings) (Second Amendment) Act, 1968 (Maharashtra Act XXXIII of 1968).
110. The Maharashtra Agricultural Lands (Ceiling on Holdings)

(Amendment) Act, 1969 (Maharashtra Act XXXVII of 1969).
111. The Maharashtra Agricultural Lands (Ceiling on Holdings) (Second Amendment) Act, 1969 (Maharashtra Act XXXVIII of 1969).
112. The Maharashtra Agricultural Lands (Ceiling on Holdings) (Amendment) Act, 1970 (Maharashtra Act XXVII of 1970).
113. The Maharashtra Agricultural Lands (Ceiling on Holdings) (Amendment) Act, 1972 (Maharashtra Act XIII of 1972).
114. The Maharashtra Agricultural Lands (Ceiling on Holdings) (Amendment) Act, 1973 (Maharashtra Act L of 1973).
115. The Orissa Land Reforms (Amendment) Act, 1965 (Orissa Act 13 of 1965).
116. The Orissa Land Reforms (Amendment) Act, 1966 (Orissa Act 8 of 1967).
117. The Orissa Land Reforms (Amendment) Act, 1967 (Orissa Act 13 of 1967).
118. The Orissa Land Reforms (Amendment) Act, 1969 (Orissa Act 13 of 1969).
119. The Orissa Land Reforms (Amendment) Act, 1970 (Orissa Act 18 of 1970).
120. The Uttar Pradesh Imposition of Ceiling on Land Holdings (Amendment) Act, 1972 (Uttar Pradesh Act 18 of 1973).
121. The Uttar Pradesh Imposition of Ceiling on Land Holdings (Amendment) Act, 1974 (Uttar Pradesh Act 2 of 1975).
122. The Tripura Land Revenue and Land Reforms (Third Amendment Act, 1975 (Tripura Act 3 of 1975).
123. The Dadra and Nagar Haveli Land Reforms Regulation, 1971 (3 of 1971).
124. The Dadra and Nagar Haveli Land Reforms (Amendment) Regulation, 1973 (5 of 1973)."

APPENDIX III.9: ARTICLE 359 IN THE CONSTITUTION OF INDIA

ARTICLE 359 IN THE CONSTITUTION OF INDIA ADOPTED ON 26 NOVEMBER 1949

359. Suspension of the enforcement of the rights conferred by Part III during emergencies:
  (1) Where a Proclamation of Emergency is in operation, the President may by order declare that the right to move any court for the enforcement of such of the rights conferred by Part III as may be mentioned in the order and all proceedings pending in any court for the enforcement of the rights so mentioned shall remain suspended for the period during which the Proclamation is in force or for such shorter period as may be specified in the order.
  (2) An order made as aforesaid may extend to the whole or any part of the territory of India.
  (3) Every order made under clause (1) shall, as soon as may be after it is made, be laid before each House of Parliament.

AMENDMENTS

38th Amendment (with effect from 1 August 1975)

7. Amendment of article 359.- In article 359 of the Constitution, after clause (1), the following clause shall be inserted, and shall be deemed always to have been inserted, namely:-

"(1A) While an order made under clause (1) mentioning any of the right conferred by Part III is in operation, nothing in that Part conferring those rights shall restrict the power of the State as defined in the said Part to make any law or to take any executive action which the State would but for the provisions contained in that Part be competent to make or to take, but any law so made shall, to the extent of the incompetency, cease to have effect as soon as the order aforesaid ceases to operate, except as respects things done or omitted to be done before the law so ceases to have effect.".

42ⁿᵈ Amendment (with effect from 3 January 1977)

53. Amendment of article 359.- In article 359 of the Constitution,-
(a) to clause (1A), the following proviso shall be added, namely:-
"Provided that where a Proclamation of Emergency is in operation only in any part of the territory of India, any such law may be made, or any such executive action may be taken, under this article in relation to or in any State or Union territory in which or in any part of which the Proclamation of Emergency is not in operation, if and in so far as the security of India or any part of the territory thereof is threatened by activities in or in relation to the part of the territory of India in which the Proclamation of Emergency is in operation.";

(b) to clause (2), the following proviso shall be added, namely:-
"Provided that where a Proclamation of Emergency is in operation only in a part of the territory of India, any such order shall not extend to any other part of the territory of India unless the President, being satisfied that the security of India or any part of the territory thereof is threatened by activities in or in relation to the part of the territory of India in which the Proclamation of Emergency is in operation, considers such extension to be necessary.".

44ᵗʰ Amendment (with effect from 20 July 1979)

40. Amendment of article 359.-In article 359 of the Constitution,-
(a) in clauses (1) and (1A), for the words and figures "the rights conferred by Part III", the words, figures and brackets "the rights conferred by Part III (except articles 20 and 21)" shall be substituted;

(b) after clause (1A), the following clause shall be inserted, namely:-
"(1B) Nothing in clause (1A) shall apply-
(a) to any law which does not contain a recital to the effect

that such law is in relation to the Proclamation of Emergency in operation when it is made; or

(b) to any executive action taken otherwise than under a law containing such a recital.".

59th Amendment (with effect from 30 March 1988)

3. Insertion of new article 359A.-(1) After article 359 of the Constitution, the following article shall be inserted, namely:-

'359A. Application of this Part to the State of Punjab. Notwithstanding anything in this Constitution, this Part shall, in relation to the State of Punjab, be subject to the following modifications, namely:-

(a) in article 352,-

(i) in clause (1),

(A) for the opening portion, the following shall be substituted, namely:-

"If the President is satisfied that a grave emergency exists whereby-

(a) the security of India or of any part of the territory thereof is threatened, whether by war or external aggression or armed rebellion; or

(b) the integrity of India is threatened by internal disturbance in the whole or any part of the territory of Punjab, he may, by Proclamation, make a declaration to that effect in respect of the whole of Punjab or of such part of the territory thereof as may be specified in the Proclamation.";

(B) in the Explanation,-

(1) after the words "armed rebellion", the words", or that the integrity of India is threatened by internal disturbance in the whole or any part of the territory of Punjab," shall be inserted;

(2) after the words "or rebellion", the words "or disturbance" shall be inserted;

(ii) in clause (9), after the words "armed rebellion", at both the places where they occur, the words "or internal disturbance" shall be inserted;

(b) in article 358, in clause (1), after the words "or by external aggression", the words "or by armed rebellion, or that the integrity of India is threatened by internal disturbance in the whole or any part of the territory of Punjab," shall be inserted;

(c) in article 359, for the words and figures "articles 20 and 21", at both the places where they occur, the word and figures "article 20" shall be substituted.'

(2) The amendment made to the Constitution by sub-section (1) shall cease to operate on the expiry of a period of two years from the commencement of this Act, except as respects things done or omitted to be done before such cesser.

63rd Amendment (with effect from 6 January 1990)

3. Omission of article 359A.- Article 359A of the Constitution shall be omitted.

APPENDIX III.10: THE CONSTITUTION (THIRTY-EIGHTH AMENDMENT) ACT, 1975

Statement of Objects and Reasons appended to the Constitution (Thirty-ninth Amendment) Bill, 1975 which was enacted as the Constitution (Thirty-eighth Amendment) Act, 1975

STATEMENT OF OBJECTS AND REASONS

The Constitution (Thirty-ninth Amendment) Bill, 1975 seeks to amend articles 123, 213, 239B, 352, 356, 359 and 360 of the Constitution.

2. Article 123 empowers the President to promulgate Ordinances when both the Houses of Parliament are not in session if he is satisfied that circumstance exist rendering it necessary to take immediate action. Corresponding powers have been conferred by the Constitution on the Governor under article 213. Similar powers have been conferred on the Administrator under article 239B when

the Legislature of a Union territory is not in session. On the plain language of articles 123, 213 and 239B there is no doubt that the satisfaction mentioned in those articles is subjective satisfaction and that it is not justiciable. There is no doubt that this was also the intention of the makers of the Constitution. However, litigation is pending involving the justificability of this issue and contentions are being raised that the issue is subject to judicial scrutiny. To place the matter beyond doubt, it is proposed to provide in the Constitution that the satisfaction of the President, Governor or Administrator shall be final and conclusive and shall not be questioned in any court on any ground.

3. Article 352 empowers the President to declare Emergency if he is satisfied that the security of India or any part of it is threatened by war, external aggression or internal disturbance. Article 356 empowers the President to assume to himself the functions of the Government of a State if the constitutional machinery in any State fails and the Government in the State cannot be carried on. Likewise article 360 empowers the President to declare Financial Emergency if he is satisfied that the financial stability of India is threatened. Here again, the issue regarding satisfaction is, on the face of the articles clearly not justiciable. However, as the validity of the Proclamation issued under article 352 has been challenged in several proceedings and as litigation of this nature involves waste of public time and money, it is proposed to amend these three articles so as to make the satisfaction of the President final and conclusive and not justiciable on any ground.

4. In addition to article 352, contentions have been raised in certain writ petitions that while the original Proclamation of Emergency is in operation no further Proclamation of Emergency could be made thereunder. In order to place the matter beyond doubt it is proposed to make it clear in article 352 that the President may issue different Proclamations on different grounds whether or not there is a Proclamation already in existence and in operation.

5. When a Proclamation of Emergency is in operation, the

President is empowered under article 359 of the Constitution to make an order suspending the right to move any court for the enforcement of such of the rights conferred by Part III as may be mentioned in that order. It was intended that the powers conferred by this article should be exercised during an emergency according to needs of the situation. On the other hand, article 358 renders the provisions of article 19 automatically inoperative while the Proclamation of Emergency is in operation, and the power to make any law or to take any executive action is not restricted by the provisions of that article. The intention underlying article 359 appears to be that when an order is made under clause (1) of that article in relation to any of the rights conferred by Part III and mentioned in the order, the order so made would have for all practical purposes the same effect in relation to those rights as article 358 has in relation to article 19. It is, therefore, proposed not to have any differences in language between article 358 and the language in respect of those rights only which may be mentioned in the Presidential Order under clause (1) of article 359.

6. The Bill seeks to achieve the aforesaid objects.

NEW DELHI; H. R. GOKHALE.

The 20th July, 1975.

THE CONSTITUTION (THIRTY-EIGHTH AMENDMENT) ACT, 1975

[1st August, 1975.]

An Act further to amend the Constitution of India.

BE it enacted by Parliament in the Twenty-sixth Year of the Republic of India as follows:-

1. Short title.-This Act may be called the Constitution (Thirty-eighth Amendment) Act, 1975.

2. Amendment of article 123.-In article 123 of the Constitution, after clause (3), the following clause shall be inserted, and shall be deemed always to have been inserted, namely:-

"(4) Notwithstanding anything in this Constitution, the

satisfaction of the President mentioned in clause (1) shall be final and conclusive and shall not be questioned in any court on any ground.".

3. Amendment of article 213.-In article 213 of the Constitution, after clause (3), the following clause shall be inserted, and shall be deemed always to have been inserted, namely:-

"(4) Notwithstanding anything in this Constitution, the satisfaction of the Governor mentioned in clause (1) shall be final and conclusive and shall not be questioned in any court on any ground.".

4. Amendment of article 239B.-In article 239B of the Constitution, after clause (3), the following clause shall be inserted, and shall be deemed always to have been inserted, namely:-

"(4) Notwithstanding anything in this Constitution, the satisfaction of the administrator mentioned in clause (1) shall be final and conclusive and shall not be questioned in any court on any ground.".

5. Amendment of article 352.-In article 352 of the Constitution, after clause (3), the following clauses shall be inserted, and shall be deemed always to have been inserted, namely:-

"(4) The power conferred on the President by this article shall include the power to issue different Proclamations on different grounds, being war or external aggression or internal disturbance or imminent danger of war or external aggression or internal disturbance, whether or not there is a Proclamation already issued by the President under clause (1) and such Proclamation is in operation.

(5) Notwithstanding anything in this Constitution,-

(a) the satisfaction of the President mentioned in clause (1) and clause (3) shall be final and conclusive and shall not be questioned in any court on any ground;

(b) subject to the provisions of clause (2), neither the Supreme Court nor any other court shall have jurisdiction to entertain any question, on any ground, regarding the validity of-

(i) a declaration made by Proclamation by the President to the effect stated in clause (1); or

(ii) the continued operation of such Proclamation.".

6. Amendment of article 356.- In article 356 of the Constitution, after clause (4), the following clause shall be inserted, and shall be deemed always to have been inserted, namely:-

"(5) Notwithstanding anything in this Constitution, the satisfaction of the President mentioned in clause (1) shall be final and conclusive and shall not be questioned in any court on any ground.".

7. Amendment of article 359.- In article 359 of the Constitution, after clause (1), the following clause shall be inserted, and shall be deemed always to have been inserted, namely:-

"(1A) While an order made under clause (1) mentioning any of the right conferred by Part III is in operation, nothing in that Part conferring those rights shall restrict the power of the State as defined in the said Part to make any law or to take any executive action which the State would but for the provisions contained in that Part be competent to make or to take, but any law so made shall, to the extent of the incompetency, cease to have effect as soon as the order aforesaid ceases to operate, except as respects things done or omitted to be done before the law so ceases to have effect.".

8. Amendment of article 360.- In article 360 of the Constitution, after clause (4), the following clause shall be inserted, and shall be deemed always to have been inserted, namely:-

"(5) Notwithstanding anything in this Constitution,-
- (a) the satisfaction of the President mentioned in clause (1) shall be final and conclusive and shall not be questioned in any court on any ground;
- (b) subject to the provisions of clause (2), neither the Supreme Court nor any other court shall have jurisdiction to entertain any question, on any ground, regarding the validity of-
  - (i) a declaration made by Proclamation by the President to the effect stated in clause (1); or
  - (ii) the continued operation of such Proclamation.".

APPENDIX III.11: ARTICLE 19 IN THE CONSTITUTION OF INDIA

A. ARTICLE 19 IN THE CONSTITUTION OF INDIA WITH AMENDMENTS UPTO 5 OCTOBER 1973

19. Protection of certain rights regarding freedom of speech, etc.-
(1) All citizens shall have the right—
  (a) to freedom of speech and expression;
  (b) to assemble peaceably and without arms;
  (c) to form associations or unions;
  (d) to move freely throughout the territory of India;
  (e) to reside and settle in any part of the territory of India;
  (f) to acquire, hold and dispose of property; and
  (g) to practise any profession, or to carry on any occupation, trade or business.

[22][(2) Nothing in sub-clause (a) of clause (1) shall affect the operation of any existing law, or prevent the State from making any law, in so far as such law imposes reasonable restrictions on the exercise of the right conferred by the said sub-clause in the interests of [23]{the sovereignty and integrity of India,} the security of the State, friendly relations with foreign States, public order, decency or morality, or in relation to contempt of court, defamation or incitement to an offence.]

(3) Nothing in sub clause (b) of the said clause shall affect the

---

[22]Subs. for '(2) Nothing in sub-clause (a) of clause (1) shall affect the operation of any existing law in so far as it relates to, or prevent the State from making any law relating to, libel, slander, defamation, contempt of court or any matter which offends against decency or morality or which undermines the security of, or tends to overthrow, the State' by the Constitution (First Amendment) Act, 1951 w.e.f. 18 June 1951.

[23]Ins. by the Constitution (Sixteenth Amendment) Act, 1973 w.e.f. 5 October 1973.

operation of any existing law in so far as it imposes, or prevent the State from making any law imposing, in the interests of [24][the sovereignty and integrity of India,] public order, reasonable restrictions on the exercise of the right conferred by the said sub clause.

(4) Nothing in sub clause (c) of the said clause shall affect the operation of any existing law in so far as it imposes, or prevent the State from making any law imposing, in the interests of [25][the sovereignty and integrity of India,] public order or morality, reasonable restrictions on the exercise of the right conferred by the said sub clause.

(5) Nothing in sub clauses (d), (e), and (f) of the said clause shall affect the operation of any existing law in so far as it imposes, or prevent the State from making any law imposing, reasonable restrictions on the exercise of any of the rights conferred by the said sub-clauses either in the interests of the general public or for the protection of the interests of any Scheduled Tribe.

(6) Nothing in sub clause (g) of the said clause shall affect the operation of any existing law in so far as it imposes, or prevent the State from making any law imposing, in the interests of the general public, reasonable restrictions on the exercise of the right conferred by the said sub-clause, and, in particular, [26][nothing in the said sub-clause shall affect the operation of any existing law in so far as it relates to, or prevent the State from making any law relating to-

---

[24]Ins. by the Constitution (Sixteenth Amendment) Act, 1973 w.e.f. 5 October 1973.
[25]Ins. by the Constitution (Sixteenth Amendment) Act, 1973 w.e.f. 5 October 1973
[26]Subs. for 'nothing in the said sub-clause shall affect the operation of any existing law in so far as it prescribes or empowers any authority to prescribe, or prevent the State from making any law prescribing or empowering any authority to prescribe, the professional or technical qualifications necessary for practising any profession or carrying on any occupation, trade or business' by the Constitution (First Amendment) Act, 1951 w.e.f. 18 June 1951.

(i) the professional or technical qualifications necessary for practising any profession or carrying on any occupation, trade or business, or

(ii) the carrying on by the State, or by a corporation owned or controlled by the State, of any trade, business, industry or service, whether to the exclusion, complete or partial, of citizens or otherwise].

nothing in the said sub-clause shall affect the operation of any existing law in so far as it prescribes or empowers any authority to prescribe, or prevent the State from making any law prescribing or empowering any authority to prescribe, the professional or technical qualifications necessary for practising any profession or carrying on any occupation, trade or business.

AMENDMENTS

44th Amendment (with effect from 20 July 1979)

2. Amendment of article 19.- In article 19 of the Constitution,-
    (a) in clause (1),-
        (i) in sub-clause (e), the word "and" shall be inserted at the end;
        (ii) sub-clause (f) shall be omitted;
    (b) in clause (5), for the words, brackets and letters "sub-clauses (d), (e) and (f)", the words, brackets and letters "sub-clauses (d) and (e)" shall be substituted.

97th Amendment (with effect from 12 January 2012)

2. Amendment of article 19 - In Part III of the Constitution, in article 19, in clause (1), in sub-clause (c), after the words "or unions", the words "or co-operative societies" shall be inserted.

APPENDIX III.12: ARTICLE 21 IN THE CONSTITUTION OF INDIA

ARTICLE 21 IN THE CONSTITUTION OF INDIA ADOPTED ON 26 NOVEMBER 1949

21. Protection of life and personal liberty—No person shall be deprived of his life or personal liberty except according to procedure established by law.

APPENDIX III.13: PROVISIONS AND AMENDMENTS RELATING TO PROCLAMATION OF EMERGENCY IN JAMMU AND KASHMIR

THE CONSTITUTION (APPLICATION TO JAMMU AND KASHMIR) ORDER, 1954 OF THE PRESIDENT OF INDIA, DATED 14 MAY 1954

2. The provisions of the Constitution which, in addition to article 1 and article 370, shall apply in relation to the State of Jammu and Kashmir and the exceptions and modifications subject to which they shall so apply shall be as follows:-

(13) Part XVIII

(a) To article 352, the following new clause shall be added,

"(4) No Proclamation of Emergency made on grounds only of internal disturbance or imminent danger thereof shall have effect in relation to the State of Jammu and Kashmir (except as respects article 354) unless it is made at the request or with the concurrence of the Government of that State.".

The Constitution (Application to Jammu and Kashmir) Amendment Order, 1975 of the President of India, dated 29 June 1975

2. In paragraph 2 of the Constitution (Application to Jammu and Kashmir) Order, 1954, in clause (a) of sub-paragraph (13) (relating to Part XVIII), in clause (4) of article 352, for the words "unless it is made at the request or with the concurrence of the Government of that State", the following shall be substituted, namely:—

"unless—
(a) it is made at the request or with the concurrence of the Government of that State, or
(b) where it has not been so made, it is applied subsequently by the President to that State at the request or with the concurrence of the Government of that State.".

Appendix IV

Correspondence

APPENDIX IV.1: LETTER OF J.P. GOYAL TO JAYAPRAKASH NARAYAN, DATED 6 JULY 1975[1]

Dear Shri Jayaprakash Narayan,

On instructions from your brother Shri Rajeshwar Prasad I came here along with your brother and Shri V.M. Tarkunde to legally advise you about the validity or invalidity of your detention and in regard to any application which you may wish to file in court against your detention—If you want to meet me, please write to me immediately on this very letter that you agree to meet me.

Yours sincerely,
J.P. Goyal
Advocate, Supreme Court
New Delhi
6-7-1975

I want very much to see Mr. Goyal as a lawyer to consult him about my case.
Sd- J.P. Narayan
6-7-1975

---

[1]Source: 'JP Papers', File 8, unpublished, Cultural Informatics Lab, Indira Gandhi National Centre for the Arts, New Delhi and Braj Kishore Memorial Institute, Patna.

APPENDIX IV.2:
LETTER OF JAYAPRAKASH NARAYAN TO M.G. DEVASAHAYAM, DATED 13 JULY 1975[1]

P.G.I. Hospital
Chandigarh
13-7-75

Dear Mr. Devasahayam,

This is to inform you that I am nominating Mr. Tarkunde, Mr. Goyal and Mr. Lekhi, all Supreme Court advocates at Delhi, as my lawyers all of whom together or any one or two of whom may be allowed to interview me. I am writing to Mr. Tarkunde informing him of this and requesting them to see me at their convenience.

I should like to repeat the request already made orally, that at least an hour be allowed for consultation with my lawyers. I shall be obliged.

Yours sincerely,
Jayaprakash

Mr. M.G. Devasahayam
Deputy Commissioner
Chandigarh

---

[1]Source: 'JP Papers', File 8, unpublished, Cultural Informatics Lab, Indira Gandhi National Centre for the Arts, New Delhi and Braj Kishore Memorial Institute, Patna.

APPENDIX IV.3: LETTER OF JAYAPRAKASH NARAYAN TO V.M. TARKUNDE, DATED 13 JULY 1975[1]

c/o Superintendent,
Sub-Jail,
Chandigarh,
13-7-75

Dear Mr. Tarkunde,

I hope you and Mr. Goyal have had consultations with other lawyers and have decided upon the right course of legal action to be taken in regard to my detention. If you have, I should like to meet you again for consultations.

I am writing to the D.C., Chandigarh, that I am nominating you, Mr. Goyal and Mr. Lekhi as my lawyers, and that all the three of you or any one or two of you should be allowed to interview me and that the time allowed should be at least an hour.

Looking forward to meeting you soon.

Your sincerely,

Jayaprakash

P.S. Please show this letter to Mr. Goyal—it is meant for him too.

Mr. V.M. Tarkunde
D-426, Defence Colony
New Delhi–24

---

[1] Source: 'JP Papers', File 8, unpublished, Cultural Informatics Lab, Indira Gandhi National Centre for the Arts, New Delhi and Braj Kishore Memorial Institute, Patna.

APPENDIX IV.4: LETTER OF DISTRICT MAGISTRATE DELHI TO J.P. GOYAL, DATED 24 OCTOBER 1975[1]

OFFICE OF THE DISTRICT MAGISTRATE DELHI
No. FPA/ADM/ND/75   Dated 24-10-75

To
    Shri J.P. Goyal, Advocate
    431, Mathura Road, New Delhi

Memo

Reference his application for interview with MISA detenu Shri Jaya Prakash Narayan lodged at Central Jail, Chandigarh.

2. This is to inform you that you are permitted to meet the above named detenu on 26-10-75 in the presence and hearing of Supdt. Jail per orders of the Distt. Magistrate Delhi. Shri Pranab Chatterji is also allowed to accompany you at the time of interview.

Sd/- Meenakshi Datta
Addl. Distt. Magistrate Delhi

Copy forwarded for information & necessary action to

1. The Supdt. of Jail, Central Jail, Chandigarh.
2. The Distt. Magistrate, Chandigarh.

Sd/- Meenakshi Datta

Allowed to meet detenu from 11.15 a.m. to 12.15 in the presence and hearing of R.D. Sharma, Asstt. Supdt Jail, since Mohinder Singh, E.M. cum Supdt. Jail is away on tour.

Sd/- D.M. Chandigarh

---

[1]Source: 'JP Papers', File 4, unpublished, Cultural Informatics Lab, Indira Gandhi National Centre for the Arts, New Delhi and Braj Kishore Memorial Institute, Patna.

Index

Absolute stay, 37
Additional District Magistrate (ADM), 63, 144
Additional Solicitor General of India, 20, 26
Advani, L.K., 38, 49, 67, 68, 135
Advocate General of Gujarat, 137
Advocate General of Haryana, 81
Advocate General of Maharashtra, 40
Advocate General of Tamil Nadu, 108, 126
Advocate General of Uttar Pradesh (UP), 10, 21
Affidavit, 10, 22, 33, 40, 90-91, 180
Ahmed, Fakhruddin Ali, 141
Akali Dal, 38, 154
Allahabad High Court, 10, 14, 15, 18, 19, 28, 37, 77, 87, 93, 95, 103
All India Convention of Lawyers, 37, 87
All India Institute of Medical Sciences (AIIMS), 59, 61, 66
All India Reporter (AIR), 16, 22, 24, 26, 27, 41, 76, 88, 100, 109, 110, 111, 112, 113, 144
Alva Commission, 61, 69
American press, 138
Ambedkar, B.R., 4
Andhra Pradesh High Court, 118, 119
Article 352 of the Constitution of India, 44, 48
Ashoka Hotel, 37, 87, 116
Attorney General of India, 15, 27, 95, 124, 137

Bakht, Sikander, 47
Bar Association of India, 128
Beg, M.H., 91, 92, 93, 106, 107, 109, 114, 131, 137, 138
Bench
  Election, 11
  Labour, 11
  Tax, 11
Bharatiya Lok Dal (BLD), 33, 38, 47
Bhushan, Prashant, 3, 8, 16, 17, 79, 80, 88, 98, 99, 132, 133
Bhushan, Shanti, 3, 9, 10, 12, 13, 15, 16, 17, 21, 28, 29, 30, 31, 32, 33, 34, 35, 36, 45, 77, 78, 79, 81, 84, 85, 86, 87, 90, 91, 92, 93, 95, 96, 101, 102, 103, 104, 105, 106, 107, 108, 110, 111, 115, 116, 117, 118, 122, 128, 129, 135, 137
Black day, 137-139
Blue Book, 18, 19
Boat Club, 31, 129
Bombay High Court, 21, 30, 139
Bombay House, 122
Bosu, Jyotirmoy, 34, 35
British press, 138
Broome, W., 10, 11, 12, 13, 14, 15, 18

Caveat filing, 28
Chandigarh High Court, 57, 121
Civil Appeal No. 887 of 1975, 46
Civil Appeal No. 909 of 1975, 46
Civil Procedure Code (CPC), 11
Congress Working Committee (CWC), 136
Constitution, 101, 104, 115, 125, 128
  Article 191, 9
  Article 192, 9
  Article 136, 22 (Editor Note)
  Article 352, 44
  Article 226, 58
  Article 32, 58
  Article 14, 76, 77, 104, 105, 107, 110, 137
  Article 329, 109
  Article 359, 87, 107
  Article 329A, 83, 107, 111

242 • *Saving India from Indira*

Article 143, 132 (Editor Note)
Article 19, 137
Article 21, 137
Article 356, 153
Article 22, No Folio before appendices
Article 358 No Folio before appendices
Article 359, 87, 107
Article 14 of, 105
Constitution (Thirty-eighth Amendment) Act, 121, 124, 135
Constitution (Thirty-ninth Amendment) Act, 101-2, 104, 105, 109
clause 4(4) of, 101
Constitution (Thirty-second Amendment) Act, 1973, 115
Constitution (Forty-first Amendment) Bill, 125
Constitution Bench, 127, 132, 133, 137
Constitution makers, 101
Coordination Committee, 38, 39
Crime Investigation Department (CID) officer, 140

Dadachanji, J.B., 29, 30, 31, 33, 36, 46, 84, 122, 126, 127,
Dandavate, Madhu, 49
Daphtary, C.K., 11, 15, 114, 115, 117, 118, 119, 120, 122, 123, 124
Defence of India Rules, 65
Delhi High Court, 56, 71, 100, 138, 145
Democracy
declaration of Emergency, 46
destruction of values, 45
Democratic values, destruction of, 44
De, Niren, 21, 27, 84, 95, 96, 97, 124, 125, 137
Desai, Morarji, 1, 3, 38, 59, 63, 84, 85, 86, 150, 154
Devasahayam, M.G., 48, 50, 51, 52, 56, 68, 69, 70, 71, 72, 73, 74
Devi, Gayatri, 78, 108
Division Bench, 127, 132
Dravida Munnetra Kazhagam (DMK), 44

Election appeal, 76

Election Bench, 11, 20
Election campaigns, 36
Election Laws (Amendment) Act, 1975, 77, 82, 83, 107, 109
Election petition, 15, 18, 119
draft of, 9
filing of, 9
Emergency, 104, 110, 128, 139
proclamation of, 54, 136
Gagrat & Co., 33
Gandhi, Indira, 9, 10, 14, 16, 19, 31, 33, 37, 38, 39, 60, 63, 65, 93, 97, 106, 108, 114, 128, 129, 136, 138, 139, 140
Gandhi, Mahatma, 48, 49, 54, 60, 65, 106, 134
Gandhi, Rajiv, 34, 147
Gandhi, Sanjay, 8, 31, 74, 97, 99, 108, 147, 139, 146, 148, 149, 150
Gandhi Peace Foundation, 43, 56, 59
Garg, N.K., 47, 55
G.B. Pant Hospital, 59
Ghatate, Dr. N.M., 49, 50, 51, 67, 68, 121, 123, 124, 135, 137, 144, 145, 154
Gokhale, H.R., 27, 29, 40, 46, 62, 63, 82, 106, 118, 138, 146, 151
Government *Gazette*, 15
Government of India, 137
Goyal, J.P., 8, 52, 58, 65, 70, 72, 73, 98, 102, 127
Gupta, C.B., 10, 84, 72
Gupte, S.V., 15, 24, 110

Habeas corpus petitions, 56, 135, 136
Haryana High Court, 121, 124
High Court
Allahabad, 10, 14, 15, 16, 18, 19, 22, 27, 37, 77, 87, 93, 95, 103
Andhra Pradesh, 118, 119
Bombay, 21, 30, 139
Chandigarh, 57
Delhi, 56
Haryana, 121, 124
Himachal Pradesh, 93
Karnataka, 135
Punjab, 121, 124

Himachal Pradesh High Court, 93
Hindustan Times, 44, 59

I. *Jagadeeswara Rao vs Union of India*, 115, 118, 121
India Gate, 31
India International Centre (IIC), 63, 91, 92, 99, 103, 104, 108, 110
Indian Administrative Service (IAS) officer, 56
Indian Evidence Act, 1872, 20
  section 123, 20
  section 162, 20
Indian National Congress (R), 9
Interlocutory stage, 16
Iyer, V.R. Krishna, 28, 31, 33, 79, 109

Jaitley, Arun, 112
Jana Sangh, 38
Janata Party, 138
  Working Committee of, 44
Judicial suicide, 134
  habeas corpus cases, 134–137

Kanwar Lal Gupta vs Amar Nath Chawla & Ors, 1975, 27, 76
Karnataka High Court, 135
Kesavananda Bharati case, 88, 102, 114, 115, 116, 119, 121, 123–128,
Khanna, H.R., 11, 77, 88, 91, 98, 106, 107, 137, 138, 145
Koirala, B.P., 66
Kripalani, J.B., 66

Labour Bench, 11
Lal, Bansi, 71, 73, 74, 151
Law Reports, 138
Lekhi, P.N., 32, 64, 72, 84, 85, 135
Limaye, Madhu, 34, 35
Lodhi Hotel, 122
Lohia, Ram Manohar, 56, 57, 58, 59, 62, 66, 72

Maharani of Jaipur, 108
Maharani of Patiala, 64, 86
Maintenance of Internal Security Act, 1971 (MISA), 43, 48, 65, 122

Malkani, K.R., 8, 47, 51, 55,
Mehta, Asoka, 38, 47, 54, 136
Mehta, Om, 45, 51, 62,
Mishra, Shyam Nandan, 34, 49, 50, 135
Mody, Piloo, 34, 38, 41, 47, 67, 68, 136

Narain, Raj, 9, 10, 12, 13, 14, 15, 16, 17, 18, 20, 21, 22, 23, 24, 26, 27, 28, 31, 32, 33, 34, 38, 39, 41, 43, 44, 45, 46, 48, 55, 57, 63, 81, 85, 86, 87, 105, 106, 108, 129, 136, 138, 140, 151, 152
Narayan, Jayaprakash, 25, 38, 39, 41, 43, 46, 48, 50, 52, 55, 56, 58, 60, 61, 62, 64, 65, 66, 69, 70, 72, 74, 86, 92, 130, 135, 136, 140, 142, 146
National Emergency, 17, 24, 44
Nayar, Kuldeep, 138, 145, 148
Nehru, Jawaharlal, 2, 5, 18, 93, 100

Office of the Prime Minister, 35Prime minister office, 35
Officer on Special Duty (OSD), 12
Opposition parties, 37, 134

Palkhivala, N.A., 4, 26, 29, 30, 31, 32, 34, 35, 36, 37, 40, 46, 116, 117, 120, 121, 122, 123, 124, 125, 127, 128, 131, 132, 137
Patnaik, Biju, 47, 55, 136
Petition
  election, 18
  writ, 27
Petitioner's counsel, 20
Pitti, Badri Vishal, 119, 120, 121, 130
Political leaders, 136
Postgraduate Institute of Medical Education and Research (PGIMER), 55
Prasad, Rajeshwar, 45, 56, 57, 58, 59, 62, 66, 72
Presidential election, 141
Prison Diary, 65
Punjab High Court, 121, 124

Ray, A.N., 20, 21, 25, 37, 78, 79, 81, 82, 86, 87, 90, 91, 92, 93, 94, 96, 100,

103, 104, 106, 107, 114, 115, 116, 117, 123, 124, 128, 133, 137, 145
Ray, Rabi, 34
Ray, Siddhartha Shankar, 27, 82
Rajmata of Gwalior, 108
Ramlila Maidan, 39
Rao, Narasimha P.V., 122
Rao, S. Ramachandra, 118, 119, 121, 122, 124, 125, 126, 133
Reddy, K. Brahmananda, 6, 45, 51, 52
Rejoinder affidavit, 33
Representation of the People (Amendment) Act, 1974, 76, 107, 109
Respondent's counsel, 20
Rule 14(4) of the Haryana rules, 47

Samyukta Socialist Party, 9, 38,
Scindia, Vijayaraje, 108
Sen, A.K., 81, 82, 90, 94, 95, 96, 98, 101
Shah Commission, 139
Shastri, Lal Bahadur, 1, 4, 18
Shekhar, Chandra, 47, 52, 54, 56, 136
Singh, Chaudhary Charan, 78
Sinha, J.M.L, 16, 22, 26, 28, 29, 30, 32, 42, 44, 46, 52, 63, 77, 81, 107, 109, 112, 129, 138, 144
Socialist Party, 5, 38, 89, 150,
Sohna Rest House, 59
Solomon, B., 9
Special leave petition (SLP), 10, 13, 14, 19, 20
Srivastava, K.N., 18, 19, 22, 26
Srivastava, R.C., 9, 10, 13, 15, 21, 28, 29, 85, 91, 103
State of Punjab vs Amar Singh Harika, 15
State of Uttar Pradesh vs Raj Narain, 20
Sugar Industry Enquiry Commission, 14
Supreme Court, 21, 27, 31, 3, 36, 38, 78, 87, 106, 110, 115, 121, 126, 138
    Bench, 138
    curse of censorship, 105-106
    decisive resolution, 38-39
    filing appeals, 29
    hearing day, 34-38
    historic election case, 101
    judgement and aftermath, 28-33
    judgement and its effect, 106-111
    petitions, 29
    physical and mental strain, 102-104
    Registrar of, 92
    validity of the Constitution, 101
    wrong decision, 104-105
Supreme Court Bar Association, 90, 91, 94, 95, 96, 104, 120
    members, 90
Supreme Court Cases (SCC), 41, 88, 110
Supreme Court judgements, 18
    Additional District Magistrate, Jabalpur vs S.S. Shukla, 137
    Indira Nehru Gandhi vs Raj Narain & Anr, 46
    Kanwar Lal Gupta vs Amar Nath Chawla & Ors, 27, 76
    Raj Kumar vs Union of India, 15

Tarkunde, V.M., 21, 46, 50, 56, 57, 58, 59, 60, 61, 62, 64, 65, 70, 72, 87, 116, 117, 123, 124, 135, 136, 136, 137, 138
Tax Bench, 11
Thakur, Karpoori, 141
The Case That Shook India, 3, 8, 16, 79, 88, 98-99, 133
The Constitution (Thirty-ninth Amendment) Act, 1975, 83
The Indian Express, 24, 44, 130
The Statesman, 32, 41, 44, 112, 131, 132
Tripathy, Satya Deo, 141

Vajpayee, Atal Bihari, 135
Vakalatnama, 28, 40
Voluminous papers, 31

Writ petitions, 27, 58